ROBERT BROWNING

Robert Browning

A COLLECTION OF CRITICAL ESSAYS

EDITED BY

PHILIP DREW

METHUEN & CO LTD

First published in 1966
by Methuen & Co Ltd, 11 New Fetter Lane, London EC4
Editorial matter © Philip Drew, 1966
Printed in Great Britain by the
Shenval Press Ltd, London, Hertford and Harlow

CONTENTS

v

CONTENTS

vi

EDITOR'S NOTE

I have standardized the use of italics and quotation marks and shifted all footnotes to the end of each article. Some authors have been kind enough to suggest slight modifications of their essays: these have been incorporated in the present text. Otherwise each essay appears in its original form. All editorial notes are in square brackets.

Copyright material is reprinted by permission of the following: HENRY JAMES: John Farquharson Ltd and the James Estate; GEORGE SANTAYANA: Charles Scribner's Sons and Messrs Constable; PERCY LUBBOCK: The Author, John Murray Ltd and the *Quarterly Review*; EDWIN MUIR: The Hogarth Press; H. S. DAVIES: The Author and Messrs Hutchinson; K. BADGER: The Author and *Boston University Studies in English*; W. C. DEVANE: The Author and the *Yale Review*; W. O. RAYMOND: The Author and *PMLA*; ROBERT LANGBAUM: The Author, Messrs Chatto & Windus, and Random House; ROBERT PREYER: The Author and *ELH*; E. E. STOLL: Doubleday & Co Inc; ROMA A. KING, JR: The Author and *Victorian Newsletter*; R. D. ALTICK: The Author and *Studies in English Literature*; ISOBEL ARMSTRONG: The Author and *Victorian Poetry*; JOHN HOWARD: The Author and *Victorian Poetry*; WATSON KIRKCONNELL: The Author and *Modern Language Notes*; F. E. L. PRIESTLEY: The Author and *University of Toronto Quarterly*; FREDERICK PAGE: Oxford University Press.

I should like to express my thanks to all those who have allowed me to reprint their work, and also to Mr Ernst Honigmann for his patient and skilful assistance as proof reader.

ABBREVIATIONS

Benziger, *Images*	James Benziger, *Images of Eternity* (Carbondale: 1962)
Chesterton, *Browning* (EML)	G. K. Chesterton, *Robert Browning* (London: 1903) – English Men of Letters series
DeVane, *Handbook*	William Clyde DeVane, *A Browning Handbook*, 2nd ed. (New York: 1955)
Duckworth, *Background*	F. R. G. Duckworth, *Browning: Background and Conflict* (London: 1931)
ELH	[Journal of English Literary History]
Honan, *Characters*	Park Honan, *Browning's Characters* (New Haven: 1961)
Langbaum, *Experience*	Robert Langbaum, *The Poetry of Experience* (London: 1957)
B. Miller, *Portrait*	Betty Miller, *Robert Browning, A Portrait* (London: 1952)
J. H. Miller, *Disappearance of God*	J. Hillis Miller, *The Disappearance of God* (Cambridge, Mass.: 1963)
MLN	*Modern Language Notes*
MLQ	*Modern Language Quarterly*
PMLA	[*Publications of the Modern Language Association of America*]
Raymond, *Infinite Moment*	W. O. Raymond, *The Infinite Moment* (Toronto: 1950)
UTQ	*University of Toronto Quarterly*
VP	*Victorian Poetry*

INTRODUCTION

I N making this collection it was not part of my purpose to present
a survey of Browning's varying critical fortunes. There is no lack
of studies of Browning's reputation or of his standing with the
public, the reviewers and the critics since he began writing: some of
the most important are referred to on p. 65. However, as the essays
presented here span some seventy-five years, they inevitably reflect changing views of the poet, and illustrate the fluctuations of
critical opinion.

I

The first section of the book begins with James's glowing but characteristically double-edged tribute, written a few weeks after the poet's
death. The other essays in this section represent the extremes of
hostile and friendly criticism by those to whom Browning was still a
modern poet. On the one hand Santayana, in what has been called
'the most devastating criticism which Browning has encountered',
attempts to demolish utterly Browning's claims to consideration as a
serious poet. Percy Lubbock on the other hand tries to establish
Browning's reputation by purely literary arguments. I think that it is
true to say that both Lubbock and Santayana were, in different ways
and for different motives, trying to eradicate the image of Browning
as seer, prophet and evangelist which had been piously constructed
and worshipped by the Browning Societies and others of like mind.

Lubbock's essay was written in Browning's centenary year, 1912.
Of Browning criticism since that date it is apparently possible to take
at least two strongly divergent views. Mr Sykes Davies, whose essay
introduces the second section, says firmly that Browning exists in 'a
sort of critical vacuum'; in his catholic anthology of critical opinions

he finds nothing written about Browning in the last fifty years worth reprinting. A completely opposite view is expressed by another contributor, that beacon of Browning studies, Professor DeVane, when he talks of 'the almost overpowering wealth and excellence of research upon Browning's poetry in the last quarter of a century', that is, up to 1956.[1] The essays collected in this book will go some way to help the reader to decide whether Davies or DeVane is right.

Perhaps it is fair to say that the defect in Browning studies taken as a whole is neither a total dearth of good material nor an embarrassing excess, but an imbalance, and one which is connected with the eccentric way in which Browning criticism has developed. To put this briefly, it seems to have happened backwards. Early criticism of Browning, that is up to 1900, tended to be total, dealing with an entity called the-man-and-his-message. This phase was followed by a number of more specialized but still fairly general studies; it is only in recent years that one has been able to look for the substantial volume of detailed studies of single poems on which the whole body of generalization would more profitably and more naturally have been built up. At last we seem to be at the stage where an informed discussion of Browning begins with the assumption that both parties will regard him initially as the maker of a number of separate poems each of which stands or falls on its own merits.

Yet, as this welcome change is comparatively recent, the acceptable essays that deal with the whole of the poet's work are still more numerous than those which confine their attention to a single poem. This collection therefore devotes rather more space to general surveys than would be ideal, and correspondingly less to particular studies.

Edwin Muir's short but penetrating critique is a good example of the way in which Browning has appealed to and influenced those whose lives are spent wrestling with words. An interest in the language rather than in, for example, the theological implications of the poems is almost the hallmark of the modern critic, and Muir ably shows how far this approach can be profitably applied to Browning.

It is surprising that Bernard Shaw was for many years a member of the London Browning Society, and attended meetings regularly, contributing to the discussions with wit and candour. On one occasion he remarked in exasperation that 'no matter what paper they had before them, in the discussion they always got into Browning's optimistic theology'.[2] This feeling will be familiar to all who have read much criticism of Browning, and much of the best recent work has concentrated on other approaches to Browning's art, yet many of Browning's greatest poems deal with the major questions of human existence, and it is idle to suppose that they can be understood without any examination of the answers he offers. The essays by Professor Badger and Professor Raymond on Browning's religion and his humanism are admirable examples of the exceptionally difficult feat of discussing the broad implications of Browning's poetry without altogether losing sight of the individual poems. Professor Badger places Browning's opinions in the context of the great religious debates of the nineteenth century, while Professor Raymond takes issue with those who, following F. R. G. Duckworth and Mrs Miller, try to construe the poet's frequent use of light symbolism into an admission of poetic disability.

Professor Langbaum and Professor DeVane contribute studies of a more purely literary kind. Professor DeVane shows how one image, that of Andromeda, powerfully moved Browning throughout his life and shines through many different poems written at many different times. Professor Langbaum's expert account of the dramatic basis of Browning's poems is an invaluable aid to the understanding of this vitally important element in the poet's work. It is especially fitting that these last two authors should be represented in this book, since each has made an outstanding contribution to Browning studies, Professor DeVane most notably with his *Browning Handbook*, a work to which the word 'indispensable' can for once be applied with complete accuracy, and Professor Langbaum with his *Poetry of Experience*, by far the most stimulating and acute contribution to Browning criticism in recent years.

The concluding section of this collection consists entirely of studies of single poems, arranged in order of publication of the poems. These essays complement and, as it were, corroborate the general

3

studies which precede them. Thus, for example, Mr Kirkconnell's essay on the *Epilogue* to *Dramatis Personae* and Professor Priestley's careful analysis of *La Saisiaz* illuminate and give body to the accounts of Browning's theology and philosophy. Similarly Professor Stoll's account of *In a Balcony* provides a particular example in the general discussion of Browning's dramatic powers. It is notable that most of these separate studies naturally begin by considering Browning as a 'maker' but move on to consider him also as a 'mage', the terms which Professor Roma A. King Jr uses in his essay on *Cleon*, where their critical applications are clearly shown.

Only Professor Preyer's essay in this section is not devoted to a single poem, since he wishes to relate all three of Browning's early narrative poems to the prevailing Romantic ideals. He pays special attention to *Pauline*, which was the subject of the most famous of all critical accounts of Browning's work, that by John Stuart Mill. Mill was sent a copy of the poem by W. J. Fox and wrote his comments in the margins. At the end he drafted his general critique, which is reprinted in this book immediately after Professor Preyer's essay. For various reasons neither the *Examiner* nor *Tait's Magazine* printed Mill's review: his annotated copy was returned to Browning, who studied Mill's observations with great care and was apparently profoundly influenced by them, for he was reported as saying in his old age that 'his early poems were so transparent in their meaning as to draw upon him the ridicule of the critics, and that, boy as he was, this ridicule and censure stung him into quite another style of writing'.

While I have tried to avoid including too many essays on the same topic or adopting the same approach, I have not attempted to make this a completely *representative* collection. I haven't, for example, felt bound to include an essay by a European scholar, or an essay on *Pippa Passes*, or an essay by a logical positivist, or an essay on Browning's knowledge of botany just for the sake of completeness and fair play: the essays I have put in are here because they are the best available: without regard to date or subject matter. It seemed, however, essential to include two or three examples of the most recent criticism of Browning to show, so to speak, where we stand at

4

present: the essays of Professor Altick and Mr Howard (1963) and Mrs Armstrong (1964) demonstrate something of the flexibility and diversity of contemporary Browning scholarship.

The mood of James's opening tribute is lightly echoed in the tail-piece, an imaginary conversation by Frederick Page, which not only evokes the atmosphere of a literary drawing-room, such as that of Alice Meynell, and the conversation of a distinguished man of letters such as Patmore, but contrives to say a great deal about the sound and movement of Browning's verse.

II

I should perhaps offer some explanation of the omissions from this collection. A number of excellent articles came to hand too late for anything more than a brief reference in a footnote. Others were excluded by difficulties over copyright, although, as my list of acknowledgements shows, authors, editors and publishers have on the whole been most generous and accommodating. I have also, with extreme regret, been forced to leave out a number of articles because of their length. I should, for example, have been particularly pleased to print some of the excellent accounts of Browning's poetry written in his own lifetime. The two celebrated articles by Milsand written in 1851 and 1856, H. Buxton Forman's extended review article on *The Ring and the Book* (1869) and the anonymous review of *Fifine at the Fair* in *Temple Bar* (1873) all make critical points of great value and show that Browning could count on certain readers for a highly informed and sympathetic response to his work, but their length made it out of the question to include them in a work of this compass. The same consideration ruled out James's article on 'The Novel in *The Ring and the Book*' and a number of other admirable studies.

Finally I must draw attention to a major weakness in this collection, that most of the essays are favourable to Browning and indeed start from the assumption that he is a serious poet of some stature. Although this is, of course, a tradition in compilations of this kind, it is a tradition with which I should willingly have broken if I

5

had been able to discover any essays offering a cogent expression of the contrary view. But, as Mr Sykes Davies has pointed out, when Browning was toppled from his pedestal as the Sage of the Age of Steam, the result was not a barrage of criticism but a scornful silence. Those who think poorly of Browning have not attacked him but ignored him; a pity, since closely reasoned critical examination, whether friendly or hostile, is precisely what Browning's poetry has most needed for seventy years. But what is there? Mr Eliot, possibly affected by his admiration for Mr Santayana, dismissed an age of English poetry by saying 'Tennyson and Browning ruminated'.[3] Dr Leavis, possibly affected by his admiration for Mr Eliot, devoted a page, and that not the most valuable page, of *New Bearings in English Poetry* to Browning. These brief unargued rejections, and their elaborations and dilutions by the pens of smaller critics, constituted for many years the sole response to Browning by a most influential body of opinion.

As this book shows, Browning has not wanted devoted and subtle interpreters, yet one fact is undeniable – that he has been virtually ignored by the dominant critical writers of our time. His influence for good or ill on the poets of this century has often been remarked. His voice is to be heard in the monologues of Pound and Eliot and Frost and Kipling, in the dramatic lyrics of Hardy, Owen and de la Mare, in the familiar verse of Graves and Masefield, and in the more recent experiments of 'the Group'. Yet, as I say, among the critics neglect of Browning has been striking. Perhaps this is the proper place to offer a few speculations about the shyness of modern writers to employ their skills on Browning's major poems.

The primary reason is, I think, that most contemporary critics (and here I am not thinking solely of literary critics) are at home only when they can confine their attention to matters of technique: their aesthetic makes no provision for assessing the importance of an artist's subject or a poet's theme. If they come into the open they are forced to admit that, according to their theory, subject is of no importance whatsoever: if they take account of subject at all they do it surreptitiously and call it by another name. But Browning cannot be apprehended by these methods. He is a prime example of the man

6

who treats words as a medium in which something meaningful can be made. To him *what* he is saying is necessarily of supreme importance. Of course, he does not naïvely suppose that a poem cannot be great unless its subject has some obvious qualities of nobility, and he continually denied that the poet was personally committed to every word of his poem, any more than the dramatist was. But the power to speak the truth, in a very simple sense of the word, was to him one vitally important touchstone of a poet. This is infuriating, because it is quite plain that he is technically one of the great masters of English: what prevents him from becoming a popular subject for analysis is his tiresome habit of using language to say something. The parallel with Milton is hard to resist.

To maintain that what Browning is saying must be taken seriously is not to concede that his poems must be handed over to the metaphysicians for dissection, as if they were nothing more than exercises in argument. They have to be taken as artifacts in words and at the same time as statements about the world conveyed through a special way of using language. For a comprehensive assessment of them a man needs to be a scholar and a poet at once, not only sensitive in his responses to words and capable of following and judging arguments which are often of considerable conceptual difficulty, but also competent to use both qualifications simultaneously throughout his reading and evaluation of the poem. Confronted with such demands many critics, understandably preferring to work an easier or more immediately rewarding vein, have moved elsewhere, sometimes with a sigh of regret, sometimes with a disparaging jibe.

As Browning wrote to Thackeray's daughter (May 9, 1873), 'Remember that everybody this thirty years has given me his kick and gone his way, just as I am told the understood duty of all highway travellers in Spain is to bestow at least one friendly thump for the Mayoral's sake on his horses as they toil along uphill.'

Whatever the reason, the *fact* of Browning's unpopularity is undeniable. The collection that follows has been undertaken in the belief that informed and impartial appraisal can do nothing but good, even if it results only in settling Browning's unpopularity on a more rational basis. My aim in short has been neither to justify nor to advertise Browning, but to revive an intelligent interest in his work and to make accessible some of the material which is most helpful for a fair examination of his poetry.

In conclusion, I may observe that Browning was himself no stranger to unpopularity, nor was he unaware of the mutability of poetic reputation, if we may judge from his poem *Earth's Immortalities – Fame*, probably written in 1844, when he was 32.

> See, as the prettiest graves will do in time,
> Our poet's wants the freshness of its prime;
> Spite of the sexton's browsing horse, the sods
> Have struggled through its binding osier rods;
> Headstone and half-sunk footstone lean awry,
> Wanting the brick-work promised by-and-by;
> How the minute grey lichens, plate o'er plate,
> Have softened down the crisp-cut name and date!

NOTES

[1] See *The Victorian Poets: A Guide to Research*, ed. F. Faverty (1956), p. 78.

[2] See D. Smalley, 'Mephistopheles at the Conventicle', *Saturday Review of Literature*, XXVII (1944), pp. 13–15.

[3] In a review of Herbert Grierson's anthology of Meta physical poetry (*Times Literary Supplement*, 1921).

I

GENERAL STUDIES
BEFORE 1914

HENRY JAMES

BROWNING IN WESTMINSTER ABBEY

THE lovers of a great poet are the people in the world who are most to be forgiven a little wanton fancy about him, for they have before them, in his genius and work, an irresistible example of the application of the imaginative method to a thousand subjects. Certainly, therefore, there are many confirmed admirers of Robert Browning to whom it will not have failed to occur that the consignment of his ashes to the great temple of fame of the English race was exactly one of those occasions in which his own analytic spirit would have rejoiced, and his irrepressible faculty for looking at human events in all sorts of slanting coloured lights have found a signal opportunity. If he had been taken with it as a subject, if it had moved him to the confused yet comprehensive utterance of which he was the great professor, we can immediately guess at some of the sparks he would have scraped from it, guess how splendidly, in the case, the pictorial sense would have intertwined itself with the metaphysical. For such an occasion would have lacked, for the author of *The Ring and the Book*, none of the complexity and convertibility that were dear to him. Passion and ingenuity, irony and solemnity, the impressive and the unexpected, would each have forced their way through; in a word, the author would have been sure to take the special, circumstantial view (the inveterate mark of all his speculation) even of so foregone a conclusion as that England should pay her greatest honour to one of her greatest poets. As they stood in the

From *The Speaker*, I (1890), pp. 10–12 (unsigned); reprinted in *Essays in London and Elsewhere* (1893) and *English Hours* (1905).

Abbey, at any rate, on Tuesday last, those of his admirers and mourners who were disposed to profit by his warrant for inquiring curiously may well have let their fancy range, with its muffled step, in the direction which *his* fancy would probably not have shrunk from following, even perhaps to the dim corners where humour and the whimsical lurk. Only, we hasten to add, it would have taken Robert Browning himself to render the multifold impression.

One part of it on such occasion is, of course, irresistible – the sense that these honours are the greatest that a generous nation has to confer and that the emotion that accompanies them is one of the high moments of a nation's life. The attitude of the public, of the multitude, at such hours, is a great expansion, a great openness to ideas of aspiration and achievement; the pride of possession and of bestowal, especially in the case of a career so complete as Mr Browning's, is so present as to make regret a minor matter. We possess a great man most when we begin to look at him through the glass plate of death; and it is a simple truth, though containing an apparent contradiction, that the Abbey never takes us so benignantly as when we have a valued voice to commit to silence there. For the silence is articulate after all, and in worthy instances the preservation great. It is the other side of the question that would pull most the strings of irresponsible reflection – all those conceivable postulates and hypotheses of the poetic and satiric mind to which we owe the picture of how the bishop ordered his tomb in St Praxed's. Macaulay's 'temple of silence and reconciliation' – and none the less perhaps because he himself is now a presence there – strikes us, as we stand in it, not only as local but as social – a sort of corporate company; so thick, under its high arches, its dim transepts, and chapels, is the population of its historic names and figures. They are a company in possession, with a high standard of distinction, of immortality, as it were; for there is something serenely inexpugnable even in the position of the interlopers. As they look out, in the rich dusk, from the cold eyes of statues and the careful identity of tablets, they seem, with their converging faces, to scrutinize decorously the claims of each new recumbent glory, to ask each other how he is to be judged as an accession. How difficult to banish the idea that Robert Browning would have enjoyed prefiguring and playing with the mystifications, the reservations, even perhaps the slight buzz of scandal, in the Poets' Corner, to which his own obsequies might give rise! Would not his great relish, in so characteristic an interview with his crucible, have been his perception of the bewildering modernness, to much of the society, of the new candidate for a niche? That is the interest and the fascination, from what may be termed the inside point of view, of Mr Browning's having received, in this direction of becoming a classic, the only official assistance that is ever conferred upon English writers.

It is as classics on one ground and another – some members of it perhaps on that of not being anything less – that the numerous assembly in the Abbey holds together, and it is as a tremendous and incomparable modern that the author of *Men and Women* takes his place in it. He introduces to his predecessors a kind of contemporary individualism which surely for many a year they had not been reminded of with any such force. The tradition of the poetic character as something high, detached and simple, which may be assumed to have prevailed among them for a good while, is one that Browning has broken at every turn; so that we can imagine his new associates to stand about him, till they have got used to him, with rather a sense of failing measures. A good many oddities and a good many great writers have been entombed in the Abbey; but none of the odd ones have been so great and none of the great ones so odd. There are plenty of poets whose right to the title may be contested, but there is no poetic head of equal power – crowned and recrowned by almost importunate hands – from which so many people would withhold the distinctive wreath. All this will give the marble phantoms at the base of the great pillars and the definite personalities of the honorary slabs something to puzzle out until, by the quick operation of time, the mere fact of his lying there among the classified and protected makes even Robert Browning lose a portion of the bristling surface of his actuality.

For the rest, judging from the outside and with his contemporaries, we of the public can only feel that his very modernness – by which we mean the all-touching, all-trying spirit of his work, permeated with accumulations and playing with knowledge – achieves a kind of conquest, or at least of extension, of the rigid pale. We cannot enter here upon any account either of that or of any other element of his genius, though surely no literary figure of our day seems to sit more unconsciously for the painter. The very imperfections of this original are fascinating, for they never present themselves as weaknesses; they are boldnesses and overgrowths, rich roughnesses and humours, and the patient critic need not despair of digging to the primary soil from which so many disparities and contradictions spring. He may finally even put his finger on some explanation of the great mystery, the imperfect conquest of the poetic form by a genius in which the poetic passion had such volume and range. He may successfully say how it was that a poet without a lyre – for that is practically Browning's deficiency: he had the scroll, but not often the sounding strings – was nevertheless, in his best hours, wonderfully rich in the magic of his art, a magnificent master of poetic emotion. He will justify on behalf of a multitude of devotees the great position assigned to a writer of verse of which the nature or the fortune has been (in proportion to its value and quantity) to be treated rarely as quotable. He will do all this and a great deal more besides; but we need not wait for it to feel that something of our latest sympathies, our latest and most restless selves, passed the other day into the high part – the show-part, to speak vulgarly – of our literature. To speak of Mr Browning only as he was in the last twenty years of his life, how quick such an imagination as his would have been to recognize all the latent or mystical suitabilities that, in the last resort, might link to the great Valhalla by the Thames a figure that had become so conspicuously a figure of London! He had grown to be intimately and inveterately of the London world; he was so familiar and recurrent, so responsible to all its solicitations, that, given the endless incarnations he stands for today, he would have been missed from the congregation of worthies whose memorials are the special pride of the Londoner. Just as his great sign to those who knew him was that he was a force of health, of temperament, of tone, so what he takes into the Abbey is an immense expression of life – of life rendered with large liberty and free experiment, with an unprejudiced intellectual eagerness to put himself in other people's place, to participate in complications and consequences; a restlessness of psychological research that might well alarm any pale company for their formal orthodoxies.

But the illustrious whom he rejoins may be reassured, as they will not fail to discover: in so far as they are representative it will clear itself up that, in spite of a surface unsuggestive of marble and a reckless individualism of form, he is quite as representative as any of them. For the great value of Browning is that at bottom, in all the deep spiritual and human essentials, he is unmistakably in the great tradition – is, with all his Italianisms and cosmopolitanisms, all his victimization by societies organized to talk about him, a magnificent example of the best and least dilettantish English spirit. That constitutes indeed the main chance for his eventual critic, who will have to solve the refreshing problem of how, if subtleties be not what the English spirit most delights in, the author of, for instance, *Any Wife to any Husband* made them his perpetual pasture, and yet remained typically of his race. He was indeed a wonderful mixture of the universal and the alembicated. But he played with the curious and the special, they never submerged him, and it was a sign of his robustness that he could play to the end. His voice sounds loudest, and also clearest, for the things that, as a race, we like best – the fascination of faith, the acceptance of life, the respect for its mysteries, the endurance of its charges, the vitality of the will, the validity of character, the beauty of action, the seriousness, above all, of the great human passion. If Browning had spoken for us in no other way, he ought to have been made sure of, tamed and chained as a classic, on account of the extraordinary beauty of his treatment of the special relation between man and woman. It is a complete and splendid picture of the matter, which somehow places it at the same time in the region of conduct and responsibility. But when we talk of Robert Browning's speaking 'for us' we go to the end of our privilege, we say all. With a sense of security, perhaps even a certain complacency, we leave our sophisticated modern conscience, and perhaps even our heterogeneous modern vocabulary, in his charge among the illustrious. There will possibly be moments in which these things will seem to us to have widened the allowance, made the high abode more comfortable, for some of those who are yet to enter it.[1]

NOTE

[1] [For James's views on Browning see also 'The Private Life' (1892), a short story in which the character of Clare Vawdrey is based on Browning; *William Wetmore Story and his Friends* (1903), especially I, pp. 171, 267, 270; II, pp. 66, 88, 226, 233, 283; 'The Novel in *The Ring and the Book*', a centenary lecture delivered to the Royal Society of Literature in 1912, revised text in *Quarterly Review*, CCXVII (1912), pp. 68–87.]

GEORGE SANTAYANA

FROM 'THE POETRY OF BARBARISM'

['The Poetry of Barbarism' first appeared in *Interpretations of Poetry and Religion* (1900), and has been frequently reprinted. It is to be found in *Essays in Literary Criticism of George Santayana*, edited by Irving Singer (New York, Scribners, 1956), pp. 149-78.

In the first part of the essay Santayana deplores the state of contemporary poetry. 'Our poets are things of shreds and patches; they give us episodes and studies, a sketch of this curiosity, a glimpse of that romance; they have no total vision, no grasp of the whole reality, and consequently no capacity for a sane and steady idealization.' Since the age lacks an adequate vision of 'beauty, order, and perfection', 'its moral strength is a blind and miscellaneous vehemence. Its poetry, in a word, is the poetry of barbarism.' Whitman and Browning are chosen to illustrate Santayana's general point. Although Whitman is clearly the less articulate, 'in Browning the barbarism is no less real though disguised by a literary and scientific language, since the passions of civilized life with which he deals are treated as so many "barbaric yawps", complex indeed in their conditions, puffings of an intricate engine, but aimless in their vehemence and mere ebullitions of lustiness in adventurous and profoundly ungoverned souls'.

Santayana next gives a general and unfavourable account of Whitman, censuring him for his superficiality, his primitiveness, and his inability to paint the ideals of 'wealth, learning and power', of 'pure goodness and pure love'.

What follows is the third and concluding section of the essay: it is printed complete.]

I F we would do justice to Browning's work as a human document, and at the same time perceive its relation to the rational ideals of the imagination and to that poetry which passes into religion, we must keep, as in the case of Whitman, two things in mind. One is the genuineness of the achievement, the sterling quality of the vision and inspiration; these are their own justification when we approach them from below and regard them as manifesting a more direct or impassioned grasp of experience than is given to mildly blatant, convention-ridden minds. The other thing to remember is the short distance to which this comprehension is carried, its failure to approach any finality, or to achieve a recognition even of the traditional ideals of poetry and religion.

In the case of Walt Whitman such a failure will be generally felt; it is obvious that both his music and his philosophy are those of a barbarian, nay, almost of a savage. Accordingly there is need of dwelling rather on the veracity and simple dignity of his thought and art, on their expression of an order of ideas latent in all better experience. But in the case of Browning it is the success that is obvious to most people. Apart from a certain superficial grotesqueness to which we are soon accustomed, he easily arouses and engages the reader by the pithiness of his phrase, the volume of his passion, the vigour of his moral judgment, the liveliness of his historical fancy. It is obvious that we are in the presence of a great writer, of a great imaginative force, of a master in the expression of emotion. What is perhaps not so obvious, but no less true, is that we are in the presence of a barbaric genius, of a truncated imagination, of a thought and an art inchoate and ill-digested, of a volcanic eruption that tosses itself quite blindly and ineffectually into the sky.

The points of comparison by which this becomes clear are perhaps not in everyone's mind, although they are merely the elements of traditional culture, aesthetic and moral. Yet even without reference to ultimate ideals, one may notice in Browning many superficial signs of that deepest of all failures, the failure in rationality and the indifference to perfection. Such a sign is the turgid style, weighty without nobility, pointed without naturalness or precision. Another sign is the 'realism' of the personages, who, quite like men and women in actual life, are always displaying traits of character and never attaining character as a whole. Other hints might be found in the structure of the poems, where the dramatic substance does not achieve a dramatic form; in the metaphysical discussion, with its confused prolixity and absence of result; in the moral ideal, where all energies figure without their ultimate purposes; in the religion, which breaks off the expression of this life in the middle, and finds in that suspense an argument for immortality. In all this, and much more that might be recalled, a person coming to Browning with the habits of a cultivated mind might see evidence of some profound incapacity in the poet; but more careful reflection is necessary to understand the nature of this incapacity, its cause, and the peculiar accent which its presence gives to those ideas and impulses which Browning stimulates in us.

There is the more reason for developing this criticism (which might seem needlessly hostile and which time and posterity will doubtless make in their own quiet and decisive fashion) in that Browning did not keep within the sphere of drama and analysis, where he was strong, but allowed his own temperament and opinions to vitiate his representation of life, so that he sometimes turned the expression of a violent passion into the last word of what he thought a religion. He had a didactic vein, a habit of judging the spectacle he evoked and of loading the passions he depicted with his visible sympathy or scorn.

Now a chief support of Browning's popularity is that he is, for many, an initiator into the deeper mysteries of passion, a means of escaping from the moral poverty of their own lives and of feeling the rhythm and compulsion of the general striving. He figures, therefore, distinctly as a prophet, as a bearer of glad tidings, and it is easy for those who hail him as such to imagine that, knowing the labour of life so well, he must know something also of its fruits, and that in giving us the feeling of existence, he is also giving us its meaning. There is serious danger that a mind gathering from his pages the raw materials of truth, the unthreshed harvest of reality, may take him for a philosopher, for a rationalizer of what he describes. Awakening may be mistaken for enlightenment, and the galvanizing of torpid sensations and impulses for wisdom.

Against such fatuity reason should raise her voice. The vital and historic forces that produce illusions of this sort in large groups of men are indeed beyond the control of criticism. The ideas of passion are more vivid than those of memory, until they become memories in turn. They must be allowed to fight out their desperate battle against the laws of Nature and reason. But it is worth while in the meantime, for the sake of the truth and of a just philosophy, to meet the varying though perpetual charlatanism of the world with a steady protest. As soon as Browning is proposed to us as a leader, as soon as we are asked to be not the occasional patrons of his art, but the pupils of his philosophy, we have a right to express the radical dissatisfaction which we must feel, if we are rational, with his whole attitude and temper of mind.

The great dramatists have seldom dealt with perfectly virtuous characters. The great poets have seldom represented mythologies that would bear scientific criticism. But by an instinct which constituted their greatness they have cast these mixed materials furnished by life into forms congenial to the specific principles of their art, and by this transformation they have made acceptable in the aesthetic sphere things that in the sphere of reality were evil or imperfect: in a word, their works have been beautiful as works of art. Or, if their genius exceeded that of the technical poet and rose to prophetic intuition, they have known how to create ideal characters, not possessed, perhaps, of every virtue accidentally needed in this world, but possessed of what is ideally better, of internal greatness and perfection. They have also known how to select and reconstruct their mythology so as to make it a true interpretation of moral life. When we read the maxims of Iago, Falstaff, or Hamlet, we are delighted if the thought strikes us as true, but we are not less delighted if it strikes us as false. These characters are not presented to us in order to enlarge our capacities of passion nor in order to justify themselves as processes of redemption; they are there, clothed in poetry and imbedded in plot, to entertain us with their imaginable feelings and their interesting errors. The poet, without being especially a philosopher, stands by virtue of his superlative genius on the plane of universal reason, far above the passionate experience which he overlooks and on which he reflects; and he raises us for the moment to his own level, to send us back again, if not better endowed for practical life, at least not unacquainted with speculation. With Browning the case is essentially different. When his heroes are blinded by passion and warped by circumstance, as they almost always are, he does not describe the fact from the vantage-ground of the intellect and invite us to look at it from that point of view. On the contrary, his art is all self-expression or satire. For the most part his hero, like Whitman's, is himself; not appearing, as in the case of the American bard, *in puris naturalibus*, but masked in all sorts of historical and romantic finery. Sometimes, however, the personage, like Guido in *The Ring and the Book* or the 'frustrate ghosts' [cf. *The Statue and the Bust*, 246] of other poems, is merely a Marsyas, shown flayed and quivering to the greater glory of the poet's ideal Apollo. The impulsive utterances and the crudities of most of the speakers are passionately adopted by the poet as his own. He thus perverts what might have been a triumph of imagination into a failure of reason.

This circumstance has much to do with the fact that Browning, in spite of his extraordinary gift for expressing emotion, has hardly produced works purely and unconditionally delightful. They not only portray passion, which is interesting, but they betray it, which is odious. His art was still in the service of the will. He had not attained, in studying the beauty of things, that detachment of the phenomenon, that love of the form for its own sake, which is the secret of contemplative satisfaction. Therefore, the lamentable accidents of his personality and opinions, in themselves no worse than those of other mortals, passed into his art. He did not seek to elude them: he had no free speculative faculty to dominate them by. Or, to put the same thing differently, he was too much in earnest in his fictions, he threw himself too unreservedly into his creations. His imagination, like the imagination we have in dreams, was merely a vent for personal preoccupations. His art was inspired by purposes less simple and universal than the ends of imagination itself. His play of mind consequently could not be free or pure. The creative impulse could not reach its goal or manifest in any notable degree its own organic ideal.

We may illustrate these assertions by considering Browning's treatment of the passion of love, a passion to which he gives great prominence and in which he finds the highest significance.

Love is depicted by Browning with truth, with vehemence, and with the constant conviction that it is the supreme thing in life. The great variety of occasions in which it appears in his pages and the different degrees of elaboration it receives, leave it always of the same quality – the quality of passion. It never sinks into sensuality; in spite of its frequent extreme crudeness, it is always, in Browning's hands, a passion of the imagination, it is always love. On the other hand it never rises into contemplation: mingled as it may be with friendship, with religion, or with various forms of natural tenderness, it always remains a passion; it always remains a personal impulse, a hypnotization, with another person for its object or its cause. Kept within these limits it is represented, in a series of powerful sketches, which are for most readers the gems of the Browning gallery, as the last word of experience, the highest phase of human life.

> The woman yonder, there's no use of life
> But just to obtain her! Heap earth's woes in one
> And bear them – make a pile or all earth's joys
> And spurn them, as they help or help not this;
> Only, obtain her!   [*In a Balcony*, 157–61]

> When I do come, she will speak not, she will stand,
>   Either hand
> On my shoulder, give her eyes the first embrace
>   Of my face,
> Ere we rush, ere we extinguish sight and speech
>   Each on each. . . .
> Oh heart! Oh blood that freezes, blood that burns!
>   Earth's returns
> For whole centuries of folly, noise, and sin!
>   Shut them in,
> With their triumphs and their glories and the rest!
>   Love is best.   [*Love among the Ruins*, 67–72, 79–84]

In the piece called *In a Gondola* the lady says to her lover:

> Heart to heart
> And lips to lips! Yet once more, ere we part,
> Clasp me and make me thine, as mine thou art.
> [222-4]

And he, after being surprised and stabbed in her arms, replies:

> It was ordained to be so, sweet! – and best
> Comes now, beneath thine eyes, upon thy breast.
> Still kiss me! Care not for the cowards! Care
> Only to put aside thy beauteous hair
> My blood will hurt! The Three, I do not scorn
> To death, because they never lived: but I
> Have lived indeed, and so – (yet one more kiss) –
>   can die! [225-31]

We are not allowed to regard these expressions as the cries of souls blinded by the agony of passion and lust. Browning unmistakably adopts them as expressing his own highest intuitions. He so much admires the strength of this weakness that he does not admit that it is a weakness at all. It is with the strut of self-satisfaction, with the sensation, almost, of muscular Christianity, that he boasts of it through the mouth of one of his heroes, who is explaining to his mistress the motive of his faithful services as a minister of the queen:

> She thinks there was more cause
> In love of power, high fame, pure loyalty?
> Perhaps she fancies men wear out their lives
> Chasing such shades. . . .
> I worked because I want you with my soul.
> [*In a Balcony*, 174-8]

Readers of the fifth chapter of this volume need not be reminded here of the contrast which this method of understanding love offers to that adopted by the real masters of passion and imagination.[1] They began with that crude emotion with which Browning ends; they lived it down, they exalted it by thought, they extracted the pure gold of it in a long purgation of discipline and suffering. The fierce paroxysm which for him is heaven, was for them the proof that heaven cannot be found on earth, that the value of experience is not in experience itself but in the ideals which it reveals. The intense, voluminous emotion, the sudden, overwhelming self-surrender in which he rests was for them the starting-point of a life of rational worship, of an austere and impersonal religion, by which the fire of love, kindled for a moment by the sight of some creature, was put, as it were, into a censer, to burn incense before every image of the Highest Good. Thus love ceased to be a passion and became the energy of contemplation: it diffused over the universe, natural and ideal, that light of tenderness and that faculty of worship which the passion of love often is first to quicken in a man's breast.

Of this art, recommended by Plato and practised in the Christian Church by all adepts of the spiritual life, Browning knew absolutely nothing. About the object of love he had no misgivings. What could the object be except somebody or other? The important thing was to love intensely and to love often. He remained in the phenomenal sphere: he was a lover of experience; the ideal did not exist for him. No conception could be farther from his thought than the essential conception of any rational philosophy, namely, that feeling is to be treated as raw material for thought, and that the destiny of emotion is to pass into objects which shall contain all its value while losing all its formlessness. This transformation of sense and emotion into objects agreeable to the intellect, into clear ideas and beautiful things, is the natural work of reason; when it has been accomplished very imperfectly, or not at all, we have a barbarous mind, a mind full of chaotic sensations, objectless passions, and undigested ideas. Such a mind Browning's was, to a degree remarkable in one with so rich a heritage of civilization.

The nineteenth century, as we have already said, has nourished the hope of abolishing the past as a force while it studies it as an object; and Browning, with his fondness for a historical stage setting and for the gossip of history, rebelled equally against the Pagan and the Christian discipline. The 'Soul' which he trusted in was the barbarous soul, the 'Spontaneous Me' of his half-brother Whitman. It was a restless personal impulse, conscious of obscure depths within itself which it fancied to be infinite, and of a certain vague sympathy with wind and cloud and with the universal mutation. It was the soul that might have animated Attila and Alaric when they came

24

GEORGE SANTAYANA

down into Italy, a soul not incurious of the tawdriness and corruption of the strange civilization it beheld, but incapable of understanding its original spirit; a soul maintaining in the presence of that noble, unappreciated ruin all its own lordliness and energy, and all its native vulgarity.

Browning, who had not had the education traditional in his own country, used to say that Italy had been his university. But it was a school for which he was ill prepared, and he did not sit under its best teachers. For the superficial ferment, the wordly passions, and the crimes of the Italian Renaissance he had a keen interest and intelligence. But Italy has been always a civilized country, and beneath the trappings and suits of civilization which at that particular time it flaunted so gayly, it preserved a civilized heart to which Browning's insight could never penetrate. There subsisted in the best minds a trained imagination and a cogent ideal of virtue. Italy had a religion, and that religion permeated all its life, and was the background without which even its secular art and secular passions would not be truly intelligible. The most commanding and representative, the deepest and most appealing of Italian natures are permeated with this religious inspiration. A Saint Francis, a Dante, a Michael Angelo, breathe hardly anything else. Yet for Browning these men and what they represented may be said not to have existed. He saw, he studied, and he painted a decapitated Italy. His vision could not mount so high as her head.

One of the elements of that higher tradition which Browning was not prepared to imbibe was the idealization of love. The passion he represents is lava hot from the crater, in no way moulded, smelted, or refined. He had no thought of subjugating impulses into the harmony of reason. He did not master life, but was mastered by it. Accordingly the love he describes has no wings; it issues in nothing. His lovers 'extinguish sight and speech, each on each'; sense, as he says elsewhere, drowning soul.[2] The man in the gondola may well boast that he can die; it is the only thing he can properly do. Death is the only solution of a love that is tied to its individual object and inseparable from the alloy of passion and illusion within itself. Browning's hero, because he has loved intensely, says that he has

25

lived; he would be right, if the significance of life were to be measured by the intensity of the feeling it contained, and if intelligence were not the highest form of vitality. But had that hero known how to love better and had he had enough spirit to dominate his love, he might perhaps have been able to carry away the better part of it and to say that he could not die; for one half of himself and of his love would have been dead already and the other half would have been eternal, having fed –

> On death, that feeds on men;
> And death once dead, there's no more dying then.

The irrationality of the passions which Browning glorifies, making them the crown of life, is so gross that at times he cannot help perceiving it.

> How perplexed
> Grows belief!
> Well, this cold clay clod
> Was man's heart:
> Crumble it, and what comes next?
> Is it God?   [*In a Year*, 75–80]

Yes, he will tell us. These passions and follies, however desperate in themselves and however vain for the individual, are excellent as parts of the dispensation of Providence:

> Be hate that fruit or love that fruit,
> It forwards the general deed of man,
> And each of the many helps to recruit
> The life of the race by a general plan;
> Each living his own, to boot.
> [*By the Fireside*, 246–50]

If we doubt, then, the value of our own experience, even perhaps of our experience of love, we may appeal to the interdependence of goods and evils in the world to assure ourselves that, in view of its consequences elsewhere, this experience was great and important after all. We need not stop to consider this supposed solution, which bristles with contradictions; it would not satisfy Browning himself, if he did not back it up with something more to his purpose, something nearer to warm and transitive feeling. The compensation for our defeats, the answer to our doubts, is not to be found merely in a proof of the essential necessity and perfection of the universe; that would be cold comfort, especially to so uncontemplative a mind. No: that answer, and compensation are to come very soon and very vividly to every private bosom. There is another life, a series of other lives, for this to happen in. Death will come, and –

> I shall thereupon
> Take rest, ere I be gone
> Once more on my adventure brave and new:
> Fearless and unperplexed,
> When I wage battle next,
> What weapons to select, what armour to indue.
>
> [*Rabbi Ben Ezra*, 79–84]

> For sudden the worst turns the best to the brave,
> The black minute's at end,
> And the element's rage, the fiend-voices that rave,
> Shall dwindle, shall blend,
> Shall change, shall become first a peace out of pain,
> Then a light, then thy breast,
> O thou soul of my soul! I shall clasp thee again,
> And with God be the rest! [*Prospice*, 21–8]

Into this conception of continued life Browning has put, as a collection of further passages might easily show, all the items furnished by fancy or tradition which at the moment satisfied his imagination – new adventures, reunion with friends, and even, after a severe strain and for a short while, a little peace and quiet. The gist of the matter is that we are to live indefinitely, that all our faults can be turned to good, all our unfinished business settled, and that therefore there is time for anything we like in this world and for all we need in the other. It is in spirit the direct opposite of the philosophic maxim of regarding the end, of taking care to leave a finished life and a perfect character behind us. It is the opposite, also, of the religious *memento mori*, of the warning that the time is short before we go to our account. According to Browning, there is no account: we have an infinite credit. With an unconscious and characteristic mixture of heathen instinct with Christian doctrine, he thinks of the other world as heaven, but of the life to be led there as of the life of Nature.

Aristotle observes that we do not think the business of life worthy of the gods, to whom we can only attribute contemplation; if Browning had had the idea of perfecting and rationalizing this life rather than of continuing it indefinitely, he would have followed Aristotle and the Church in this matter. But he had no idea of any-thing eternal; and so he gave, as he would probably have said, a filling to the empty Christian immortality by making every man busy in it about many things. And to the irrational man, to the boy, it is no unpleasant idea to have an infinite number of days to live through, an infinite number of dinners to eat, with an infinity of fresh fights and new love-affairs, and no end of last rides together.

But it is a mere euphemism to call this perpetual vagrancy a development of the soul. A development means the unfolding of a definite nature, the gradual manifestation of a known idea. A series of phases, like the successive leaps of a water-fall, is no development. And Browning has no idea of an intelligible good which the phases of life might approach and with reference to which they might con-stitute a progress. His notion is simply that the game of life, the exhilaration of action, is inexhaustible. You may set up your tenpins again after you have bowled them over, and you may keep up the sport for ever. The point is to bring them down as often as possible with a master-stroke and a big bang. That will tend to invigorate in you that self-confidence which in this system passes for faith. But it is unmeaning to call such an exercise heaven, or to talk of being 'with God' in such a life, in any sense in which we are not with God already and under all circumstances. Our destiny would rather be, as Browning himself expresses it in a phrase which Attila or Alaric might have composed, 'bound dizzily to the wheel of change to slake the thirst of God'.[3]

Such an optimism and such a doctrine of immortality can give no justification to experience which it does not already have in its de-tached parts. Indeed, those dogmas are not the basis of Browning's attitude, not conditions of his satisfaction in living, but rather over-flowings of that satisfaction. The present life is presumably a fair average of the whole series of 'adventures brave and new' which fall to each man's share; were it not found delightful in itself, there would be no motive for imagining and asserting that it is reproduced *in infinitum*. So too if we did not think that the evil in experience is actually utilized and visibly swallowed up in its good effects, we should hardly venture to think that God could have regarded as a good something which has evil for its condition and which is for that reason profoundly sad and equivocal. But Browning's philosophy of life and habit of imagination do not require the support of any metaphysical theory. His temperament is perfectly self-sufficient and primary; what doctrines he has are suggested by it and are too loose to give it more than a hesitant expression; they are quite powerless to give it any justification which it might lack on its face.

It is the temperament, then, that speaks; we may brush aside as unsubstantial, and even as distorting, the web of arguments and theories which it has spun out of itself. And what does the temperament say? That life is an adventure, not a discipline; that the exercise of energy is the absolute good, irrespective of motives or of consequences. These are the maxims of a frank barbarism; nothing could express better the lust of life, the dogged unwillingness to learn from experience, the contempt for rationality, the carelessness about perfection, the admiration for mere force, in which barbarism always betrays itself. The vague religion which seeks to justify this attitude is really only another outburst of the same irrational impulse.

In Browning this religion takes the name of Christianity, and identifies itself with one or two Christian ideas arbitrarily selected; but at heart it has far more affinity to the worship of Thor or of Odin than to the religion of the Cross. The zest of life becomes a cosmic emotion; we lump the whole together and cry, 'Hurrah for the Universe!' A faith which is thus a pure matter of lustiness and inebriation rises and falls, attracts or repels, with the ebb and flow of the mood from which it springs. It is invincible because unseizable; it is as safe from refutation as it is rebellious to embodiment. But it cannot enlighten or correct the passions on which it feeds. Like a servile priest, it flatters them in the name of Heaven. It cloaks

29

irrationality in sanctimony; and its admiration for every bluff folly, being thus justified by a theory, becomes a positive fanaticism, eager to defend any wayward impulse.

Such barbarism of temper and thought could hardly, in a man of Browning's independence and spontaneity, be without its counterpart in his art. When a man's personal religion is passive, as Shakespeare's seems to have been, and is adopted without question or particular interest from the society around him, we may not observe any analogy between it and the free creations of that man's mind. Not so when the religion is created afresh by the private imagination; it is then merely one among many personal works of art, and will naturally bear a family likeness to the others. The same individual temperament, with its limitations and its bias, will appear in the art which has appeared in the religion. And such is the case with Browning. His limitations as a poet are the counterpart of his limitations as a moralist and theologian; only in the poet they are not so regrettable. Philosophy and religion are nothing if not ultimate; it is their business to deal with general principles and final aims. Now it is in the conception of things fundamental and ultimate that Browning is weak; he is strong in the conception of things immediate. The pulse of the emotion, the bobbing up of the thought, the streaming of the reverie – these he can note down with picturesque force or imagine with admirable fecundity.

Yet the limits of such excellence are narrow, for no man can safely go far without the guidance of reason. His long poems have no structure – for that name cannot be given to the singular mechanical division of *The Ring and the Book*. Even his short poems have no completeness, no limpidity. They are little torsos made broken so as to stimulate the reader to the restoration of their missing legs and arms. What is admirable in them is pregnancy of phrase, vividness of passion and sentiment, heaped-up scraps of observation, occasional flashes of light, occasional beauties of versification – all like

> the quick sharp scratch
> And blue spurt of a lighted match.
> [*Meeting at Night*, 9–10]

There is never anything largely composed in the spirit of pure beauty, nothing devotedly finished, nothing simple and truly just. The poet's mind cannot reach equilibrium; at best he oscillates between opposed extravagances; his final word is still a *boutade*, still an explosion. He has no sustained nobility of style. He affects with the reader a confidential and vulgar manner, so as to be more sincere and to feel more at home. Even in the poems where the effort at impersonality is most successful, the dramatic disguise is usually thrown off in a preface, epilogue or parenthesis. The author likes to remind us of himself by some confidential wink or genial poke in the ribs, by some little interlarded sneer. We get in these tricks of manner a taste of that essential vulgarity, that indifference to purity and distinction, which is latent but pervasive in all the products of this mind. The same disdain of perfection which appears in his ethics appears here in his verse, and impairs its beauty by allowing it to remain too often obscure, affected, and grotesque.

Such a correspondence is natural: for the same powers of conception and expression are needed in fiction, which, if turned to reflection, would produce a good philosophy. Reason is necessary to the perception of high beauty. Discipline is indispensable to art. Work from which these qualities are absent must be barbaric; it can have no ideal form and must appeal to us only through the sensuousness and profusion of its materials. We are invited by it to lapse into a miscellaneous appreciativeness, into a subservience to every detached impression. And yet, if we would only reflect even on these disordered beauties, we should see that the principle by which they delight us is a principle by which an ideal, an image of perfection, is inevitably evoked. We can have no pleasure or pain, nor any preference whatsoever, without implicitly setting up a standard of excellence, an ideal of what would satisfy us there. To make these implicit ideals explicit, to catch their hint, to work out their theme, and express clearly to ourselves and to the world what they are demanding in the place of the actual – that is the labour of reason and the task of genius. The two cannot be divided. Clarification of ideas and disentanglement of values are as essential to aesthetic activity as to intelligence. A failure of reason is a failure of art and taste.

The limits of Browning's art, like the limits of Whitman's, can therefore be understood by considering his mental habit. Both poets had powerful imaginations, but the type of their imaginations was low. In Whitman imagination was limited to marshalling sensations in single file; the embroideries he made around that central line were simple and insignificant. His energy was concentrated on that somewhat animal form of contemplation, of which, for the rest, he was a great, perhaps an unequalled master. Browning rose above that level; with him sensation is usually in the background; he is not particularly a poet of the senses or of ocular vision. His favourite subject-matter is rather the stream of thought and feeling in the mind; he is the poet of soliloquy. Nature and life as they really are, rather than as they may appear to the ignorant and passionate participant in them, lie beyond his range. Even in his best dramas, like *A Blot in the 'Scutcheon* or *Colombe's Birthday*, the interest remains in the experience of the several persons as they explain it to us. The same is the case in *The Ring and the Book*, the conception of which, in twelve monstrous soliloquies, is a striking evidence of the poet's predilection for this form.

The method is, to penetrate by sympathy rather than to portray by intelligence. The most authoritative insight is not the poet's or the spectator's, aroused and enlightened by the spectacle, but the various heroes' own, in their moment of intensest passion. We therefore miss the tragic relief and exaltation, and come away instead with the uncomfortable feeling that an obstinate folly is apparently the most glorious and choiceworthy thing in the world. This is evidently the poet's own illusion, and those who do not happen to share it must feel that if life were really as irrational as he thinks it, it would be not only profoundly discouraging, which it often is, but profoundly disgusting, which it surely is not; for at least it reveals the ideal which it fails to attain.

This ideal Browning never disentangles. For him the crude experience is the only end, the endless struggle the only ideal, and the perturbed 'Soul' the only organon of truth. The arrest of his intelligence at this point, before it has envisaged any rational object, explains the arrest of his dramatic art at soliloquy. His immersion in the forms of self-consciousness prevents him from dramatizing the real relations of men and their thinkings to one another, to Nature, and to destiny. For in order to do so he would have had to view his characters from above (as Cervantes did, for instance), and to see them not merely as they appeared to themselves, but as they appear to reason. This higher attitude, however, was not only beyond Browning's scope, it was positively contrary to his inspiration. Had he reached it, he would no longer have seen the universe through the 'Soul', but through the intellect, and he would not have been able to cry, 'How the world is made for each of us!' [*By the Fireside*, 241]. On the contrary, the 'Soul' would have figured only in its true conditions, in all its ignorance and dependence, and also in its essential teachableness, a point against which Browning's barbaric wilfulness particularly rebelled. Rooted in his persuasion that the soul is essentially omnipotent and that to live hard can never be to live wrong, he remained fascinated by the march and method of self-consciousness, and never allowed himself to be weaned from that romantic fatuity by the energy of rational imagination, which prompts us not to regard our ideas as mere filling of a dream, but rather to build on them the conception of permanent objects and overruling principles, such as Nature, society, and the other ideals of reason. A full-grown imagination deals with these things, which do not obey the laws of psychological progression, and cannot be described by the methods of soliloquy.

We thus see that Browning's sphere, though more subtle and complex than Whitman's, was still elementary. It lay far below the spheres of social and historical reality in which Shakespeare moved; far below the comprehensive and cosmic sphere of every great epic poet. Browning did not even reach the intellectual plane of such contemporary poets as Tennyson and Matthew Arnold, who, whatever may be thought of their powers, did not study consciousness for itself, but for the sake of its meaning and of the objects which it revealed. The best things that come into a man's consciousness are the things that take him out of it – the rational things that are independent of his personal perception and of his personal existence. These he approaches with his reason, and they, in the same measure, endow him with their immortality. But precisely these things – the objects of science and of the constructive imagination – Browning always saw askance, in the outskirts of his field of vision, for his eye was fixed and riveted on the soliloquising Soul. And this Soul being, to his apprehension, irrational, did not give itself over to those permanent objects which might otherwise have occupied it, but ruminated on its own accidental emotions, on its love-affairs, and on its hopes of going on so ruminating for ever.

The pathology of the human mind – for the normal, too, is pathological when it is not referred to the ideal – the pathology of the human mind is a very interesting subject, demanding great gifts and great ingenuity in its treatment. Browning ministers to this interest, and possesses this ingenuity and these gifts. More than any other poet he keeps a kind of speculation alive in the now large body of sentimental, eager-minded people, who no longer can find in a definite religion a form and language for their imaginative life. That this service is greatly appreciated speaks well for the ineradicable tendency in man to study himself and his destiny. We do not deny the achievement when we point out its nature and limitations. It does not cease to be something because it is taken to be more than it is.

In every imaginative sphere the nineteenth century has been an era of chaos, as it has been an era of order and growing organisation in the spheres of science and of industry. An ancient doctrine of the philosophers asserts that to chaos the world must ultimately return. And what is perhaps true of the cycles of cosmic change is certainly true of the revolutions of culture. Nothing lasts for ever: languages, arts, and religions disintegrate with time. Yet the perfecting of such forms is the only criterion of progress; the destruction of them the chief evidence of decay. Perhaps fate intends that we should have, in our imaginative decadence, the consolation of fancying that we are still progressing, and that the disintegration of religion and the arts is bringing us nearer to the protoplasm of sensation and passion. If energy and actuality are all that we care for, chaos is as good as order, and barbarism as good as discipline – better, perhaps, since impulse is not then restrained within any bounds of reason or beauty. But if the powers of the human mind are at any time adequate to the task of digesting experience, clearness and order inevitably supervene. The moulds of thought are imposed upon Nature, and the conviction of a definite truth arises together with the vision of a supreme perfection. It is only at such periods that the human animal vindicates his title of rational. If such an epoch should return, people will no doubt retrace our present gropings with interest and see in them gradual approaches to their own achievement. Whitman and Browning might well figure then as representatives of our time. For the merit of being representative cannot be denied them. The mind of our age, like theirs, is choked with materials, emotional, and inconclusive. They merely aggravate our characteristics, and their success with us is due partly to their own absolute strength and partly to our common weakness. If once, however, this imaginative weakness could be overcome, and a form found for the crude matter of experience, men might look back from the height of a new religion and a new poetry upon the present troubles of the spirit; and perhaps even these things might then be pleasant to remember.[4]

NOTES

[1] [This refers to the essay, 'Platonic Love in Some Italian Poets', also to be found in Singer's collection, pp. 94–111: the poets in question are Dante, Guido Cavalcanti, Michelangelo, and Lorenzo de' Medici.]

[2] [Line 16 of 'Not with my Soul, Love' (*Ferishtah's Fancies*, 1884) reads 'Sense quenching Soul!']

[3] [cf. *Rabbi Ben Ezra*, 183–6, 'Not even while the whirl was worst, / Did I, to the wheel of life / With shapes and colours rife, / Bound dizzily, – mistake my end, to slake Thy thirst.']

[4] [Browning is defended against Santayana in: Helen Dryer Woodard, 'Santayana on Robert Browning: a Pessimist Criticism', *Poet-Lore*, XII (1901), pp. 97–111; Chesterton, *Browning* (EML), pp. 183–6; Margaret Sherwood, *Undercurrents of Influence in English Romantic Poetry* (1934), pp. 323–50; K. L. Knickerbocker, 'Robert Browning: a Modern Appraisal', *Tennessee Studies in Literature*, IV (1959), pp. 1–12. See also W. O. Raymond, 'Browning's *The Statue and the Bust*', *UTQ*, XXVIII (1959), pp. 233–49; R. W. Hartle, 'Gide's Interpretation of Browning', *U. of Texas Studies in English*, XXVIII (1949), pp. 244–56; J. H. Miller, *Disappearance of God*, pp. 81–156.]

PERCY LUBBOCK

ROBERT BROWNING

I T is a hundred years since Browning was born, but less than half
that time since his work began to find a place, create an influence,
become a familiar and treasured possession, in the English mind.
If we would review the meaning which it now has for us, it is obvious that the centenary of his birth is an altogether arbitrary
moment to choose for the task. A completed century does indeed
carry with it, by a long habit of association, a sort of moral
meaning, of which we reasonably forget that it springs from nothing
more moral than a mere system of notation; but our date, though
it has thus a relation to Browning's biography, has none to the history
of his work or his influence, the beginning of which can be fixed
at no definite point. Yet the custom of considering a man's
work on such an occasion has a certain convenience which is none
the worse for being no more than practical. Although of Browning
at any rate – who at fifty-five could still throw his challenge to the
British public with no assurance that it would 'like him yet' [cf.
The Ring and the Book, XII, 835] – it cannot be said that his
poetry has rested long enough in British memories for its place and
quality to be now matters adjudged, there has been, even in his case,
time for the evaporation of many misconceptions from which no
critical sense (not to speak of the merely British) can free itself
without help from time. Uncritical blame, unreasonable objections,
dispose of themselves readily enough; but even the more baffling
obscurations of praise – praise rightly addressed but spreading too
wide, concealing its object, praise which bewildered by eddying al-

From *The Quarterly Review*, CCXVII (1912), pp. 437–57.

together away from the mark, in some quite other direction – may well have been dispersed by now. It is certainly not for their much indebted successors to disparage the first of the faithful, the earliest tenders of the shrine, who indeed reacted in their own sense no more freely than was needed to put an end to neglect and repel prejudice. They produced a body of criticism and annotation which must help later critics at all points, and not least where they least feel able to subscribe to it. At the same time, if Browning's centenary is a convenient moment at which to speak of his poetry, it is so because conditions, as they say of the weather, may be held to be now normal. Browning may be attacked or praised, but in either case the gusto born of the consciousness that we are opposing here a coterie, there the world at large, has long ceased to flutter the nerves of criticism. *Pippa Passes, Men and Women, The Ring and the Book,* now belong to us all; and we may read them more simply at least, if not more searchingly, than was once possible. At any rate it is quite certain that we do read them, and that there will be a ready welcome for the new and handsome edition which is being issued under the superintendence of Mr F. G. Kenyon.[1] The aspect of these volumes is as admirable as the tact which has gone to the making of the illustrative and biographical notes, few but fit, with which each is introduced. Our view of Browning has changed its angle in the twenty and more years since his death; but it has never shifted away from him, and we may try to summarise what we see.

The change of angle has, in the first place, certainly seemed to show us that Browning, 'ever a fighter' as he declared himself [*Prospice*, 13], was involved by fate in a more insidious conflict than he perceived, and that all unawares he failed to make good his position in it. The battle of life, as enacted on the surface, was a straightforward engagement enough; and indeed, to turn from the clash and clatter of the exhortations, the renunciations, the defiances voiced in so many of his poems, to the extraordinary felicity of his actual circumstances from first to last, is to feel that the vigorous rain of blows misses its echo on the defences of the adversary, for the sufficient reason that the adversary has never presented himself. Browning was armed and eager, but it so happened that there were no giants in his path to slay. Privation, or what to his simple demands would have been privation, never came near him. No necessity, no disability, not even any self-contradiction of his own temperament, interfered with his life-long dedication to his proper work; the pang of expression thwarted, for whatever reason, seems to have been quite unknown to him. He knew great sorrow, but not the cruelties of sorrow bitter and unnatural. Within and without, his life was one of the most singularly fortunate that genius can ever have known. This must be insisted on, not in the least for the disparagement of his spirit and courage – for in spite of a little unnecessary bluster and a few protestations that might have been taken for granted, these had a soundness and sanity which disaster could only have tempered more finely – but in order to emphasise the point that his destiny might seem to have drawn aside and held back on purpose to give him room for a complete realisation of himself. Moreover, he was not of those who need pressure from without, some stricter schooling than uninterrupted liberty and felicity, to evoke the best of their mind and strength. His was a strength that could do no less than exercise itself to the full, a mind which, so far as concerned activity, was its own discipline. And besides, it is to be remarked that one dangerous indulgence was withheld until long past the time when it might have been a danger; and that was such a favouring audience as, for example, counted for so much in Tennyson's later development. Browning's originality flowed from the very first in such deeply-cut lines that indulgence of this kind would probably indeed never have affected him to his hurt; but the want of it may be noted as yet a further chance in favour of a serene unhampered use of his gift. Browning, if any poet who ever lived, could be himself.

And yet, for all that, one needs only to re-read his work, only to feel its matchless energy, its various power, its swift and sudden beauty, close in upon the mind and call out with undiminished keenness the old responses; no less unmistakable, in the end, than its power and virtue is the sense that it has not in fact developed in harmony with itself. There was an undertow the effect of which can be discerned here and there throughout his work, and which finally mastered and redirected the conflicting impulse that was surely more thoroughly and originally his own. Browning had little to fear from any confessed hostility of fate; but fate had planned a more ingenious device than an open attack. This prodigal, restless, inquisitive mind, passionately awake, instantly appreciative of the gifts of life, was thrown into a time when appreciation, curiosity, creative energy, could indeed find as ample material and as free a play as at any moment in history, but always on a condition liable in the circumstances to be very dangerous to them. The condition was that they should justify themselves to the age's rather vulgar conception of moral and material usefulness – a condition, as it is not now the mode to question, entirely rational in itself, but which presupposes a more disciplined self-criticism than was abroad at that remarkable moment.

Browning, while it would have been impossible for open pressure to have deflected him from what he proposed to do, was by the very nature of his endowment particularly exposed to the invisible pressure of the moral atmosphere in which he might find himself. All his affinities brought him out into the open. Far from taking shelter from life, he had not even his back to the wall; he stood forward with life all round him. He flung his mind wide to it and absorbed it, delighted with its staring colours, fascinated by its grotesque shapes and contrasts. These he could deal with, we know how consummately; but with the rest he appropriated moral and intellectual standards which needed a different treatment, one which it was not in him to give. He could not criticise them; that is why we are able to say that the first impulse we distinguished, the impulse to fasten, in an ecstasy of perception, on things seen, and to represent them in all their sharpness, was more truly characteristic. When he became a moralist he could only bring to the task the same energy; and all his acuteness in disentangling the moods of men and women, all his quickness in seizure and presentation, availed nothing beside the fact that, though he could dramatise their application, he could not really criticise the standards themselves which were offered him. Anarchy in the ideal world troubled him as little (or rather pleased him as much) as the fantastic jumble of objects displayed in the market-place, when 'June was the month, Lorenzo named the Square' [*The Ring and the Book*, I, 90]; indeed they both affected him in much the same way. As he stands before the booths, we may feel with him the easy sweep of vision with which he takes in the scattered unrelated fragments, and the glow of exhilaration with which they are noted, absorbed, fastened in the brain. Their trivial incongruity is a stimulus and a challenge, a brisk crossplay of suggestion, where the delight lies, not in the quality of the suggestion, but in the sense of the rapid brushing of all manner of unexpected points of life. So in the world of ideas his delight was in the process itself, in the mercurial dance of thought, till thought will accept no other fulfilment than to go dancing on for ever. Thus Browning could be satisfied with the self-stultifying conclusion that energy was its own end and conflict its own eternal reward. He could celebrate the antagonism between good and evil without caring for the implication that, if it is the fight itself which is the one essential, the names of the antagonists could be exchanged without spoiling the moral.

Browning, in short, was a spiritual adventurer born out of due time. His rich endowment, the seething flood of originality which was set in such contrast with the broadly civilised tradition that Keats had established and Tennyson was already adorning, seems designed for a different opportunity than that which it received. In these days, when we are forbidden to use the old labels which were once so helpful, when no edges may remain definite and no classification unqualified, it is possibly rash to speak of the Renaissance as a time when an exceptional burst of sight and sound gave, for those who were fit for it, a unique opportunity for seeing and hearing. Let us at least make the claim that, if ever there was a time resembling in this respect our old-fashioned idea of the Renaissance, that would have been the moment for Browning as for no other poet since Shakespeare. To picture a world of new learning, with possibilities of spiritual flight suddenly thrown open in every direction, new discoveries with the turning of a page, new castles of imagination at the hearing of a word, new sympathies and curiosities at the chance sight of a face, is to feel that among poets of later times it is Browning whom we would set there if we could, he who would respond to it most freely and reproduce it most worthily. At such a moment there could be little time for sitting in judgment or weighing moral values. To represent would be the only preoccupation, the only regret that the stream passed so swiftly that the spectator could not make sure of missing nothing. Browning's quick-eyed vigilance, his tireless nerves, his very unfastidiousness – how perfectly they would there be in place! Our sense of what Browning was, of what he has meant to us and what we owe him, expresses itself adequately perhaps in the mere wish that he might have had Shakespeare's chance.

This we may say without exaggerating the extent to which his own chance was unfortunate. Whatever it lacked, the age to which he was born was certainly not an age of exhausted vitality or starved refinements; and, indeed, it has its obvious points of likeness to the picture just suggested. At any rate it amassed its abundance of impressions and ideas with the stout appetite of heroes. But it was not an adventurous time, and it strikes us rather as jovially or heavily feasting on the profusion spread out before it, than as dashing irrepressibly forth to discover and explore. We feel that in the Elizabethan consciousness, for example, there was a temper, nervous and robust at the same time, which is not to be found either in the robust self-satisfactions or in the nervous self-denunciations of the middle decades of the nineteenth century. Genius was lavished upon those decades as it has only been at the most magnificent moments in the history of art; and if, in the curious loss of the sense of formal beauty, it could be little trained in habits of discipline, that again could be matched at such moments. It is not the pervading want of discipline, but the pervading want of enterprise, which is of importance when we consider the effect of his time on Browning. It was not in his nature to sit still while good things were set before him. He would be out, rummaging, ransacking, probing, long before the board was spread. But he finds himself, as he turns over the glittering heaps, in a world which, in imposing the demand that things should be useful, gets itself into a false position by adding that they must be definitely and patently useful, and that too this very minute; in other words, the moral of any artistic transaction must be immediately definable and applicable, it being oddly assumed that this aspect of the case, the one demanding for true judgment the widest knowledge and synthetic power, was just that which anybody could ban or bless offhand.

Into this world Browning, then, brings his vibrating sensitiveness to all that is being said or done or exposed around him, and his urgent curiosity as to what is being thought. He hears an anecdote, and the picture embodying it surges into his mind with the effect of a sudden sound. He intercepts a glance, and the story it tells is before him in an instant, or would be, but that already another explanation has substituted another motive, to be ousted as quickly in its turn. He lights upon old books, and a dark phrase or a detail of obscure legend strikes the same spark with as little difficulty. He even at first seems to have no time to feel and live, in any rarer sense, on his own account. 'It is his way,' his wife later on could still write of him, 'to *see* things as passionately as others feel them'; and certainly, in his earlier years at any rate, he could close tightly with experience, master its reality, on terms which would have kept another mind in a state of sterile detachment. But his lighting power of assimilation, doubled with this power of doing without any keenly intimate life of his own, could not help him to the judging and appraising of values, if he should wish to proceed beyond the mere representation of them. And here comes in that unsuspected pressure of the atmosphere in which he lived. I am not, of course, alluding to any direct demand from imperious auditors, for we are still at the time when 'he who praised and read and wrote/Was apt to find himself the self-same me' [*The Ring and the Book*, I, 1384–5]; but to the diffused spirit which was just the one thing he could not see, and which, therefore, had him at discretion. It is as though the injunction to moralise as well as dramatise, to reason as well as represent, were conveyed to him in his sleep, so that he woke up thinking it was his own idea; where, if it had been offered him openly, he would simply have seized and dramatised the demand itself. Add to this that the spirit, as we have said, was decidedly unenterprising, easily satisfied, and as easily bullied; and it will be seen that it was no happy influence for a dramatist. As it was, Browning led it a pretty dance, and made it somewhat breathlessly recognise that at any rate all its first judgments were wrong. But he was in the position of his own Blougram, offering arguments good enough for his critic, and lacking the stimulus of a capable opponent, who would not be bewildered by being caught out on separate points, and who might have demanded a more embracing synthesis.

A point already so freely conceded as that Browning was no philosopher need not be further laboured; but it would be impossible to speak of him to any purpose without in some measure dealing with it, if only because the concession has sometimes been made with what is surely too little discretion. We need not claim, in granting it, that Browning's very inconsistency and incompleteness of thought make him somehow more intimately a poet than those who have desired to complete the broken arcs and to formulate a more final end than his mere glorification of the means. If we believe in poetry at all, we must say that it transcends all other search for truth, but not that it transcends by evading it. Moreover, Browning considered himself, and in a sense was, pre-eminently a dramatist; and the quality of his drama is closely involved with the ease with which he satisfied himself intellectually, compared with his inexhaustible voracity for types and motives and instances. His plays, strictly so-called, are not perhaps much read; but the reason for this would appear to be that no modern poetic plays are read. The assertion that they are unfitted for the stage and would be ineffective there must no doubt be accepted in the practically complete absence of any evidence for or against it; for a playgoer will hardly maintain that their obvious dramatic weakness, in some respects, is proof in itself. But, granted the point, if we are never to expect to see embodied their equally obvious interest and beauty, that might surely be an additional reason for reading them. When we have done so, we find that they have a charm which it would seem a good little problem for the stage to try to reproduce; also, what is to our immediate point, they have a great deal to tell us about Browning.

In the first place, their position as a more or less compact group in the earlier period of his writings (the last of them is dated 1846), while it shows his eventual decision, for whatever reason, that the play-form was not for him, shows also the enterprise, the masterly self-possession with which he started on his work. If the faults of his plays were the faults of immaturity, they would not be worth lingering over; for a youthful poet is a youthful poet, and though he may tell us about youth (if that is what we are asking for), he will not necessarily tell us much about himself individually. But Browning, at any rate after *Pauline*, was never youthful in this sense; he had entered into complete control of himself and his manner in more than time to be able to sit down at four-and-twenty and produce a fully elaborated play 'on commission'; writing blank verse as unmistakably his own, for its fearless attack, its resilience, its sound texture, as the verse of *The Ring and the Book*. And more than this, his plays have a decorative economy which is perhaps the quality we should least expect in the first flowering of so exuberant a genius as his. *Colombe's Birthday*, for example, whatever else may be said of it, is an admirable piece of decoration, fitted securely into its frame, entangled with no more material than it needs, and worked out with a freshness and sweetness which make it one of the most lovable of all his productions. If some of the plays do not trace themselves so surely, there is the same lucidity of design in two such touching motives of irony as *King Victor and King Charles* and *A Soul's Tragedy*. With these before us we cannot say that Browning had not mastered the dramatic form in so far as that demands the orderly and gradual figuration of an idea. The notion that he could never tell a story without turning it upside down at the start and forgetting to right it again, was doubtless born (and no unnatural birth) of our struggles, early and late, to understand the story of *Sordello*; but beyond *Sordello* it has little or no application. It is true that in the more complicated situations of plays like *Strafford* or *The Return of the Druses*, the curve is not so firmly followed as in those just mentioned; while in one, *A Blot in the 'Scutcheon*, the sombre beauty of the treatment only exposes pitilessly the hapless absurdity of the plot. Yet with every reservation made, it is not in the shaping or the handling of these plays that we shall find Browning by temperament at cross-purposes with drama.

That which surely, whether consciously or no, turned him from the set play-form to the dramatic monologue with which he had

44

started, was his lack of power to grasp a character, as opposed to his immense and varied power to grasp a mood. It is not for nothing that in most of his plays unity of time is so closely observed, the action being often practically continuous, or at most contained within a limited number of hours. This device does not, of course, in true drama, meet the difficulty of the writer who sees his personages only in the light of the particular situation, but it disguises it. Character is character and mood is mood, however short or long the exposure; and tragic drama absolutely demands the figure in the round, even though we may immediately be concerned with but one aspect of it. To say that Browning's plays are undramatic by reason of their allusive quickness and the difficulty of following it without time for reflection, is beside the point; for there is nothing essential in such ineffectiveness as would be abolished by a sharpening, however unexpected, of our wits. The point would rather be that, whereas the language, the arrangement, the apparatus, are all sturdily dramatic, the figures themselves, so nimble and lively and intelligent as they are, are embodied only by the exigencies of the moment, seem struck into life by the momentary embarrassment or felicity, and so cannot hold our attention as lives to be lived. Such a contention as this naturally could not be made good except with elaborate examination and quotation from the works themselves, impossible here; but it will be borne out if we feel that the pleasure they have given in the reading has been essentially the pleasure of watching moment break in on moment, each caught up so responsively by these finely-tuned intelligences; the dissatisfaction at the end of it all, hardly to be avoided, being due to the fact that we have been more conscious of this play of events on them, the agile interlacing of action and re-action, than of the men and women, the human stuff in whose interest the scene was set. It is delightful to wonder what Colombe, Luitolfo [in *A Soul's Tragedy*], Luria, will do, they are so certain to do something rare and surprising and poignant. What they were before, what they will be presently, in what sense they have developed, are questions which are allowed to drop, and which, when it is all over, reappear still unanswered.

It will be seen, then, what was meant by the suggestion that

45

Browning's drama is concerned with the admitted bluntness of his constructive ideas. Just as, speaking generally, we find him perceiving like an angel and rationalising like the very human Briton he was; so, on that side of character-drawing which is analysis, he cannot be surpassed for certainty and swiftness of touch, while, when it comes to the synthetic grasp of the myriad fragments, he fails us. There is not a case which, as it arises, he cannot instantly take possession of. A single hint, and he is off along the line it suggests and back again with a dozen of its implications. But his own interest in the question at issue is so keen that it positively weakens his sense of its dramatic value. The particular dilemma presents itself to him less as a matter involved in certain lives and brought about by certain circumstances than as one to be instantly confronted and resolved. All the wits of all the people concerned dart forward to the work; the resolution is exquisitely accomplished, and the maze of fine feelings and perceptions, intricate as it often becomes, never cheats the attention it asks for, but proves to have been traced with perfect lucidity. And if again and again we feel that what the action lacks is not beauty or order, but simply weight – if we enjoy watching these spiritual intrigues disentangled and forget all about the human beings who are doing it – that is because Browning himself has seen the innumerable ways in which they would act and react upon each other so much more clearly than he has seen their own substance. He was, indeed, later to show a power of character-drawing beyond anything to be found in the plays: Guido and Pompilia and Caponsacchi are characters conceived and held in the fullest sense; and it might seem that the lack of any figures to put beside them from the plays is merely a mark of immaturity. Already, however, in *Paracelsus*, and again in *Pippa Passes*, Browning had shown that he worked more happily in a mixed manner – a loose structure approaching the device of the monologue, or a simple juxtaposition of scenes, unified by a lyrical embroidery running round and through them. The different problems thus arising, to be considered in a moment, were more suited to his hand; and after *Luria* he never wrote another play.[2]

All this does not for a moment mean that he was not in a more restricted sense a dramatic poet, or that he was ever interested in his intrigue to the point of forgetting that he was speaking 'in character'. His handling of these cases is not abstract; it is always in sharp concrete terms of human beings. We touch here upon a not unknown confusion of criticism in dealing with dramatic and creative genius. It is sometimes suggested, for example, that Shakespeare's amazing power of creating character is expressed by saying that he utterly identifies himself with every one of his own inventions, himself slipping through our fingers (as at any rate he used to slip) and defying our definition of his own qualities. It is rather Browning who identifies himself with his characters, with the double result that his drama is incomplete, and that no poet has written his own temperament more legibly over all his work. The creative writer is, in fact, creative exactly in so far as he refrains from merging himself in his productions. He keeps outside them; it is his detachment from them that enables him to seize them so firmly; they are far more to him than mere agents in the particular matter he is exhibiting. It is when he tries to portray himself, or rather such a character as lies nearest to his own sympathies, that the result is apt to be unsatisfying. It was not because Browning failed to feel with his characters, but exactly because he felt with them too promptly and easily, that his drama wants body. He became them so thoroughly that he could not see them. It will be noted, then, how right was the instinct which led him once for all away from the play to the dramatic monologue, the dramatic idyl, the dramatic lyric. This was the field in which everything that was fine and just in his plays could be utilised, and where that which in them was shortcoming became the appropriate and the harmonious.

The monologue is essentially a picture, and there seems no end to the pictorial effects which Browning could obtain through verse. They sprang up under his hand so readily that it is easy to overlook the tact and delicacy of adjustment which was needed for such poems as *The Bishop orders his Tomb at St Praxed's* or *How it strikes a Contemporary*. The form which Browning used to such splendid purpose is by no means a simple one, though it arises naturally enough. If other literary divisions, as lyric, elegy, epigram, have their

47

counterparts in the passing moods of the day, moods which may visit any man from moment to moment, the monologue stands for the pleasant hour of rumination, an hour which certainly has as good a claim to be translated into art as any of the twenty-four. So are born poems like how many of Browning's most beautiful and best beloved – *By the Fireside*, *Two in the Campagna*, *Love among the Ruins* – it is enough to name their names; the inrush into the mind, as we do so, of warmth and colour and serenity may show us how near these things lie to the moments which are the pith and core of life. From this mood of impassioned reflection, then, springs the monologue, readily taking to itself a more and more dramatic shape – so much so that we hardly notice the difficulty it assumes when in place of the drift and eddy of meditation or soliloquy it represents spoken words addressed to a silent interlocutor. On one side it is still reflective, still half-lyrical; on the other, as it deals with a defined situation or incident, it has to make some sort of terms with the dramatic proprieties which it has already flouted by its postulated restrictions. Its artificiality – the tirade which we are to imagine as listened to but never answered, the dialogue of which we are only to hear one side – is obviously very great; and this artificiality, instead of being its own rococo effect, is to be veiled and disguised, so that, while we feel the presence of the silent partner in the debate, we may not be embarrassed by his lack of response. It should be but a few situations, one might suppose, and those subdued in tone, which could be capable of being so treated. Browning, however, in the high manner of genius so distracting to the wistful critic, takes in hand this fragile toy, treats it with entire liberty, puts it to impossible uses, and achieves with it a succession of splendid living poems in which the monologue finally becomes everything that it could not be. It riots in *Fra Lippo Lippi* as easily as it dreams in *Andrea del Sarto*; it converses (as one may almost say) in *Mr Sludge*, '*the Medium*' as naturally as it muses to itself in *Prince Hohenstiel-Schwangau*. He has not overstepped the limitations of the monologue, which remain where they were; but he has shown us, as a poet will, that, though we may point out what success demands, we may never say that the demand is an impossible one.

Among these superb pictures of temperament and manners there is not one which does not show to the full those two sides of Browning's genius which are his passionate appreciation of things seen and his instant sympathy with a condition of mind. Now it is the mind of a particular time and place, as in *The Bishop orders his Tomb*, in which the mark of a whole culture upon a whole century is given in little more than a hundred packed lines; and in half the space almost as much as is done in *My Last Duchess*. Now it is the mind of all times and all places, wherever the instinctive mixture of respect and suspicion and patronage is called out by the presence of a real living poet whom we may pass walking in the street. Now, sharply individualised, it is the mind of the suspected or detected prevaricator, scouring itself in the luxury of sincerity. The closely knit lucidity, the relieved colour, the brilliant life of these things, are beyond praise; and it may be remarked, as bearing on a previous suggestion that in all the best of them the initial germ is in the figure of the imagined speaker himself, not in the case he is to plead or the doctrine he is to preach. The question is not what there is to be said for spiritualism, but what Mr Sludge would or could say; not whether Bishop Blougram is justified, but how he would justify himself. The distinction is in any case vital for dramatic force, which is, of course, prejudiced by the least hint that the helpless speaker is being used as a mouth-piece. It is especially important in Browning's case, since for him to pass from the special pleading of an observed or invented personage to speculation on his own account, is simply to leave the region where he is supreme and unapproached for that in which he is, to say the most of it, but one of all the rest. So early as *A Death in the Desert* we see the beginning of the temptation which was to take him so far away from his best work. By the time he reached *Fifine at the Fair*, he could show what havoc might be made of a fine poem, vigorously and vividly attacked, by shifting the centre of gravity from the speaker to the subject he is debating. Even of *La Saisiaz* we can say that, if he had put it into the mouth of an imaginary inquirer and kept it there, it would have been a poem.

How Browning, in years of continuous work at the very top of his power, concentrated all the forces and all the subtleties of the monologue to fill the daring design of *The Ring and the Book*, is a subject that asks for other and worthier treatment than can here be given; it is better passed over altogether than trifled with in a paragraph. It is, moreover, the easier to omit it that my object has been rather to emphasise certain aspects of Browning's poetry than to examine particular poems; and in this connection *The Ring and the Book* would give only fuller, weightier, more magnificent illustrations of points I have already been concerned with. It has everything in the world to say to the dramatic and pictorial scope of his poetry, gathering up as it does all the keenness of delineation, all the abounding energy, all the ripeness of style and diction, which are to be found in the rest of his work, into one supreme culmination. But it stands apart from the considerations for which the pages here available must be saved, for which, moreover, much else that it would be easy to linger over must be sacrificed. The whole question, for instance, how and where Browning found his subjects (as to which *The Ring and the Book* is almost alone in explaining itself) attracts by its many obscurities, and would lead seductively on to his power of awaking the past by means of an erudition doubtless more curious than exhaustive. His language, his metres, his very rhymes, might furnish points of departure for developments which still wait to be worked out, bearing upon his detachment from what in his day was the main stream of poetry. But his purely lyrical poems, hardly touched on yet, compel with beauty of so rare a quality that other issues must be left.

There is and there ever will be but one biography of Browning which tells us about him to any purpose, and that is his own works. We shall never know, we who can only know him there, how it may have been that the author of *Love among the Ruins*, *Any Wife to any Husband*, *Confessions*, was so completely hidden behind the sound conventional figure made familiar to us by many sketches from many of his friends; for even they at the most can only tell us that so it was. It is not surely because we are so innocent as to expect a poet always to exhibit a rolling eye and a frenzied gait, that this blankness strikes us as an enigma. We know that a poet does not eat his supper

in a room
Blazing with lights, four Titians on the wall,
And twenty naked girls to change his plate.
            [*How it strikes a Contemporary*, 75–7]

But the man who went up and down Valladolid had, we remember, something in his mien which curiosity, a little to its discomfort, could not altogether fathom.

Oh, you might smile! There wanted not a touch,
A tang of . . . well, it was not wholly ease
As back into your mind the man's look came.
                          [ibid., 47–9]

The touch, the tang, seems never to have been discerned in the case of the poet who went up and down London – not even, we may add, when it was in an atmosphere richer in its admonitions than that of Bayswater, not even when it was Rome or Florence that he went up and down. The outer and inner Browning will not, when all is said, form a single picture; and we shall never get near his poetry by trying to reach it through his life.

The deadlock can be admitted, but it cannot be passed by or forgotten; when all is said we shall always try to say more. It is not merely the heights and the depths of the play of emotion in Browning's lyrics that force us into the dilemma; it is not that he could identify himself with the sweep of passion, when life is stripped of its everyday meanings to be glorified with a new one. To understand and express the passion which, far from owning any connection with daily things, is the negation of them, seems in the circumstances a less unlikely feat than to do what Browning did. Before trying to define what that was, it is worth dwelling on the kind of lyrical expression which is most akin to what we call the normal, the central, and (in no depreciatory sense) the conventional. The treatment of passionate love as though nothing in life rhymed with it but nightingales' songs and the flush of roses and the silver of moonlight, is often derided as the traditional extravagance of poets, more often indulged as a fantasy appropriate to their romantic needs. Men and women – such would be the implication – exchange their loves to a sterner tune than the nerves of poets could endure; they know that real life is not so romantically staged, and they do not ask that it should be. There could not, as a matter of fact, be a greater fallacy. It is not only the legendary poet, it is the most prudent and approved of normal hearts which, when its hour strikes, cannot find anything in the world to harmonise with itself but that which lies above the roof and outside the four walls of ordinary life. To escape from life is nothing; everybody has done so for a moment, the poet only for a little longer than the rest. They return, and sooner or later the poet returns; but it is futile to say that until he does so he is moving in regions too impalpable for others. The poet might round on us and say that he has been but following our own lead. The night of stars, the nightingale in the cedar, were what we ourselves demanded and all we seemed able to understand. We shall have to rise to further flights than the romance which thus uttered itself, if we are to be shown the more difficult secrets of a poet's insight. Not the evasion of life, which anyhow claims us again soon enough, but the translation of the whole of it to the level of passion – that was Browning's achievement, and it has almost been his alone.

No one else, not Shakespeare himself, has written poetry of this order in an atmosphere where life – life which, whatever happens, has to be lived from day to day – can be sustained and continued. Nothing in the necessities of ordinary existence is contradicted by these poems at their greatest intensity. If in Browning's plays we scarcely feel the characters to survive the intrigue in which they are presented, in his lyrics we find a contrast to this in the sense that the pictured mood is nowhere severed from what came before or is to follow after. Browning called his lyrics dramatic, meaning that they were not direct, but imaginative expressions. But his concern here is not with the characters who speak, only with the phase through which, as they speak, life is passing; and the phase may be what it will – a flame of rapture, or the darkest shadow of humiliation and self-abasement – life still asserts itself and goes forward. The passion that can have no imaginable issue but doom and annihilation he did indeed represent; but he represented it with a difference which becomes plain if we put *In a Gondola* or *Porphyria's Lover* beside *In a Year or Two in the Campagna* – an exquisitely poised and fantastic piece of rococo beside the sudden kindling of an experience which has struck home, it matters not whether actually or by imagination. The tortuous and not very happy poem *Dîs Aliter Visum*, shows a man and woman on the brink of a happiness which might have been seized and appropriated, but is allowed to slip precisely because the man, 'who is old and knows too much', cannot believe in the possibility of keeping the succeeding years, stretching ahead, at the pitch of the single lyrical hour on the cliff-top. He is right, if the poets are to be trusted; such an hour can only be prolonged at the cost of the wrench of disillusion. He was wrong, the woman tells him years later; such hours are nothing if they cannot be worked into the whole fabric and given a meaning. This is what Browning does, not by the mere domestication of such raptures, not by taming them to suit the fireside and the family circle, but simply by keeping them clear of the influences of decay.

His, in short, is the passion which has not for an instant shrunk from the work of understanding itself. There is, to our misfortune, nothing in life which makes this an inevitable venture. Indeed, there is nothing so easy to misunderstand as that which everybody knows, nothing which so readily acquiesces in conventional judgments as that which everybody possesses the means to judge. So, for example, of art, the expression of a pleasure shared by all, we make a private and incalculable inspiration, revealed only to a chosen few. And so, too, of passion. Here, indeed, with the best will in the world to misapprehend, we cannot refuse to confess its universality, but we easily make up for that by denying its continuity with life – deepest of pleasures, loveliest of life's ornaments, but a thing which has its places and its seasons, and which in other places and different seasons will be certainly intrusive and probably mischievous. To Browning it is, indeed, a beauty and a delight; but it is both of these in a way and for a reason that conventional standards will little help us to appreciate. We must shift our view, and see it, not as one of life's good things, but as the rhythm by which all good things are unified and made significant. There is only one means of attaining this clarity; and the first step is to control the lazy prepossession that there is anything worth understanding which can be understood without labour or thought. In nearly the whole of Browning's poetry there is no touch that is either hysterical or sentimental; and we may measure, if we can, the difference in the colour of life which is induced by such freedom. If, in a few well-known pieces, sentiment may seem to be played with a little insincerely, if, in a few others, the exuberance is lacking in simplicity, these are momentary interruptions in the steady comprehension with which the working of passion in human life is faced. Sentimentality never fronts the real issue at all: hysteria clouds it. Browning's grave and searching realism evades no difficulties here, and never condescends to the idea that beauty is exquisite or pleasure rare if either is thought of as separable from the sum of life.

Thus it is, then, that he is able to linger among the emotional refinements and ingenuities which he so loves to explore, without forfeiting in their minuteness the ardour and glow of passionate beauty. His passion is living and enduring because it has understood that nothing can endure – however brilliant its moment of climax – which is discontinuous with all else. There are features in his work, obvious enough, which have suggested to some an affinity between his treatment of these themes and that which is to be seen in the lyrical poems of Donne; and indeed, if we must have an anti-type in literature to Browning's lyric, it is there if anywhere that we shall find it.[3] But Donne, precisely, bringing the same fire to the same intricacies of experience, shows only too often how easily the simplicity of true passion may be damaged in the quest for an ever closer notation of the labyrinth. His overcharged brain drives him into an extravagance of discrimination before he has reached the inner lucidity which alone ensures proportion. Browning, with a brain far inferior, indeed, for keenness and force, could yet indulge to all lengths its subtlety of perception, without losing his relation to reality, because he had once for all achieved simplicity first. And if it was this that gave him his control over complexity, it is to this, and to nothing less, that is due the entirely unique savour of his style. Browning's handling of words, in the best of his lyric poetry, becomes more and more of a wonder, the deeper they fix themselves in the mind; and we end – where we do not perhaps begin – by discovering, under their appearance of informality, how instantly sensitive they prove themselves to his touch. Their response is so quick that the movement by which they slip into their places escapes us; they do not make the gesture, of one sort or another, that in other writers enables us to watch the process of expression. It is an artless judgment which concludes that with Browning there was no process, that language was an obstacle to his bursting thought, which he broke down unscrupulously, careless so long as his thought got through. Language, rather, obeyed the candour of his passion, and answered by yielding him effects of beauty which, when we look at the extreme simplicity of the means, it seems impossible to analyse.

To every lover of these poems a different instance will at once present itself. They hang in the memory irresistibly and (as it may often appear) unaccountably. They persist when a hundred things, of which we more clearly understand the beauty, droop and lose their charm. There are stanzas of *By the Fireside*, of *James Lee's Wife*, of *Mesmerism*, of *Love among the Ruins*, of a score more, which seem to have caught us by accident, for nothing that they say or any way in which they say it; it happened so. They have music without any recognized harmonies; loftiness without any heightened expression; pathos without pathetic device; passion without a passionate word. Where we can definitely point to the means, as we can, for example, in *The Last Ride Together*, *Evelyn Hope*, *May and Death*, and a few others, we probably feel in the end that the ring of the poem is not entirely true. The poems that last, the poems that we never exhaust, seem mysteriously to have caught a note of style for which no precept can be laid down, but which can be described by saying that it possesses the fringe of values, the associated harmonics, of the *spoken* word. Between writing and speaking (by which, it should possibly be noted, I do not at all mean oratory or recitation) there lies a chasm which tempts an effort to sound and measure it. Mere differences between the formal and the informal, the plain and the coloured, are negligible when it comes to the discrimination between the moral and emotional values of a word picked up from a written page, and those which it bears when a voice utters it as the immediate symbol proposed by the brain. These values Browning incessantly captures

E

for the written word; if a quotation is desired it might be any of a hundred, and may be this:

> But he looked upon the city, every side,
>   Far and wide,
> All the mountains topped with temples, all the glades'
>   Colonnades,
> All the causeys, bridges, aqueducts – and then,
>   All the men!   [*Love among the Ruins*, 61–6]

'All the men!' It is not a line in a written poem; it is a *remark*, suddenly dropped to us by an urgent and present imagination, to which the listener reacts as instinctively as to an unexpected voice. And here is another, sharper and finer in its subdued sadness:

> Was it something said,
>   Something done,
> Vexed him? was it touch of hand,
>   Turn of head?
> Strange! that very way
>   Love begun:
> I as little understand
>   Love's decay.
>   [*In a Year*, 9–16]

A direct association, not a transmitted portrayal of passion and beauty – this is what we seem to find; and it holds us till we may likely be surprised to see how acute a divergence of mind and temperament has been altogether forgotten. Browning, in many articles of his creed, and not those which he would have felt to be least important, is very remote from us now. Yet of the poetry of the nineteenth century there is none which has had more continuous power over new generations, and certainly none which appeals to nearly so great a diversity of spirit. Lovers of Browning are of no definite sort or complexion, and they do not, perhaps, always love each other. But they have all discovered, and they perpetually renew the discovery, that the mind can pour itself into the endless variety of these poems, sure of finding support and comprehension and fulfilment.[4]

NOTES

[1] [*The Works of Robert Browning*, ed. F. G. Kenyon, Centenary edition in ten volumes (London, 1912), of which this essay is a review.]

[2] [For the plays cf. Honan, *Characters*, especially Chapters II and III, pp. 41–103.]

[3] [cf. Joseph E. Duncan, 'The Intellectual Kinship of John Donne and Robert Browning', *Studies in Philology*, L (1953), pp. 81–100.]

[4] [cf. Chesterton, *Browning* (EML), especially Chapters II, VI and VII.]

II

GENERAL STUDIES
AFTER 1914

HUGH SYKES DAVIES

BROWNING

BEING now within a stone's throw of laying down the awkward duties of the anthologist, perhaps I may be forgiven for indulging, by way of a last fling, in some slight expression of my own opinions. Great care has been taken to keep them out of the other introductions in this volume, and to utter nothing but the generalities of accepted opinion, or at most very lightly to underline what emerged from the array of criticism before me.

This temptation, to try my hand at the business myself, is the stronger in the case of Browning, because I cannot help being conscious of a sort of critical vacuum around him. In some thirty years spent attentively on the fringes of the literary world there has come out to me not a single whisper of Browning mattering much to anyone in those solemn inner circles which revolve ceremonially around the Graven Imagery of modern poetry. If he has been mentioned at all, it has been in passing, and generally neither for praise or blame, but incidentally to the last degree. There would seem to be no 'Browning problem', no critical issue. For a whole generation, he has been left to the romantic publicity of that Wimpole Street job, and to his readers.

Readers he certainly has. The whole body of poetry-readers nowadays is but a small one, and a relatively large part of it is to be found in the upper forms of schools, in the English departments of univer-

From *The Poets and their Critics* (1962), Vol. II, pp. 296–300. The book is a collection of critical opinions by various authors on the major English poets from Blake to Browning: this passage is Mr Sykes Davies' introduction to the section on Browning.

sities and training colleges. It is here, in this relatively large part of the absolutely minute body, that Browning has his readers, that he gives his obviously genuine pleasure. And one can see why. The moods of youth will sometimes fall in with the melancholy languors of Tennyson's most personal note; but much more often they will respond to the vigour and impetus of Browning's characteristic zest for the surface of life. And Tennyson, when his personal note is not being heard, is a Bardic pomposity the more ridiculous (as Henry James so delicately hinted) because it tottered and titubated on such high stilts; the young never easily stomach false dignity. Browning, on the other hand, and again in the light of James' penetrating description, was 'as little as possible a Bard'. The fault into which he characteristically falls is sheer tediousness. He can be very boring, but not embarrassingly ridiculous. It is a fault, moreover, into which he does not always fall. The best pieces from *Men and Women* are nearly free from it; [*The Bishop Orders his Tomb at*] *St Praxed's Church* is, for what it does, a pretty compressed piece of writing.

But when we read Browning are we reading poetry? Or are we reading him primarily because it is poetry? Those are the really dubious points, for it must be granted at once that with many of his young readers the real attraction is in the incident, the character, the gusto of the monologue. And this, after all, is an attraction by no means special or proper to poetry, for it is one shared with prose fiction, and also with drama.

It is precisely because he had moved so far into the proper territory of the novel that he still has his readers; because he was the Victorian poet who most completely fell in with – surrendered to, if you like – this new and overwhelming literary impetus. And it is for the same reason that his best critics are novelists like Henry James[1] and his friend Percy Lubbock.[2] Their critical weapons, sharpened in the first serious attack in Britain on the problems of prose fiction, enabled them to analyse Browning with a sureness and delicacy that was quite beyond their poetically trained colleagues. They dissect his approach to character, his presentation of it, both in its strengths and its limitations; and they comment no less adequately on his 'philosophy of life', his slightly shaky 'moral and intellectual

62

standards'. But on his 'poetry' they are naturally less convincing. James has a fine remark about 'the world of Expression at any cost'; and Lubbock has a good, if only half-developed, point, about the 'fringe of values, the associated harmonics, of the *spoken* word'. But between them they offer nothing more.

Lubbock's point, taken a little further, may enable us to define more exactly what elements or aspects of poetry Browning did not surrender, but firmly kept with him, as he made his incursion into the territory of prose fiction. Above all, he kept the weapon of metre, as a norm of rhythmical movement to be established in order that it could be on occasion disarrayed. And by this norm of rhythm, and the disruptions which only a norm makes possible, he was able to approximate on paper, with remarkable closeness, to spoken English. The problem to be solved here is, perhaps, one peculiar to English, or at least peculiarly acute in our language. For in our natural speech, in the only rounded fullness of which any language is ultimately capable, we make enormous use of intonation, inflection, variations of vocal emphasis; and not merely as means of decoration or amusement but as the essence of the communication. The notation of mere writing, inadequate in principle and in all languages, is therefore specially incapable of transferring English speech to the dead and silent page. But something, even much, can be done if this bare notation is supplemented by the lavish and skilful management of metre, with its norms of rhythm and its departures from them; by this means, the intonation, the emphasis of the internal voice of the reader, can be made to fall, as often as not, where the writer needs it to fall. And in this kind of management Browning was so skilful and so lavish that any young writer, either in prose or in verse, does well to take him as a principal object of study. It is, I take it, tolerably clear that Henry James learned from him not a little, and exactly in this matter of spoken rhythms, of syntax flexibly moulded to the intonations and emphases of the sounding voice. This is not to say, of course, that we should try to write like Browning, or even like James; only that there is much to be learned from both, and from their remarkable connection. Lubbock's prose offers a good example of the happier effects of such tuition, in its style no less than its content.

But when we have noted that this element of poetry, at least, Browning took with him into the foreign territory, we have noted all. That special and magical cultivation of the word itself, which in recent years has come to be regarded as the distinctive weapon of poetry, he did not possess, and so could not take with him. He possessed it neither in its Shakespearean or Metaphysical form, of coruscating imagery, wit, and richness of association, nor in that other form, even less definable, of surface plainness resting directly upon a dense compression of feeling and thought, of which Jonson was an early example, Wordsworth a later and richer. And it is because the whole movement that we call modern poetry has rested on one or both of these highly special forms of imaginative wording that Browning counts for so little with those who make it. Nor is there any reason to suppose that he will come to play a larger part. For poetry, once prose fiction had occupied, or usurped, so much of its ancient provinces, in narrative and the depiction of character, has perforce – and no doubt rightly – concentrated its forces upon what it, and it alone, can do. And this happens to be the one thing that Browning could not do.

It is exactly this that seems to me to make his work so much deserving of study; – that it illustrates, and so clearly comments upon, that decisive shift which took place in his day between the territories held by the two chief forms of literature, those of poetry and of prose fiction. It was the shift noted, a little hesitantly, by Trollope – who might, if he wished, have had the material of *The Ring and the Book* for prose fiction, for Browning offered it to him – but he 'couldn't manage it'. In that very interesting, and characteristically unclever chapter of the *Autobiography* on 'The Art of Fiction', Trollope points the contrast between poetry, widely respected, but little read, and fiction, widely read, but little respected, and he makes this puzzled protest: 'He who sits down to write his tale in prose does not dream that the poet's honour is within his reach; – but his teaching is of the same nature, and his lessons tend to the same end . . . and that will be the greatest teacher who will spread such truth the widest.' The fact, more outrageously stated, was that in the course of the nineteenth century poetry ceased to be the greatest literary force exerted upon the imagination of Britain; and what poetry had ceased to be, prose fiction became.

It is in the light of this crucial change that is best seen that crisis in the nature and conception of poetry which seems to me to emerge so clearly from the whole of this collection of criticism. And it is illuminated for us, not only by the ultimate untenability of Tennyson's posture of the Sage who was also the Bard, but even more by Browning's desertion, so much more tenable, into the other camp – on to 'the novelist's side of the street', as Henry James put it. The provinces, so to speak, and the forms of government, both of modern poetry and of the modern novel, are by implication defined in this parting of the ways between the two great Victorians. And the essential difference is, that while modern poetry has not much use for Tennyson, the modern novel has a great deal of use for Browning, much of which has still to be made.[3]

NOTES

[1] [See pp. 11–16.]
[2] [See pp. 36–57.]
[3] [cf. Hugh Sykes Davies, *Browning and the Modern Novel* (The St John's College, Cambridge, Lecture, 1961–2, University of Hull Publications, 1962). Studies in the course of Browning's reputation abound. Among them may be noted: T. R. Lounsbury, *The Early Literary Career of Robert Browning* (1911); M. B. Cramer,'Browning's Friendships and Fame Before Marriage (1833–1846)', *PMLA*, LV (1940), pp. 207–30, and 'What Browning's Literary Reputation Owed to the Pre-Raphaelites, 1847–1856', *ELH*, VIII (1941), pp. 305–21, and 'Browning's Literary Reputation at Oxford, 1855–1859', *PMLA*, LVII (1942), pp. 232–40; C. C. Watkins, 'Browning's "Fame Within these Four Years" [1861–5]', *Modern Language Review*, LII (1958), pp. 492–500; B. R. McElderry, Jr., 'Browning and the Victorian Public in 1868–69', *Research Studies of the State College of Washington*, V (1937), pp. 193–203, and 'Victorian Evaluation of *The Ring and the Book*', *RSSCW*, VII (1939), pp. 75–89; Helen P. Pettigrew, 'The Early Vogue of *The Ring and the Book*', *Archiv für das Studium der neurem Sprachen und Literaturen*, CLXIX (1936), pp. 36–47; Boyd Litzinger, *Time's Revenges: Browning's Reputation as a Thinker, 1889–1962* (Knoxville: 1964); Duckworth, *Background*, Part I; D. C. Somervell, 'The Reputation of Robert Browning', *Essays and Studies*, XV (1929), pp. 122–38; Louise Greer, *Browning and America* (1952). The main interests of academic writers on Browning can be assessed from Raymond, *Infinite Moment*, Chap. XI, 'Browning Studies in England and America, 1910–1949', pp. 193–231, and W. C. DeVane, 'Robert Browning' in *The Victorian Poets: A Guide to Research*, edited by Frederic E. Faverty (Harvard U.P., 1956), pp. 58–83.]

EDWIN MUIR

ROBERT BROWNING

ABT VOGLER is a good example of Browning's poetic method and also of a fault into which it sometimes led him: what is usually described as his optimism. In *Abt Vogler*, as in most of his poems, he starts with a fact of experience – in this case the evocation of music from a musical instrument – and follows it to see where it will lead him. He follows it within a simple, impressive framework which is his world of imagination; and no matter in what direction the inquiry may lead him, it is bound to reach and rest upon one of the four truths which to him were the corner-stones of that world. These four truths or affirmations, which depend upon and follow from each other, are – the uniqueness of personality, the imperfection of human life, the desire of the imperfect being for perfection, and the presence of God. These are traditional truths, and all Browning's poetry is in a sense an illustration of them, or rather a description of moments in which one or another of them is realised in ordinary experience.

Browning's inquiry into life ends at some such point; but it may begin anywhere. In general, the farther from the end it begins, the better the result is likely to be. The poems in which he states a point of view quite different from his own, as in *Cleon, Caliban upon Setebos*, and that very fine poem, *An Epistle of Karshish*, are his best, for they call out and exercise his imagination. Where he has to state a point of view virtually his own, he acquires a false confidence, as in *Rabbi Ben Ezra* and to some extent in *Abt Vogler*; the figure who is ostensibly monologising fades into that of the author; and we are

From *Essays on Literature and Society* (Hogarth Press, 1949), pp. 103–109.

confronted with Browning himself and his chief fault, which is to 'greet the unseen with a cheer' [*Epilogue* to *Asolando*] and bluff himself by a display of pious geniality into mystical high spirits. When he says in this mood, ' . . . All we have willed or hoped or dreamed of good shall exist' [*Abt Vogler*, 73], he is not uttering a mystical truth, but expressing his own sanguine and belligerent character. He has given us his impression of that character in the *Epilogue* to *Asolando*:

> One who never turned his back but marched breast forward,
>   Never doubted clouds would break,
> Never dreamed, though right were worsted, wrong would triumph,
> Held we fall to rise, are baffled to fight better,
>   Sleep to wake.

This belligerent confidence, a quality of character, was accepted by Browning's contemporaries as optimism. But the great majority of his poems, and the best of them, do not end in belligerent confidence. His character, and his personal philosophy when he stated it, were optimistic; but his world of imagination was not: for the qualities which made up that world were not all comforting. The uniqueness and separation of the individual, the imperfection of human life, are not comforting. One of his finest short poems, *Two in the Campagna*, describes the desire of a lover to be completely united in soul and mind with his mistress, and his frustration:

> Just when I seemed about to learn!
>   Where is the thread now? Off again!
> The old trick! Only I discern –
>   Infinite passion, and the pain
> Of finite hearts that yearn.

If we judge Browning by his best work, then it is as absurd to call him an optimist as it would be to call Dante an optimist because the *Divine Comedy* begins in Hell and ends in Heaven. What happened to him when he spoke directly of his hopes was that he forgot the more formidable elements in his imaginative world. He had to enter into the lives of people quite unlike himself before he could realise all the obstacles to his easy faith in things. But this is what he did; his work consisted in this.

To understand Browning's originality one has to replace him in his age, an age when the tradition of romantic poetry was generally accepted, and poetry had become overwhelmingly contemplative, and contemplative of a set order of things, such as youth, age, life, death, love, joy, grief. These things were seen as states in an unchanging light; as simple and profound things, not as complex things containing contradictions and subject to change and development. The mood of this poetry is perfectly expressed in Tennyson's lines:

> The woods decay, the woods decay and fall,
> The vapours weep their burthen to the ground,
> Man comes and tills the field and lies beneath,
> And after many a summer dies the swan.
>
> [*Tithonus*]

The task of the poet was to contemplate such things. Browning instead set himself to enter into them and discover where they would lead him. To call his method dramatic is somewhat to misstate it. The pattern of drama is created by the action. Browning's pattern, as we have seen, was laid up in heaven: the action might receive confirmation from it, but could not create it. This pattern existed for him by an act of faith before he entered into his characters; and each of these was merely a thread by following which he reached some point in the pattern, and in reaching it confirmed concretely the truth of his faith in it. There is this sense of metaphysical activity behind the scenes in all his poetry. The confirmation demanded as many *independent* witnesses as possible. These had to be men and women who had tested themselves against life, and who therefore belonged to all sorts of active callings, as painters, musicians, craftsmen, priests, soldiers, revolutionaries, impostors, lovers, husbands, wives. The particular response, the demonstration of the special kind of truth which fascinated Browning, could not have been elicited from them in the actual moment of action. He did not try to write drama and fail; he tried to do something different, with complete success. He was concerned with the *dramatis personae* rather than with the play; he set himself to find out what the *dramatis personae* really thought of the play, privately. The form he invented for discovering this was the dramatic monologue which he perfected in the three volumes written in his fresh maturity: *Dramatic Romances and Lyrics* [1845], *Men and Women* [1855], and *Dramatis Personae* [1864]. He used it later, on a vast scale, in *The Ring and the Book* [1868-9]; and the five chief monologues in that long poem contain, perhaps, his greatest poetry.

But if Browning had not been intensely interested in men and women as well as in their place in the pattern, his work would not have its endless fascination and variety. His interest was shown in two ways: in a love for the curious, and in a love for the violently ordinary. He wrote about Paracelsus, Master Hugues of Saxe-Gotha, Abt Vogler and Ben Karshook. He wrote also on such subjects as 'Up at a Villa – Down in the City', 'By the Fireside', 'Any Wife to any Husband', 'Respectability', 'How it strikes a Contemporary', 'Popularity', 'Nationality in Drinks', and 'Mr Sludge, "The Medium" '. His taste for the ordinary shocked his contemporaries more than his taste for the odd and the remote; for it brought unexpected material into his poetry, and along with it, to deal with it, a vast new vocabulary in which the conventional poetic vocabulary of the time was swamped and drowned. The nature of his interest in mankind made this vocabulary necessary; for it was not an interest in human states, such as grief or happiness, but rather in human activity; and all human activity is technical, and demands from the poet a technical interest. Browning had this technical interest in a high degree; when he wrote of painters, or priests, or lovers, or impostors, he wrote with a professional appreciation of the importance of their modes. As love was to him the highest activity of which human beings were capable, he devoted his most intense imaginative consideration to it. He wrote, unlike the romantic poets, as a practised lover; and his subject was neither happy nor unhappy love, but love as an experience, a love both ideal and physical, whose reality was bound up with its permanence. Even his most spontaneous lyrics give an impression of experience; but his greatest love poetry is reflective, as in *Two in the Campagna* and *By the Fireside*.

Of a special kind of poetry he was incapable. He was unable to

69

relapse into the passive and receptive states which give a quite different response to life from his own. He could not have seen with composure Tennyson's man come and till the field and lie beneath; he would have concentrated on the tilling of the field, with an agricultural passion. But what his imagination did grasp, that is the various branches of the technique of living, it grasped with a knowledge which no other modern poet has equalled.

All Browning's work is an inquiry beginning with a Perhaps and converging circuitously upon one of the cardinal truths in which he believed. The metrical forms which he uses sometimes fit with astonishing felicity the spirit of this inquiry; they have a tentative and casual music in which the thought seems to be experimentally finding its proper expression: almost a hand-to-mouth music. He was particularly fond of the five-line stanza which he used in *Two in the Campagna* and *By the Fireside*, a stanza in which the last line seems to be carelessly improvised in response to an afterthought. Except when he is using a long heavy line for some dignified theme, the greatest virtue of his verse is naturalness and lightness:

> How say you? Let us, O my dove,
>   Let us be unashamed of soul,
> As earth lies bare to heaven above!
>   How is it under our control
> To love or not to love? [*Two in the Campagna*]

This is almost a chance music, cast off in the heat of the inquiry. Of this free, faintly interrogative, street music, he was a master; and he used it with consummate ease and variety. His blank verse had a variety beyond that of any other poet of his age. A few passages from *The Ring and the Book*, where it displays all its qualities, will show what he could do with it:

> And where was I found but on a strange bed
> In a strange room like hell, roaring with noise,
> Ruddy with flame, and filled with men. . . . [III, 1150–2]

> Launching her looks forth, letting looks reply
> As arrows to a challenge. . . .   [V, 900–1]

Found myself in my horrible house once more,
After a colloquy . . . no word assists!
With the mother and the brothers, stiffened me
Straight out from head to foot as dead man does,
And, thus prepared for life as he for hell,
Marched to the public square and met the world. . . .
                                    [V, 1269–74]

The two, three creeping house-dog-servant-things
Born mine and bred mine. . . .   [IV, 1077–8]

Be as the angels rather, who, apart,
Know themselves into one, are found at length
Married, but marry never. . . .   [VII, 1833–5]

As in his arms he caught me, and, you say,
Carried me in, that tragical red eve,
And laid me where I next returned to life
In the other red of morning, two red plates
That crushed together, crushed the time between,
And are since then a solid fire to me. . . . [VII, 1579–84]

The imagery in these passages, and Browning's imagery in general, derives its force from its psychological truth, not from its formal beauty. It shows the depths to which Browning's imagination could pierce; it is sufficient to demonstrate that his view of life cannot be adequately defined as optimism. His variety is another matter; in that, he is second among English poets to no one but Shakespeare and Chaucer.[1]

NOTE

[1] [For other accounts of Browning's diction cf. Bernard Groom, *On the Diction of Tennyson, Browning and Arnold*, Society for Pure English Tract, LIII (1939); Josephine Miles, *The Primary Language of Poetry in the 1740s and 1840s*, Univ. of Calif. Pubs. in English, Vol. XIX, No. 2 (1950); J. H. Miller, *Disappearance of God*, esp. pp. 115–24. On *By The Fireside* see Geoffrey Tillotson, 'A Word for Browning', *Sewanee Review*, LXXII (1964), pp. 389–97.]

KINGSBURY BADGER

'SEE THE CHRIST STAND!':
BROWNING'S RELIGION

I

ROBERT BROWNING's religion – how definite and how Christian was it? For a full century now readers of Browning's poetry have differed widely in their interpretations, so widely that one critic has called Browning's religion 'a vague subjective theism in which Christian belief counted for little or nothing'[1] and another has called it 'essentially positive, and Christian without being orthodox'.[2] To one critic Browning is a barbarous poet whose faith 'has far more affinity to the worship of Thor or of Odin than to the religion of the Cross;'[3] to another 'not only is he the prophet of a liberal religion, but his poetry has been an instrument of grace'.[4]

According to one reading of his writings, Browning was a religious reactionary. Although not a regular church-goer, he reacted so strongly to the scepticism of his day that he grew steadily more orthodox, until he finally 'drifted towards the Anglican Church'.[5] We see a man grieving over his mother's death and conscience-stricken over having followed the Unitarian heresy and left his mother's evangelical Christianity, being led back to faith by his strong-minded and deeply religious, if non-sectarian, wife.[6] We hear him tell us, in his *Christmas-Eve and Easter-Day*, how he examined 'the various modes of man's belief'. After having found love persistent in the very midst of ignorance and corruption, and after praying that even the erring Göttingen professor might one day know 'the God of Revelation', he returned to Zion Chapel and declared, 'I

From *Boston University Studies in English*, I (1955–6), pp. 53–73.

choose here.' Such faith as this, faith in his mother's God and his mother's Savior, he expressed in poem after poem. Is it not true that only after the recovery from atheism described in *Pauline* and the reconversion described in *Christmas-Eve and Easter-Day* was Browning able to complete his *Saul* with verses rising to the magnificent affirmation 'See the Christ stand'? Browning was certainly a Christian. We may even go so far as to say with William L. Phelps, 'Of all true English poets, he is the most definitely Christian'[7] – provided we are willing to overlook Donne, Herbert, Hopkins, and possibly T. S. Eliot. Or we may find truth in Thomas Hardy's caustic comment: 'The longer I live, the more does B[rowning]'s character seem the literary puzzle of the 19th Century. How could smug Christian optimism worthy of a dissenting grocer find a place inside a man who was so vast a seer and feeler when on neutral ground?'[8]

According to a far different reading of Browning, the poet tended, or 'drifted', towards extreme liberalism in religion. Always an inquirer and never a sectarian or leaner upon creeds, in later years, says Mrs Sutherland Orr, he used language 'more habitually that of a Theist than that of a Christian';[9] moreover, to Robert Buchanan's point-blank question as to whether he considered himself a Christian, Browning replied with a thunderous 'No'.[10] We must realize that the narrator or soliloquist in dramatic poems is not the author himself and that the soliloquist in *Christmas-Eve and Easter-Day* is quite as critical of the attitudes of the dissenters and Roman Catholics as of sceptics or Biblical critics. If we may say of Browning that 'he at least believed in Soul, was very sure of God' [*La Saisiaz*, 604], we cannot truthfully add any more than that he believed in the incarnation of Love. He did believe in a Supreme Being, but his Trinity was the metaphysical Power, Intelligence, and Love, rather than the theological Father, Son, and the Holy Ghost. The philosopher Josiah Royce, who maintains that Browning 'was certainly no orthodox believer', says: 'It is noteworthy, moreover, that the incarnation has small connection, in his mind, with the other articles with which the faith of the church has joined it.'[11] Clearly he did not regard himself as a penitent sinner, did not believe in original sin,

73

eternal punishment, atonement through vicarious suffering on the cross, and did not interpret the Bible literally. Did he not say, both in *Christmas-Eve and Easter-Day* and the *Epilogue* to *Dramatis Personae*, that he preferred to worship outside church walls? Moncure D. Conway, a Unitarian friend, was also of the opinion that 'Browning was not conventionally orthodox'; but he was disturbed because Browning 'was only clear in criticizing my positions, and I could not get him to define his own positions'.[12]

According to a third reading of his poetry, Browning was always indefinite and vague about his religion, principally because he was inhibited and confused. We are told by such psychographers as F. R. G. Duckworth that, in addition to his feeling of inferiority and his jealousy of his wife's success as a writer, Browning was hampered in his expression by the warring elements of 'the mystic and the poet of action'.[13] All attempts at clarity, therefore, succeeded in expressing religious truth only obliquely, or 'broken into prismatic hues', not directly with the 'white light' of personal conviction. Did he not write to Miss Barrett in 1845, 'I only make men and women speak – give you truth broken into prismatic hues, and fear the pure white light, even if it is in me, but I am going to try'?[14] Try he did; but because he did not take a sectarian stand, says Duckworth, he took no stand at all, and because he wrote on religion almost exclusively in the dramatic mode, he did not express his own convictions. Professor Hoxie N. Fairchild's charge of vagueness carries with it also an insinuation of heresy, though, in contrast with Duckworth, he finds Browning *too* objective. In his discussion of *La Saisiaz*, Professor Fairchild tries to prove that, in 1877, Browning did not believe in revelation. There seems to be abundant evidence, writes Professor Fairchild, that, after emerging from his phase of Shelleyan atheism, Browning 'moved from a liberal sort of nonconformity to a vague subjective theism in which Christian belief counted for little or nothing', thus illustrating a 'drift' which was 'a characteristic Victorian phenomenon'.[15] No less severe is the criticism of the philosopher George Santayana. Rational philosopher that he is, Santayana objects to what he calls Browning's 'contempt for rationality' and to the 'vague religion' by which he attempts to justify his view of life as 'an adventure, not a discipline'. 'In Browning', he says, 'this religion takes the name of Christianity, and identifies itself with one or two Christian ideas arbitrarily selected; but at heart it has far more affinity to the worship of Thor or of Odin than to the religion of the Cross.'[16] So speaks a philosopher whose intellect will not allow him to accept literally and dogmatically the Catholicism for which his heart yearns, to whom it is a constant delight to remind us that Christianity rightly conceived is an ecclesiastical tradition of asceticism rather than a way of life attributed to Jesus of Nazareth.

Among the reasons for this wide divergence in interpretations of Browning's religion, the principal one, not diminished by prejudice on the part of his readers, is probably difficulty in fully comprehending the complex pattern of intellectual conflicts in Victorian times. Another reason may be ambiguity caused by Browning's free use of words with Christian designation – *incarnation, divinity, salvation, Christ* – which has made it as easy for orthodox Christians to find support for their preconceptions as it is for religious liberals to discover what they have conceived to be unmistakable signs of narrow conventional belief. What is more, this free use of Christian terms has laid the poet open to the charges both of writing with uncertainty or vagueness and of holding decidedly extra-Christian views. But certainly one of the leading reasons for disagreement regarding his religion has been failure to understand Browning's peculiar response to the Biblical criticism of his day.

It is common knowledge that Browning, after his return to theistic belief, continually defended religion against the onslaughts of rationalism in general and 'higher' (historical) Biblical criticism in particular. Strongly convinced with his Rabbi Ben Ezra that 'earth changes, but thy soul and God stand sure' [l. 159], he never thought for a moment that human life might be governed wholly by mechanical laws or blind natural forces, was never disturbed by the findings of the geologists and biologists. But the question before us is this: did Browning's return to belief in 'God and truth and love', first described in *Pauline*, mean eventual return to evangelical Christianity? Did it mean effecting some sort of compromise with orthodox Christian views? Did it mean return to Unitarianism or advance in

75

some other liberal direction, or just what did it mean? Before we can begin to answer questions by defining Browning's position, it will be necessary to sketch the general background of conflict, and to consider his intellectual preparation for the trial that was to come with Biblical criticism. Then it will be necessary to reinspect a number of key poems in the full context of Victorian literature and thought.

II

What the Victorians called rationalism, Germanism, or 'higher' criticism of the Bible struck England belatedly but with tremendous force. Among the countless books reflecting the investigations of this new science, the most powerful before Matthew Arnold's *Literature and Dogma* (1873) and Mrs Humphry Ward's *Robert Elsmere* (1888) were David F. Strauss's *Life of Jesus Critically Examined* (1845), *Essays and Reviews* (1860) by 'the Seven against Christ', and Ernest Renan's *Life of Jesus* (1863). The first was said by the high churchman Henry P. Liddon to have 'shocked the conscience of all that was Christian in Europe',[17] and the second was said by Disraeli to have 'convulsed Christendom' and 'shaken down the spire of Chichester Cathedral'.[18] For such examination of the Scriptures as these books contained – examination in the light of philology, comparative religion, and scientific historical investigation generally – Englishmen were ill-prepared, if prepared at all, though Browning, as we shall see, was well aware of what was going on.[19] Not only did he probably read Strauss, and certainly Renan, but he knew personally Max Müller, Matthew Arnold, Mrs Humphry Ward, Benjamin Jowett, and Mark Pattison, the last two being among the contributors to *Essays and Reviews*. Bishop Colenso he mentions in *Gold Hair*:

> The candid incline to surmise of late
> That the Christian faith proves false, I find;
> For our Essays-and-Reviews' debate
> Begins to tell on the public mind,
> And Colenso's words have weight.[20]

To understand what scientific examination of the Bible meant to the Victorians, we must recall that the cardinal principles of the

Reformation were reverence for an authoritative Bible and the right of private judgment. But since the safety of the first was now being threatened by the exercise of the second, in order to protect the authoritative Bible (and what else was authoritative to Protestants?) freedom of inquiry, interpretation, and expression of opinion had to be strictly limited. The great alternative, then, became acceptance of the authority of church tradition or braving the perils of reason alone, in other words, an alternative between Catholicism (Roman or Anglican) and private judgment. Unfortunately, some men tried to cling to belief in cover-to-cover inspiration of the Scriptures rather than accept either alternative. It was long before clergymen and laymen were ready to accept Lessing's and Coleridge's conception of progressive revelation, even after Carlyle had begun to write about the Bible of History.[21] The dilemma was indeed serious, once Biblical criticism began to dissolve the historical foundations of the Bible; if a man could not accept an infallible Bible any more than an infallible church, he had to struggle with the doubts imposed by reason. To be sure, those whose religion could be based not upon an inerrant Bible but upon either the dictates of church authority or reason enlightened by scholarship were better able to assimilate the results of textual and historical criticism than were those without such resources. Much of the most agonizing doubt and disbelief was reflected in the writings of men like Francis Newman, James A. Froude, John A. Symonds, and Arthur Hugh Clough, who had been brought up in strict evangelical dependence upon a God-dictated, literally interpreted Bible or of those who, like Joseph Blanco White and Mark Pattison, reacted strongly from the pietism of the Oxford Movement. The Tractarians, though they did seek historical understanding by studying the Church Fathers and did base their beliefs on a tradition broad and authoritative enough for some men, turned their backs upon inevitable developments, thus intensifying the doubts of those who were seeking definite answers to the questions being raised by Biblical scholars in Germany, France, and finally England. In summary, we may say that, save for the extreme, unthinking accepters of authority, those who were hit hardest by Biblical criticism were the orthodox Christians of the 'fundamentalist' sort and that the liberals, or men like John Stuart Mill who were brought up with no creed, were relatively unharmed. No wonder, then, that Robert Browning, no literalist and no believer in church dogmas founded upon historical facts, should not only have averted the frequently experienced soul-crises but also have thriven on the conflict of his time.

The Brownings were unquestionably liberal in the sense that they were free to think without dogmatic restraints. If we read the well-known letters in which Miss Barrett states her non-sectarian belief and Robert answers, 'What you express now, is for us both,' we see that both of them were broad in their sympathies but determined to accept no formulas, whether Roman Catholic, Puseyite, or even dissenting.[22] In answer to those who contend that Mrs Browning brought Robert back, not merely to stronger religion but to orthodoxy, the best we can do is read carefully the complete works of both with special attention to Mrs Browning's liberal views. But it will be necessary to make allowance for her use of traditional language, especially when writing to friends who, like Fanny Haworth, had become disturbed and confused in their thinking. Mrs Browning's interest in spiritualism, which she gave up towards the end of her life, and which Robert never shared, seems to have grown out of her desire to combat the rationalists and satisfy with evidence of revelation those who doubted the reality of spiritual forces in life. To Fanny Haworth she wrote in 1861:

But the whole theory of spiritualism, all the phenomena, are strikingly *confirmatory* of revelation; nothing strikes me more than that. Hume's argument against miracles (a strong argument) disappears before it, and Strauss's conclusions from *a priori* assertion of impossibility fall in pieces at once.[23]

Here Mrs Browning is defending, not orthodox, but liberal belief. To her as to her husband, revelation meant the disclosure of God as Power and Love rather than oral or literary expression of Divine Will by an anthropomorphic God; and incarnation meant the revelation of this same Power and Love through any human personality, rather than the assumption of human form, at only one time in history, by a Divine Being. It is disastrous, she believes, to draw a line between the natural and the supernatural, as she tells us in *Aurora Leigh*:

> Natural things
> And spiritual – who separates those two
> In art, in morals, or the social drift,
> Tears up the bond of nature, and brings death.[24]

One of Mrs Browning's strongest convictions was that a second Reformation was needed to free religion from lifeless creeds, formalism, and superstition and bring it abreast of modern knowledge, that there might be 'expansion according to the needs of man'. In another letter to Fanny Haworth she wrote:

> We are entering on a Reformation far more interior than Luther's; and the misfortune is, that if we don't enter, we must drop under the lintel. Do you hear of the storms in England about 'Essays and Reviews'? I have seen the book simply by reviews in abstract and extract. I should agree with the writers in certain things, but certainly not in all. I have no sort of sympathy with what is called rationalism, which is positivism in a form. The vulgar idea of miracles being put into solution, leaves me with the higher law and spiritual causation; which the rationalists deny, and which you and I hold faithfully. But whatever one holds, free discussion has become necessary. That it is full of danger; that in consequence of it, many minds will fall into infidelity, doubt, and despair, is certain; but through this moral crisis man must pass, or the end will be worse still. That's my belief, I have seen it coming for years back.[25]

She was certain, she said, that no truth could be dangerous in the long run.[26] Even though she frequently expressed, both in her poems and her letters, belief in the divinity of Jesus, she said nothing about believing that Jesus is God or the second Person of the Trinity. Robert Browning, we gather from remarks made to Mrs Orr, believed just as strongly in the divinity of Jesus, though he did not identify Him with the Deity; and he counteracted his clearly stated agnosticism regarding the Christian scheme of salvation with his positive faith in the revelation of Divine Love:

> I know the difficulty of believing. .... I know all that may be said against it [the Christian scheme of salvation] on the ground of history, of reason, of even moral sense. I grant even that it may be a fiction. But I am none the less convinced that the life and death of Christ, as Christians apprehend it, supply something which their humanity requires, and that it is true for them.[27]

79

He then proceeded to say why in his judgment humanity required Christ:

The evidence of Divine power is everywhere about us; not so the evidence of Divine love. That love could only reveal itself to the human heart by some supreme act of *human* tenderness and devotion; the fact, or fancy, of Christ's cross and passion could alone supply such a revelation.[27]

This idea of the need of incarnation occupied Browning's mind for many years, but especially during the forty years between *Christmas-Eve and Easter-Day* and *Asolando*, after he had become familiar with the writings of Strauss and Renan. He was greatly interested in the ancient world just before and at the time of Jesus, wondering, though not inquiring scientifically as the Biblical critics did, how the story of Jesus struck his contemporaries. In *Cleon*, *Karshish*, *A Death in the Desert*, and '*Imperante Augusto Natus Est*', we find this wondering about an event which 'may be a fiction' but which, 'fact or fancy', 'humanity requires'.

The one doctrine of religion that supplies what humanity requires is the doctrine of incarnation, the central doctrine, though no dogma, of Browning's religion. As a monist who has reached certainty in his belief in Soul and God, Browning has also come to believe, by 'instinct confirmed by reason', that Love is the central energy of God's being and man's; but although 'evidence of Divine Power is everywhere about us,' says Browning, evidence of Divine Love is not to be perceived in external nature; it can be revealed to the human heart only 'by some supreme act of *human* tenderness and devotion'. Now God obviously cannot perform any *human* act at all without entering into a human soul. Revelation of God as Love, then, means the manifestation of Love in a soul or souls of human beings; it means incarnation not in the sense of God's becoming a supernatural man, for there is no distinction between natural and supernatural, but in the sense of manifestation of God as Love in natural man or men. Josiah Royce has expressed the idea in this way: 'To say God is Love is, then, the same as to say God is, or has been, or will be incarnate, perhaps once, perhaps – for so Browning's always monistic intuitions about the relation of God and the world suggest to him – perhaps always, perhaps in all our life, perhaps in all men.'[28] People of lower mentality and morality – Caliban, Guido, and the intolerant believer with whom Ferishtah argues in *The Sun* – may conceive of God as only Power; but not so David, Caponsacchi, and Pompilia. Rightly conceived as the central energy of God's being and man's, Love is something greater than affection or benevolence; it is all of the passion, development, spiritual striving, morality, ideality of human life.

A mind like Browning's, fed in early youth by Shelley, Voltaire, and the Unitarian preacher W. J. Fox, and then matured through continual study of the development of souls – 'little else is worth study', he said in the dedication letter at the head of *Sordello* [1863 version] – until he was sure of God, could not be shocked by the Christ-Myth of the Biblical critics of the Strauss school. In fact, these Biblical critics, with but little interest in Love, were only negative literalists; whereas the orthodox literalists said that the letter and the event were true, the Biblical critics only said that they were not. What the German historian F. A. Wolfe had done with Homer by making the Greeks the authors of his epics, Browning was prepared to see the critics of the Bible try to parallel in their treatment of the author of the Fourth Gospel; for as he tells us in his poem *Development* Browning was familiar with higher criticism of Homer. It may be, too, that he had heard of Lessing's idea of progressive revelation, but certainly he had his own idea of progressive revelation.[29] In any case, religion has its roots in life, is experiential, is based on 'instinct confirmed by reason';[30] and that which is based on experience rather than upon creeds or accounts of historical events cannot be shaken by the questioning of creeds or analysis of contradictory accounts of historical events. Browning had no fear that the Biblical critics could really shake religious faith.

III

By the year 1849, when Browning was writing his *Christmas-Eve and Easter-Day*, John Henry Newman's all-or-nothing, authority-or-doubt alternatives had pushed James A. Froude and Mark Pattison, among others, into scepticism; and it had taken the leading Tractarian himself all the way over to Rome. John Henry's brother Francis had written his *Phases of Faith* (1848), which, like W. R. Greg's *The Creed of Christendom* (1851), described the broadening of faith caused by wide reading of Biblical critics, including Strauss. Carlyle, who had already shaken off what he called 'the rags of Houndsditch', was to proclaim his emancipation in his *Life of John Sterling* (1851). Arthur Hugh Clough, never in danger of becoming a Newmanite, had been perplexed by Biblical criticism, had refused to sign the Thirty-Nine Articles, and had resigned both his tutorship and fellowship at Oxford. Arthur's college friend and Matthew Arnold's younger brother Tom had had his faith badly shaken, particularly by Strauss's *Life of Jesus*. No doubt about it, rationalism was a serious threat to Christian belief, and Strauss was among the greatest of culprits.

Christmas-Eve and Easter-Day was begun either very late in 1849 or very early in 1850 and published April 1, 1850. By Christmas Eve of 1849 Strauss's shocking ideas were seeping down to the general reading public of the middle classes. Whether or not Browning was aware of it, many of Strauss's ideas had been anticipated for Englishmen in a book by George Eliot's friend Charles Hennell, *An Inquiry concerning the Origin of Christianity* (1838), for the German edition of which Strauss had written a foreword; and at least two translations of *The Life of Jesus* had appeared in English before George Eliot's translation. Among numerous expositions of Strauss appearing in English an outstanding one was James Martineau's in the *Westminster Review* for April 1847, a magazine which the Brownings read frequently, at least before they left England. On Christmas Eve of 1848 Thomas Cooper, the Chartist, had begun his series of popular lectures on Strauss; and on Christmas Eve of 1849 he was not only in the midst of a repetition of that series but also engaged in preparing the lectures for publication in *Cooper's Journal*, beginning January 3, 1850, under the title 'Critical Exegesis of the Gospel on the Basis of Strauss's *Leben Jesu*'. Also, Charles Kingsley, about to read divinity with a young Cambridge student by discussing Strauss's book, decided after having read *Cooper's Journal*, to attack the German critic and argue him down before he did further harm among the workingmen. It may be, and in fact seems likely, that the

Brownings, already familiar with some of Clough's poetry, met the poet in Florence in the autumn of 1849, at which time he was working on his *Epi-Strauss-ium, Easter Day, 1849*, and *Dipsychus*, all of which have 'a strong Strauss-smell' about them.

For Browning's reading of Strauss's *Life of Jesus* we have only the internal evidence of a few of his poems, of which only *Bishop Blougram's Apology* mentions him by name, although Browning does mention Strauss, and also Renan, in his letters. Probably Browning read George Eliot's translation of *The Life of Jesus*, which was published in the spring of 1846, a few months before the Brownings left England for Italy; and just as probably he attended some of Philip Harwood's six lectures on 'German Anti-Supernaturalism' delivered at his friend W. J. Fox's South Place Chapel in 1845. That he knew the book well, however, may be seen by studying the poet's allusions to it. *The Life of Jesus Critically Examined* is, of course, a criticism of the Gospels, not a biography of Jesus. Strauss's purpose was to show that the Gospel narratives were based upon Old Testament types and prophecies. Taking a position between the allegorists from Origen onward and the naturalistic rationalists, including the English deists and such German critics as Reimarus and Paulus,[31] Strauss tries to show that the Christ of the Gospels was a true product of the Hebrew mind, a product mythical rather than historical, formed both by the preconceptions of Hebrew tradition and the impressions left by the character, actions, and fate of Jesus.

Browning's expression of his stand in a day when Catholicism, dissent, and rationalism strongly opposed each other began in his *Christmas-Eve and Easter-Day* with discussion of each of those positions in turn. He takes the reader on an imaginary expedition, on Christmas Eve of 1849, to London, Rome, and Göttingen. Driven by rain-gusts into Zion Chapel Meeting, the soliloquist – too egotistical and bigoted to be Browning himself – sits hip to haunch with the 'placid flock' of dissenters listening to the garbling of texts by their zealous, aspiring, but foggy-brained 'pastor vociferous', until, with disgust and anger seizing him by turns, he finally suits action to desire and escapes down long avenues of reverie, or sleep. First he fancies himself meditating on God under a lunar-rainbow in the street outside the chapel; then he fancies he is led by the Master first to view the raree-show at St Peter's in Rome and then to listen to a dry rationalist lecture at the University of Göttingen.

A strange story this is, indeed. But what is most important about it is that it presents not only the three major religious positions of Browning's time, 'broken into prismatic hues', but also both the soliloquist's and his own views. As his friend Joseph Milsand pointed out, Browning was being 'simultaneously lyrical and dramatic, subjective and objective'.[32] He was quite familiar with dissenting chapels and had attended the Duomo in Pisa, if not yet St Peter's in Rome. Although he had never been to Göttingen, he had already become pretty familiar with the attitude of such a professor as he portrayed. It should be noted especially that, critical of all three positions, he nevertheless discerns genuine faith in the power of love in human life at all three celebrations of Christmas Eve.

As the soliloquist listens to the discourse of the Strauss-like professor, he is bored more than disturbed by the professor's thought, but Browning wants the reader to see how essentially unreligious, however admirable intellectually, is the professor's thought. Not having the scholarship to meet the professor on his own ground of Biblical exegesis, he can nevertheless show that such critics are on the wrong ground and therefore should not matter to anyone with religious faith. The professor, after a few introductory remarks on the early history of Christianity, begins his rational exercise:

> Inquiring first
> Into the various sources whence
>   This Myth of Christ is derivable;
> Demanding from the evidence,
>   (Since plainly no such life was liveable)
> How these phenomena should class.[33]
> [*Christmas-Eve*, XV]

Here the speaker definitely echoes Strauss, first, with the concept of the *mythus*; second, with the statement that no such life as that of Jesus, with its supernatural events, is liveable; and third, with his classification of the various kinds of myths of which the larger myth of Christ consists. Strauss states in the Introduction to his *Life of*

Jesus that among the 'criteria by which to distinguish the unhistorical in the Gospel narrative', the very first is that an account must be declared unhistorical 'when the narration is irreconcilable with the known and universal laws which govern the course of events'.[34] Here is the well-known premise excluding all miracles. Elsewhere in the Introduction Strauss discusses lengthily 'the various sources whence this Myth of Christ is derivable'; and the whole book is devoted to illustration of the way the myths – evangelical, pure, and historical – have grown from those sources.[35]

The Göttingen professor concedes, as he proceeds with his discourse, that Christ may have lived, but he declares that nothing really matters except 'the idea' of Christ, though of course for practical purposes one might as well accept the popular story –

> understanding
> How the ineptitude of the time,
> And the penman's prejudice, expanding
> Fact into fable fit for the clime,
> Had, by slow and sure degrees, translated it
> Into this myth, this Individuum, –
> Which, when reason had strained and abated it
> Of foreign matter, left, for residuum,
> A Man![36]   [XV]

How both myths and legends grow, 'like a snowball growing', can be seen in Strauss's Introduction; they grow, says Strauss, from idea into myth or from fact into fable, steadily expanding.[37] Toward the end of the book, while discussing Schleiermacher's attempt to reconcile the Church's conception of a sinless God-Man, an ideal Christ, with the historical man Jesus, Strauss declares that 'such a Christ never existed but in idea' and continues as follows:

The attempt to retain in sublimation the ideal in Christ with the historical, having failed, these two elements separate themselves: the latter falls as a natural residuum to the ground, and the former rises as a pure sublimate into the ethereal world of ideas. Historically Jesus can have been nothing more than a person.[38]

This residuum-man both the Göttingen professor and his prototype would have us consider a fine person, or at least so one would

suppose until they had finished explaining him away. The professor
says,

> – a right true man, however,
> Whose work was worthy a man's endeavour:
> Work, that gave warrant almost sufficient
> To his disciples, for rather believing
> He was just omnipotent and omniscient,
> As it gives to us, for as frankly receiving
> His word, their tradition, – which, though it meant
> Something entirely different
> From all that those who only heard it,
> In their simplicity thought and averred it,
> Had yet a meaning quite as respectable:
> For, among other doctrines delectable,
> Was he not surely the first to insist on
> The natural sovereignty of our race?[39]
> [XV]

Strauss likewise lays far less stress on the power of Jesus' personality to impress the minds of his disciples than on the power of
their own expectations and ideas, as well as those of their contemporaries, to exalt the personality of their Master. He describes the
historical Jesus as:

a person, highly distinguished indeed, but subject to the limitations
inevitable to all that is mortal: by means of his exalted character, however,
he exerted so powerful an influence over the religious sentiment, that it
constituted him the ideal of piety; in accordance with the general rule,
that an historical fact or person cannot become the basis of a positive
religion until it is elevated into the sphere of the ideal.[40]

The professor's lecturing had been worse, thought the soliloquist, than the preaching of the poor, blundering minister in the
dissenters' chapel. The theology of the minister in Zion Chapel
might have been confused, and the doctrines of the Catholics in
St Peter's might have been full of 'errors and perversities'; but at
least they left one air to breathe instead of holding one in the 'exhausted air-bell of the critic'. [XVI] The professor, with his loveless
learning and bare-bones morality, with his blindness to the incarnation of Love in Jesus, seemed not to realize that, instead of saying,
'Believe in abstract good and justice and truth,' Jesus said,

86

'Believe in me,
Who lived and died, yet essentially
Am Lord of Life.'[41]   [XVII]

The good professor could send his audience home with nothing
more vital than this: 'Go home and venerate the myth.'[42] [XVIII]
Such advice was a satirical epitome of Strauss's 'Concluding
Dissertation,' in which he had attempted to 're-establish dogmatically
that which had been destroyed critically'.

It is really not Strauss's historical demolition that Browning objects to; it is rather the purely intellectual, emotion-starved, un-
poetic substitute that he offers for the Christ of the Evangelists.
Browning sees the need for

something more substantial
Than a fable, myth or personification.[43]
                [XXII]

Douglas Bush expresses it in this way:

Browning could not take historical criticism as final, because human
reason and knowledge are limited and fallible and because the real
evidence is within the soul. He sees the divinity of Christ and the transforming power of human and divine love as facts of experience which
mere biblical scholarship cannot overthrow. Thus, in spite of his antagonism to Strauss, Browning's attitude was not altogether different, though
his positive faith was less intellectual and more fervent.[44]

Since Browning's religious faith grew out of an intuitive sense of
the power and love of God revealed in human life, as well as in
external nature, he could not agree with the Catholic any more than
with the rationalist. Just why he could not is made clear in the broadly
satirical *Bishop Blougram's Apology.*

Bishop Blougram and his literary friend Gigadibs discuss religion
over their wine, their discussion centering principally on the question
as to whether it is preferable to live a life of 'faith diversified by
doubt', as the former does, or of 'doubt diversified by faith', as the
latter does. The Bishop, a eupeptic *bon vivant* and a powerful polemi-
cal writer who has distinguished himself by his part in the Tractarian controversy, dominates the discussion with what might be
called his apologia. He might have been another Strauss, he says,

G   87

had he continued along the path of his flair for Biblical criticism, but he realized that 'there's still that plaguey hundredth chance/Strauss may be wrong' [587-8]. Anticipating Gigadibs' reply, he puts these words into his mouth and then answers them:

> As well be Strauss as swing 'twixt Paul and him.
> It's not worth having, such imperfect faith,
> No more available to do faith's work
> Than unbelief like mine. Whole faith, or none! [595-8]

Bishop Blougram's answer is this:

> Softly, my friend! I must dispute that point.
> Once own the use of faith, I'll find you faith.
> We're back on Christian ground. You call for faith:
> I show you doubt, to prove that faith exists.
> The more of doubt, the stronger faith, I say,
> If faith o'ercomes doubt.[45]   [599-604]

Here is the same conclusion regarding the role of doubt as that reached by John in *A Death in the Desert*, except — and this is all-important to Browning — John is sincere; whereas Blougram is a casuist and an opportunist who 'believed, say, half he spoke' [980] and 'said true things, but called them by wrong names' [996]. Here is also Strauss's conclusion, but the rationalist is arguing for purely intellectual religion just as the Bishop argues for dogmas, neither one drawing his faith from the springs of Power and Love. Strauss says in his *Life of Jesus*:

To all belief not built on demonstration, doubt is inherent, though it may not be developed; the most firmly believing Christian has within him the elements of criticism as a latent deposit of unbelief, or rather as a negative germ of knowledge, and only by its constant repression can he maintain the predominance of his faith, which is thus essentially a re-established faith. And just as the believer is intrinsically a sceptic or critic, so, on the other hand, the critic is intrinsically a believer.[46]

The trouble with Bishop Blougram, as Browning sees him, is that he is a man who, like Cardinal Wiseman and others, bases his religious belief on authority and dogmas rather than upon life. Then he rationalizes doctrines to convince himself and the common believer,

employing such pious frauds as the 'winking Virgin' [cf. 699]. He
may be a good fellow, but he is a charlatan.

In the brilliant dramatic poem *A Death in the Desert* Browning
answers Strauss and other Biblical critics by asking them to listen to
the words of the 'beloved disciple' himself. In a document presumably written by one of John's disciples we read the story of John's
ministry. Already, some sixty years after the crucifixion, John fore-
sees 'the Lord's life/Forgotten or misdelivered' [167–8]. Doubt is
spreading, despite his labors in preaching and writing his gospel
and epistles; and he can easily foresee the day when men will ask,
'Was John at all, and did he say he saw?' [197]. John's life-work will
all have been in vain, unless men can keep ever before them the
'one historic fact – the Life and Death of Christ', puzzling no more
over the miracles.

> I say, that miracle [restoring sight to a blind man] was duly
>   wrought
> When, save for it, no faith were possible.[47] [466–7]

But he has stopped preaching miracles, convinced that

> Wonders that would prove doctrine, go for nought.
> Remains the doctrine, Love.[47]   [375–6]

This – John's one doctrine, Browning's, and Christ's – is all that
men need. Man has fire and cherishes it because he knows its worth,
though he no longer believes the fable of Prometheus and, with the
sophist, 'laughs the myth of Aeschylus to scorn' [287]. Does man
know the value of Love? 'Could he give Christ up were His worth as
plain?' [297]. Someday, when John's book was critically examined,
even as the fable of Prometheus was examined, its author would be
charged with falsehood, and the great basic truth of God's Love
manifest in Christ would be questioned along with the details of the
Gospel account. Men would say,

> But this was all the while
> A trick; the fault was, first of all, in thee,
> Thy story of the places, names and dates,
> Where, when and how the ultimate truth had rise,
> – Thy prior truth, at last discovered none,
> Whence now the second suffers detriment.[48] [519–24]

Then if people wanted to know why he, John, had not averted 'the after-doubt', they must be answered,

> God's gift was that man should conceive of truth
> And yearn to gain it, catching at mistake,
> As midway help till he reach fact indeed.[48] [610–12]

IV

The concept of God as Love, a concept which Browning fails to find in the minds of the rationalist Strauss or the epicure Blougram, any more than in the Bishop of St Praxed's, informs a large number of Browning's poems. Significantly enough, though, it can be found in the minds or hearts of churchmen and laymen both.

To Browning God as Love, whether revealed in Jesus or in any other person, is to be found not necessarily in dogmas and church formularies, but certainly in human experience. The two lovers in *Two in the Campagna* feel the power of God as Love when they feel –

> Infinite passion, and the pain
> Of finite hearts that yearn.

David finds that only when inspired by Love can his singing rescue Saul as from the dead.[49] The Arab physician Karshish is delighted, in spite of himself, with the sudden thought that Lazarus may have been raised from the dead by the Love of God in Jesus. It is true that he explains what happened as a resuscitation by natural means, much as Venturini, Paulus, and other Biblical critics of the 'naturalistic' school had done;[50] yet he cannot help exclaiming,

> The very God! think, Abib; dost thou think?
> So, the All-Great, were the All-Loving too –
> So, through the thunder comes a human voice
> Saying, 'O heart I made, a heart beats here!
> 'Face, my hands fashioned, see it in myself!
> 'Thou hast no power nor mayst conceive of mine,
> 'But love I gave thee, with myself to love,
> 'And thou must love me who have died for thee!'
> The madman saith He said so: it is strange.
> [*An Epistle*, 304–12]

The trouble with Brother Lawrence's cloister-mate and with Guido was not that they disbelieved in the Trinity, the Virgin Birth, the Assumption of the Virgin, or in any other church dogma; their trouble was that they had not known the revelation of Love and that, consequently, their aggressions could issue in hate. The salvation of Caponsacchi and Pompilia was effected neither by law nor by ecclesiasticized Christianity but by Love. A Cleon or a Saul was to be saved, not by any kind of transaction but only by a transmutation. Redemption of even a Guido was possible if he could feel the power of Love:

> So may the truth be flashed out by one blow,
> And Guido see, one instant, and be saved.[51]
>
> [*The Ring and the Book*, X, 2127–8]

But Guido fails to feel this truth until, having called upon all the other powers he knows about, he finally perceives Love in Pompilia, Browning's most glorious creation of a character in whom Love is incarnate.

Because Browning found ample evidence of religion in human experience, he did not need either the external evidence of miracles or the facts of history to strengthen his faith. As he says in *Easter-Day*, it might be comforting to find 'some mummy-scrap' declaring Moses lived, or explaining Jonah's whale, but no –

> The human heart's best; you prefer
> Making that prove the minister
> To truth; you probe its wants and needs,
> And hopes and fears, then try what creeds
> Meet these most aptly, – resolute
> That faith plucks such substantial fruit
> Wherever these two correspond,
> She little needs to look beyond,
> And puzzle out who Orpheus was,
> Or Dionysius Zagrias.[52]   [VII]

Browning himself must be speaking in *The Ring and the Book* when the Pope utters his prophetic words about an age to come, after his death, whose mission shall be 'to shake this torpor of assurance from our creed'. As he sees it, triumph over paganism has been followed by slavish adherence to creeds and belief in the letter of the Scriptures. Must it be necessary in the next age, he asks,

> to break up this the new –
> Faith, in the thing, grown faith in the report –
> Whence need to bravely disbelieve report
> Through increased faith i' the thing reports belie?[53]
>
> [X, 1865–8]

NOTES

[1] H. N. Fairchild, '*La Saisiaz* and *The Nineteenth Century*', *Modern Philology*, XLVIII (1950), p. 105.

[2] Louis Cazamian in E. Legouis and L. Cazamian, *A History of English Literature* (New York: Macmillan, 1929), p. 1232.

[3] George Santayana [see above, p. 29].

[4] Legouis and Cazamian, p. 1232. Edward Berdoe finds in Browning's poetry what his age most needed, 'faith which is adequate to and consistent with its intellectual culture', and which indicates 'the direction in which we must look for the religion of the future'. *Browning's Message for His Time* (New York: Macmillan, 1891), p. 104.

[5] DeVane, *Handbook*, p. 199. DeVane recommends A. C. Pigou, who says, 'for practical purposes, he (Browning) accepted the main doctrines of Christianity', *Robert Browning as a Religious Teacher* (London: Clay, 1901), p. 43.

[6] Betty Miller's psychographic biography seems to have been written mainly to show that Browning had little mind of his own (*Portrait*, pp. 173 ff.). A. W. Crawford, 'Browning's *Christmas-Eve*', *Methodist Review*, CX (1927), describes Browning's return to creedal religion and his acceptance of his wife's religious leadership.

[7] *Browning: How to Know Him* (Indianapolis: Bobbs Merrill, 1915), p. 298.

[8] Letter to Edmund Gosse, quoted from Wilfred Partington's *Thomas J. Wise in the Original Cloth*, by Betty Miller, p. 174.

[9] 'The Religious Opinions of Robert Browning', *Contemporary Review*, LX (1891), p. 885.

[10] Orr, p. 879.

[11] 'Browning's Theism', *Boston Browning Society Papers* (New York: Macmillan, 1897), p. 25.

[12] *Autobiography, Memories and Experiences* (Boston: Houghton, Mifflin, 1904), p. 31.

[13] *Background*, Ch. IX.

[14] *Letters of Robert Browning and Elizabeth Barrett Barrett, 1845–1846* (New York: Harper, 1898), I, 6. [See W. O. Raymond, p. 110 below.]

[15] Fairchild, p. 105. In his conclusion about revelation, Fairchild agrees with Mrs Orr, who wrote (pp. 880–1), 'The one consistent fact of Mr Browning's heterodoxy was its exclusion of any belief in Revelation.'

[16] Santayana, p. 29 above.

[17] H. P. Liddon, *The Divinity of Our Lord* (London: Rivington, 1867), p. 209.

[18] G. E. Buckle, *Life of Benjamin Disraeli* (New York: Macmillan, 1916), IV, p. 326.

[19] The best works on Browning and Biblical criticism are these: W. O. Raymond, 'Browning and Higher Criticism', *PMLA*, XLIV (1929), pp. 590–621 [reprinted in *Infinite Moment*, pp. 19–51]; and DeVane, *Handbook*. A brief general discussion of the inter-relationship of Biblical criticism and Victorian literature is the Introduction to C. F. Harrold and W. H. Templeman, *Victorian Prose* (New York: Oxford, 1938). For some aspects of the subject, see my 'Mark Pattison and the Victorian Scholar', *MLQ*, VI (1945), pp. 423–47; 'Arthur Hugh Clough as Dipsychus', *MLQ*, XII (1951), pp. 39–56; and 'The Ordeal of Anthony Froude, Protestant Victorian', *MLQ*, XIII (1952), pp. 41–55. For the theological aspects, see the following: V. F. Storr, *The Development of English Theology in the Nineteenth Century, 1800–1860* (New York: Longmans, Green, 1913); L. E. Elliot-Binns, *Religion in the Victorian Era* (London: Lutterworth, 1936); Albert Schweitzer, *The Quest of the Historical Jesus* (New York: Macmillan, 1910); C. C. McCown, *The Search for the Real Jesus* (New York: Scribner, 1940); and R. W. Boynton, *Beyond Mythology* (New York: Doubleday, 1951).

[20] In his *The Pentateuch and the Book of Joshua Critically Examined* (1862–4), J. W. Colenso, a mathematician and bishop, advanced views on the authorship and contradictions of the Pentateuch generally accepted today but then considered rank heresy. For a list of writings called forth by Colenso's book, see J. F. Hurst, *History of Rationalism* (New York: Easton and Mains, 1865), pp. 599–602. [See also A. O. J. Cockshut, *Anglican Attitudes* (1959), pp. 62–125.]

[21] See G. E. Lessing, *The Education of the Human Race*; Coleridge, *Confessions of an Inquiring Spirit*; and Carlyle, *Miscellaneous Essays*.

[22] *Letters, 1845–1846*, II, pp. 427–8, 434.

[23] F. G. Kenyon, ed., *The Letters of Elizabeth Barrett Browning* (New York: Macmillan, 1897), II, p. 422.

[24] Mrs Browning, *Poetical Works* (New York: Dodd Mead, 1884), V, p. 294.

[25] Kenyon, II, p. 422.

[26] Kenyon, II, pp. 420, 426–7.

[27] Orr, p. 879.

[28] Royce, p. 25. See also Henry Jones, *Browning as a Philosophical and Religious Teacher* (Glasgow: Maclehose, 1891), Ch. VI; E. M. Naish, *Browning and Dogma* (London: Bell, 1906), pp. 150–2; Raymond, pp. 615–21. [Philip Drew, 'Henry Jones on Browning's Optimism', *VP*, II (1964), pp. 29–41.]

[29] J. C. Collins, in *Posthumous Essays* (ed. by L. C. Collins), points to interesting parallels in Browning's and Lessing's writings.

[30] *Letters, 1845–1846*, II, p. 434.

[31] See Albert Schweitzer's discussion of these men in his *Quest of the Historical Jesus*, Chapters II–V.

[32] Quoted from J. M. Cohen, *Robert Browning* (London: Longmans, Green, 1952), pp. 96–7. [See J. Milsand, 'La Poésie Expressive et Dramatique en Angleterre', *Revue Contemporaine*, XXVII (1856), pp. 511–46.]

[33] Browning, *Poetical Works* (ed. Birrell, 1896, 1914, etc.), I, p. 490.

[34] D. F. Strauss, *Life of Jesus Critically Examined*, tr. George Eliot (London: Swann, Sonnenschein, 1906), pp. 87–8.

[35] Strauss, pp. 69–92.

[36] R. Browning, I, p. 490. Strauss says (pp. 780, 782), 'as subject of the predicate which the church assigns to Christ, we place, instead of an individual, an idea', and 'by the church the evangelical narratives are received as history; by the critical theologian, they are regarded for the most part as mere mythi'.

[37] Strauss, Sec. 14 of the Introduction, especially p. 82.

[38] Strauss, 'Concluding Dissertation: The Dogmatic Import of the Life of Jesus', p. 773.

[39] R. Browning, I, p. 490.

[40] Strauss, p. 773.

[41] R. Browning, I, p. 492.

[42] Strauss says (p. 757) that the critic of the nineteenth century is intrinsically a believer who is 'filled with veneration for every religion, and especially for the substance of the sublimest of all religions, the Christian'; and again (p. 776) he says, 'The facts are become superannuated and doubtful, and only for the sake of the fundamental ideas, are the narratives of these facts an object of reverence.'

[43] R. Browning, I, p. 495.

[44] *Science and English Poetry* (New York: Oxford, 1950), p. 132.

[45] R. Browning, I, p. 536.

[46] Strauss, p. 757.

[47] R. Browning, I, p. 590.

[48] R. Browning, I, pp. 588, 590, 591. Browning may have recalled Strauss's many discussions of the author of the Fourth Gospel, and he certainly was aware of the importance attached to that book by many others of the Biblical critics (see particularly *Life of Jesus*, Part II, Ch. VII). DeVane thinks that *A Death in the Desert* reflects also Browning's readings of Renan's *Life of Jesus*, as well as Strauss's *New Life of Jesus* (*Handbook*, pp. 295–8). Certainly Browning read Renan, who speaks in *Epilogue* to *Dramatis Personae* as the representative of the rationalist position; and in a letter to Miss Blagden, Browning discusses Renan's criticisms of *John* specifically (E. C. McAleer, *Dearest Isa* (Austin: University of Texas, 1951), p. 180).

[49] It is true, as DeVane says (pp. 256–7), that 'the writing of *Christmas-Eve and Easter-Day* (1850) pressed him to solve the religious questions which troubled him, and gave him his clue to the conclusion of *Saul*'. We need not conclude, however, that his solution was belief in the special divinity, or Deity, of Jesus. We may say, rather, that God incarnate in David was a prophecy of God incarnate in Jesus and that both were prophecies of God incarnate in all, or any, men.

[50] For Venturini's and Paulus's explanations, called 'naturalistic', see Schweitzer, Chapters. II–V.

[51] R. Browning, II, p. 245.

[52] R. Browning, I, p. 498.

[53] R. Browning, II, p. 242. Browning anticipates by ten years Matthew Arnold's words ('The Study of Poetry', *Essays in Criticism – Second Series*, par. 1): 'Our religion has materialized itself in the fact, in the supposed fact; it

has attached its emotion to the fact, and now the fact is failing it. . . . The strongest part of our religion today (1879) is in its unconscious poetry.' [For other accounts of Browning's religious ideas, see: Hoxie N. Fairchild, *Religious Trends in English Poetry*, Vol. IV (1957), pp. 132–67; H. C. Duffin, 'Mysticism in Browning', *Hibbert Journal*, LIII (1955), pp. 372–5; Benziger, *Images*, pp. 164–97; J. H. Miller, *Disappearance of God*, pp. 1–16, 81–156.]

WILLIAM C. DEVANE

THE VIRGIN AND THE DRAGON

IN Browning circles, the year 1946 was one of jubilation. There were ceremonies in London and Florence, abroad, and at home the autumnal but vigorous Browning Societies of such cultural centres as Boston, New York, and Los Angeles were in high celebration, for on September 12, one hundred years ago, Robert Browning, the poet, snatched Elizabeth Barrett, considerably more renowned than himself in her day, from her parental home in Wimpole Street, married her before a handful of witnesses in Marylebone Church, and carried her off to the sun-drenched shores of Italy. On Browning's part as well as Miss Barrett's their flight was an act of decision and courage, and also of entirely legal and moral romance. Legend has endowed their act with qualities and colors which truth compels us to modify and subdue. Romance is swift and dangerous; Miss Barrett took a year and a half to come to her decision, and the only real danger lay in the condition of her health. Mr Barrett, her father, was surely not the unique prehistoric monster he has been painted.

The episode, however, catches neatly in its totality the character of the hero of the affair, 'that infinitely respectable rebel', Robert Browning. It was an event that could have happened in quite the way it did only in the benign and domestic reign of Queen Victoria. A half-century earlier, a Shelley or a Byron would have dispensed with the services of the church and the clergy, and a century later the romance would probably have been the fifth or sixth on each side. But here was a marriage made in heaven, or as we say colloquially, 'for keeps'. The success of the marriage has become proverbial, a

From *Yale Review*, XXXVII (1947), pp. 33–46.

legend to posterity. That Browning was at all times conscious of the full implications of his deed, and had in prophetic fashion anticipated and shaped the event itself will be seen from what follows. My present comments fall into three parts, which might be called anticipations of romance, the reality of marriage, and the afterglow of romance.

It ought to be clearly understood that Browning was ready for his moment when it came to him in his thirty-fifth year. He had long dreamed how the event should happen, and had constructed or found a private myth by which the event was to be controlled and shaped. Browning's private myth is a singularly revealing one, reflecting perfectly his romantic, dramatic, and strong-minded character. This myth was the legend of Andromeda. In Greek legend Andromeda was the daughter of Cepheus and Cassiopeia; she lived on the shores of Asia Minor, not far from Joppa. To satisfy Poseidon, the god of the sea, who had been offended by Andromeda's father, she was chained to a rock to be sacrificed to a sea monster. Perseus, the great Athenian hero, was returning from Ethiopia, where he had slain the Gorgon, when he found her in this predicament. He slew the dragon, set the maiden free, and married her in spite of the fact that she had been promised to another prince. She became the ancestress of a great and famous family by Perseus, and Sophocles and Euripides, among others, made the legend of Andromeda the subject of their tragedies. Incidents in the story were represented in numerous works of ancient art.

So great was the fame of Andromeda in the ancient world of the Near East that at her death, as Ovid tells it, she was translated to a constellation in the sky. But as so often happened, the legend was too humanly useful to die or leave the earth, and was merely transferred to a Christian hero and heroine. We know, as a matter of fact, very little about the life of St George, patron saint of England, Aragon, and Portugal. He seems to have flourished mightily in the third century A.D., and then to have suffered martyrdom at Lydda in Palestine about the year 300. The connection of St George with the dragon, familiar since the *Golden Legend* of Jacobus de Voraigne, can be traced to the close of the sixth century. At Arsuf or Joppa, neither of them far from Lydda, Perseus had slain the sea monster that threatened the virgin Andromeda, and George, like many another Christian saint, entered into the inheritance of veneration previously enjoyed by a pagan hero. There is no more curious accident in the annals of hagiography than that St George should have become the patron saint of England. He was, as we have noted, not English or even European by birth. The veneration of St George in Europe was one of the results of the Crusades, for the Crusaders it was who brought back his effigy from Asia Minor. When Eleanor of Aquitaine married Henry II of England in 1152, and went with him to England, she carried with her on her shield the effigy of the saint, who in due course of time became England's patron saint. From about the beginning of the fifteenth century, St George's Day, April 23, has been one of the greatest feasts of the English church. The Red Cross of St George has been for 500 years the great English national emblem, and still shines resplendent at the centre of the Union Jack. Almost every painter of Europe has given us a representation of St George's struggle with the dragon. The Red Cross Knight of the first book of Spenser's *Faerie Queene* is the most famous literary treatment of the subject.

It is clear that the Perseus–Andromeda legend and the St George legend are cognate, and, as we shall see, Browning will move from one to the other with that assurance. It is only necessary to say here that there were extant many debased forms of the legend, and Browning felt free to make use of them as well.

Readers of Browning's letters and biography will remember that the young poet always wrote at a desk over which there hung a copy of Caravaggio's picture of Andromeda, 'the perfect picture', as he called it. As he wrote his first poem, *Pauline*, in the winter of 1832–3, he glanced up at the picture, and recorded what he saw in verse:

> Andromeda!
> And she is with me: years roll, I shall change,
> But change can touch her not – so beautiful
> With her fixed eyes, earnest and still, and hair
> Lifted and spread by the salt-sweeping breeze,
> And one red beam, all the storm leaves in heaven,

Resting upon her eyes and hair, such hair,
As she awaits the snake on the wet beach
By the dark rock and the white wave just breaking
At her feet; quite naked and alone; a thing
I doubt not, nor fear for, secure some god
To save will come in thunder from the stars. [656–67]

The years rolled, but Browning did not change as much as he imagined he would. Two years before the end of his career, that is, in 1887, in the *Parleying with Francis Furini*, he employed for the last time the myth of Andromeda. Furini, the obscure Italian painter, becomes the stalking horse for Browning's defense of nude paintings, and specifically a defense of his son, Pen Browning, whose colossal figures in the nude had been subjected to prudish contemporary criticism. The emphasis in the *Parleying* is upon the nakedness of Andromeda and the goodness of the flesh, but the setting is the same; the blackness, with the single beam of light, the sea and the wind. A little further in the poem the myth of Andromeda is applied differently; this time Andromeda represents Browning's own faith, standing precariously upon the rock of consciousness amidst the growing darkness of the sky and the waters waste and wild, and awaiting destruction from the monsters of new scientific thought, or rescue from heaven.

Early and late, then, Browning uses the Andromeda myth to express his faith. But these brackets must by no means be thought to be empty. In one form or another, the Andromeda pattern may be traced all through the poet's life and works. In the Forties, Count Gismond was the Perseus to rescue the maligned lady of the romance; the ancient Gipsy rescued the Duchess in *The Flight of the Duchess*; in *My Last Duchess* no god came to the rescue of outraged innocence. That was an exception, and the lady of *The Glove* fared better in spite of the established story to the contrary. But Browning had good reason to make the Perseus of this latter story attractive and young, for the poem was written in 1845 under the eye of Miss Barrett. It was a short step from writing these things and thinking habitually in these terms, to performing them in actual life, so we are not surprised when in 1846 Browning plays the part of

Perseus to Miss Barrett's Andromeda, with only the part of the dragon left over for the unfortunate and misunderstood Mr Barrett. Such a stroke as that might well confirm a man's belief in his role for life. In Browning's Italian days, the Perseus–Andromeda pattern finds a more subtle expression – all the obvious rescues have been accomplished – but after Mrs Browning's death, the pattern becomes prominent again in retrospect. This is especially true in *The Ring and the Book*, where Browning is striving to build his masterpiece on a huge scale, and to make it a masterpiece peculiarly his own. Here we see Pompilia–Mrs Browning–Andromeda rescued from the dragon Guido by Caponsacchi–Browning–Perseus, first; and later when truth or justice is endangered, Pope Innocent, the Vicegerent of God, is the rescuer.

But this is to anticipate those middle years of Browning's life, mainly spent in Italy, when his romance turned into the reality of marriage. The fine poetic flowering of these years is given to us in *Men and Women*, published in 1855, nine years after his marriage and his flight to Italy, and it is the thinking and feeling of those two superb volumes that I wish to examine at this point. For it is in *Men and Women* that Browning ceases to be the romantic young man, and turns his heart and intelligence to the scrutiny of the relationship in marriage of man to woman and woman to man. Here the poet is not the romantic dreamer, but the observer and the recorder, and assuredly the moralist. To paraphrase King Lear, 'he takes upon him the mystery of things, as if he were God's spy' – a passage from Shakespeare's play which Browning used and was particularly fond of. And in these golden volumes of 1855 we get those amazing insights into the human heart upon which Browning's immortality as a poet must in large part ultimately rest.

The first effect of Elizabeth Barrett upon the poetry of her husband was not a happy one. In some of the earliest letters which Elizabeth Barrett wrote to Browning in 1845 she begins to manage and reform him. It seems a malady incident to being a good woman. Miss Barrett is a little unhappy about her suitor's interest in the theatre, and his lack in recent years of evangelical fervor in chapel attendance; she is profoundly uneasy over Browning's habitual poetical technique – she constantly urges him to drop his dramatic mask and speak out in the first person singular, to find, as she might put it, his own voice. She is also eager to have him speak directly upon religious and moral topics especially and become a prophet to his age. Being an obedient husband, he tried his best to be the kind of poet his wife wanted him to be. And so, in 1850, he published the first volume since his marriage, *Christmas-Eve and Easter-Day*, in which he spoke in the first person upon the problems of religious faith and doubt in contemporary terms. In spite of many splendid passages the result was not significant for its day, and is even less so for ours.[1] *Christmas-Eve and Easter-Day* must be reckoned a failure also on commercial grounds, for it sold only two hundred copies.

But, happily, Mrs Browning got preoccupied with other things, and in those seemingly idle, sun-lit years as the poet strolled about the streets and environs of Florence with Flush at his heels, Browning worked out his poetic salvation. The cares and joys of motherhood absorbed Mrs Browning, and before long she was also writing about Italian liberty and constructing *Aurora Leigh*. It was a release for Browning which he never acknowledged, and perhaps never recognized. But then as he walked about Florence he thought of many things – of the kind of poetry he could write, and only he; of the great artists of earlier times, the musicians and painters, and their relations to their women, of the true function of the poet, and, above all, of the intimate relation between man and woman in the blessed state of matrimony. There was no rebellion towards his wife in him, but rather a profound gratitude and wonder at his own good fortune. In the poem *By the Fireside*, he watched her as she sat –

> Musing by fire-light, that great brow
> And the spirit-small hand propping it. . . .

And to himself he said:

> . . . If I tread
> This path back, is it not in pride
> To think how little I dreamed it led
> To an age so blest that, by its side,
> Youth seems the waste instead? [XXV]

For art's sake, the poet transfers the perfect meeting of lovers'
spirits in this poem to a forest scene, high in the Apennines. It
really just took place in London's dreary Wimpole Street. For that
high rare communion of hearts he is everlastingly grateful –

> You might have turned and tried a man,
>   Set him a space to weary and wear,
> And prove which suited more your plan,
>   His best of hope or his worst despair,
> Yet end as he began.
>
> But you spared me this, like the heart you are,
>   And filled my empty heart at a word.
> If two lines join, there is oft a scar,
>   They are one and one, with a shadowy third;
> One near one is too far.
>
> A moment after, and hands unseen
>   Were hanging the night around us fast;
> But we knew that a bar was broken between
>   Life and life: we were mixed at last
> In spite of the mortal screen.
>
> The forests had done it; there they stood;
>   We caught for a moment the powers at play:
> They had mingled us so, for once and good,
>   Their work was done – we might go or stay,
> They relapsed to their ancient mood. [XLV–XLVIII]

But such a communion of spirit most men never know, or if they
know it, they know it fleetingly and rarely. It is the lot of most of
us to live alone, and between us there flows the unplumbed, salt
estranging sea. In *Two in the Campagna* the lovers never meet, in
spite of the speaker's strong desire:

> No. I yearn upward, touch you close,
>   Then stand away. I kiss your cheek,
> Catch your soul's warmth, – I pluck the rose
>   And love it more than tongue can speak –
> Then the good minute goes.

These are but two poems in *Men and Women*, volumes which give us the anatomy of married love. Look for a moment at the titles of the poems: *Love among the Ruins, A Lovers' Quarrel, A Woman's Last Word, Any Wife to any Husband, A Serenade at the Villa, A Pretty Woman, Respectability, A Light Woman, The Statue and the Bust, Love in a Life, Life in a Love, The Last Ride Together, Andrea del Sarto, In Three Days, In a Year, Women and Roses, The Guardian Angel, One Way of Love, Another Way of Love, Misconceptions, One Word More.* Not all the experiences recorded in these poems happened in their fulness to Browning, of course; from his own relations with his wife he picked up a hint here and a suggestion there, and his friends and acquaintances did not escape his scrutinizing eye. Not since John Donne had any such intimate revelation of married love been given us. In the full scope we see love triumphant, and love rejected; love eager and young, and love satiated; love a strong support, and love betrayed; love making heroes of men, and love enslaving and corrupting them. The poet's theme is love in all its guises. If at one end of the human scale, love is a foretaste of heaven, at the other end it can be a foretaste of hell. From the whole we gradually ascertain the unforgivable sin against love – the sin that is committed by the lovers of *The Statue and the Bust.* For those lovers, profoundly committed in their hearts to their love for each other, never dare to take the illicit step which would unite them. Indecision, respect for convention, and cowardice are the qualities of their failure –

> The counter our lovers staked was lost
> As surely as if it were lawful coin:
> And the sin I impute to each frustrate ghost
>
> Is – the unlit lamp and the ungirt loin. . . . [244–7]

A colder and more exact judgment would have been kinder to these lovers; but to the generous and impulsive poet, their failure was anathema. These lovers are really lost souls:

> So! While these wait the trump of doom,
> How do their spirits pass, I wonder,
> Nights and days in the narrow room?

Still, I suppose, they sit and ponder
What a gift life was, ages ago,
Six steps out of the chapel yonder.

Only they see not God, I know,
Nor all that chivalry of his,
The soldier-saints who, row on row,

Burn upward each to his point of bliss – [2] [214–23]

This theme of 'love not taken when it is at hand' is the subject of many poems in the poet's next volume, *Dramatis Personae*, of 1864.

But the golden time of Browning's life and genius comes to an end in 1861, for in that year Mrs Browning died. From that time to the end of his life, his comments upon love are the remembrance of things past. We now enter his third phase in these matters, and it is a phase in which he reverts to his first or Andromeda phase, with experience and memory added. Earlier in this essay I mentioned the large pattern of *The Ring and the Book*, of 1868, where Browning attempted to build his masterpiece on an epic scale, and to make it a work in technique and substance peculiarly his own. In *The Ring and the Book*, we see Pompilia rescued from the dragon Guido by Caponsacchi in the first instance; and later when truth or ultimate justice is endangered, Pope Innocent comes to save it.

But to point to these large patterns in *The Ring and the Book* is to give the barest indication of the manner in which the myth of Andromeda (with which Mrs Browning is now completely identified) had penetrated and shaped the conscious thinking and the deeper unconscious feeling in the poet's greatest single achievement. I wish now to look at the prevalence, or rather the all-pervasiveness, of the Andromeda legend through certain books of *The Ring and the Book* – including with the Andromeda myth its Christian cognate, the legend of St George and the dragon. In those books of *The Ring and the Book* where the speakers give favourable judgments upon Pompilia and Caponsacchi, I have counted at least thirty references to the Andromeda and its cognate myth, not counting such facts as this – that Browning, for all his accuracy and care in consulting the Astronomer Royal upon the condition of the moon on the night of

Pompilia's flight, April 29–30, 1697, at the last moment changed the
date, but not the moon, so that the flight would fall on April 23,
St George's Day. By the light or cynical speakers in *The Ring and
the Book*, the flight of Pompilia and Caponsacchi is usually referred
to in the terms of the story of Helen and Paris, *De Raptu Helenae*;
and Guido's pursuit is likened humorously to Vulcan pursuing Mars
to get back his Venus. But it is not too much to say that whenever
Browning is representing, favorably to Pompilia and Caponsacchi --
and that is a great deal of the time – the great scene at the inn at
Castelnuovo where the real conflict between the opposing forces
takes place, he habitually and consistently thinks of it in the terms of
the Andromeda situation, with Caponsacchi as Perseus, Pompilia as
the manacled victim, and Guido as the dragon. Moreover, the scene
is generally set as nearly as possible with the colors he imagined in
the Andromeda scene. Caponsacchi thus pictures Pompilia in that
moment at the inn:

> She started up, stood erect, face to face
> With the husband: back he fell, was buttressed there
> By the window all aflame with morning-red,
> He the black figure, the opprobrious blur
> Against all peace and joy and light and life.
> [VI, 1523–7]

And Pompilia speaking of the same scene describes Guido as 'the
serpent towering and triumphant' [VII, 1589]. When the Pope
thinks of Pompilia in the clutches of Guido, he uses a figure appropriate to Andromeda's plight:

> Such denizens o' the cave now cluster round
> And heat the furnace sevenfold: time indeed
> A bolt from heaven should cleave roof and clear place,
> Transfix and show the world, suspiring flame,
> The main offender, scar and brand the rest
> Hurrying, each miscreant to his hole: then flood
> And purify the scene with outside day –
> Which yet, in the absolutest drench of dark,
> Ne'er wants a witness, some stray beauty-beam
> To the despair of hell.   [X, 994–1003]

When Browning himself describes the same situation – Pompilia
in the power of Guido and his family – he says:

> . . . These I saw,
> In recrudescency of baffled hate,
> Prepare to wring the uttermost revenge
> From body and soul thus left them: all was sure,
> Fire laid and cauldron set, the obscene ring traced,
> The victim stripped and prostrate: what of God?
> The cleaving of a cloud, a cry, a crash,
> Quenched lay their cauldron, cowered i' the dust the crew,
> As, in a glory of armour like Saint George,
> Out again sprang the young good beauteous priest
> Bearing away the lady in his arms. . . . [I, 577–87]

Indeed, so steadily is the Perseus–St George legend used in *The
Ring and the Book* that we may know what to think of each speaker
by the treatment he accords the myth, and by what version of the
myth he employs. The speaker in *The Other Half-Rome*, favorable
to Pompilia, gives the legend a Christian character, but he only
faintly realizes his figure. When he has sketched the miraculous
rescue of Pompilia by Caponsacchi, he turns upon his auditor:

> How do you say? It were improbable;
> So is the legend of my patron-saint. [III, 1050–1]

In Caponsacchi's monologue the scene of Andromeda's distress
before the rescuer comes is set again and again – in the box at the
theatre with Guido lurking in the background, and in the window of
her house, for example – and always in the same terms of darkness
and light. Of course, Caponsacchi was only a partially effective
Perseus or St George, and being modest, cannot refer to himself in
such terms, except ironically, as he does here when he is addressing
the judges:

> I rise in your esteem, sagacious Sirs,
> Stand up a renderer of reasons, not
> The officious priest would personate Saint George
> For a mock Princess in undragoned days.
> [VI, 1769–72]

But there is nothing, or very little, to keep Pompilia in her monologue from speaking of Caponsacchi as Perseus or St George, and she constantly refers to him as such. One of the legends in the tapestries in her house, she recalls, had as its subject 'the slim young man / With wings at head, and wings at feet, and sword / Threatening a monster' [VII, 390–2]. And, of course, though she cannot call herself Andromeda, she constantly recognizes herself in the role of the helpless and innocent victim, and Caponsacchi as the heaven-sent rescuer.

The characters of evil import in *The Ring and the Book* use the same essential myth, but use it in a debased form or for a base purpose. Thus Guido uses it when in his defense he gives an account of one of his ancestors who met death in the region where Perseus and St George had performed their exploits:

> One of us Franceschini fell long since
> I' the Holy Land, betrayed, tradition runs,
> To Paynims by the feigning of a girl
> He rushed to free from ravisher, and found
> Lay safe enough with friends in ambuscade
> Who flayed him while she clapped her hands and laughed:
> Let me end, falling by a like device.   [V, 1418–24]

The keen intelligence of Guido sees the matter clearly, whatever he may make of it, but the dim mind of Bottinius, the lawyer for Pompilia's cause, can only arrive at this approximation of the Andromeda myth in his defense of Pompilia's conduct in arranging for her flight:

> 'Methinks I view some ancient bas-relief.
> There stands Hesione thrust out by Troy,
> Her father's hand has chained her to a crag,
> Her mother's from the virgin plucked the vest,
> At a safe distance both distressful watch,
> While near and nearer comes the snorting orc.
> I look that, white and perfect to the end,
> She wait till Jove despatch some demigod;
> Not that, – impatient of celestial club
> Alcmena's son should brandish at the beast, –
> She daub, disguise her dainty limbs with pitch,
> And so elude the purblind monster! Ay,

The trick succeeds, but 'tis an ugly trick,
Where needs have been no trick!' . . .
Trick, I maintain, had no alternative.
The heavens were bound with brass, – Jove far at feast . . .
With the unblamed Aethiop, – Hercules spun wool
I' the lap of Omphale, while Virtue shrieked –
The brute came paddling all the faster. You
Of Troy, who stood at distance, where's the aid
You offered in the extremity? . . .
   He,
He only, Caponsacchi 'mid a crowd,
Caught Virtue up, carried Pompilia off. . . .
   . . . what you take for pitch
Is nothing worse, belike, than black and blue,
Mere evanescent proof that hardy hands
Did yeoman's service, cared not where the gripe
Was more than duly energetic. . . . [IX, 967–1008]

All this is sufficiently far from that other admirer of Euripides
who thought in his youth that 'if Virtue feeble were, Heaven itself
would stoop to her', but it is characteristic of Browning and will serve.
It must not be imagined that Browning dropped the Perseus–
Andromeda conception of life after *The Ring and the Book*.[3] Perhaps
the most direct and poignant use of the theme of rescue in all the
poet's writings occurs in *Balaustion's Adventure*, two years later,
where Browning gives us a transcript of Euripides' *Alcestis*. There,
it will be remembered, Heracles rescues the lady from death itself.
Both overtly and covertly the poem is bound to the memory of the
poet's dead wife. But this is only one instance among a dozen. In the
Parleying with Francis Furini at the end of his life, as we have seen,
Browning made another frank avowal of his myth, and utilized it
this time as an explanation of his religious faith. How closely Mrs
Browning had become a part of that total faith one may easily see.

By the time that Browning was writing his *Parleying with Francis
Furini*, in 1887, the bright world of his youth had taken on a sombre
hue. In the death of Mrs Browning he had suffered an irreparable
loss, and after 1861, for all his dining out and being lionized, he was
often a lonely man. In the realm of his faith, too, the shocks had
come. The fierce assaults of the Higher Criticism upon the literal

authority of the Bible had undermined and doomed the evangelical position in which Browning had been bred. Science, moreover, had shaken his faith in his dearly loved doctrine of progress, or at least had changed that conception from the triumphal march of an earlier notion to the long, slow evolution of man with many setbacks and retrogressions. Economically and industrially, too, the lines of the graph no longer strained to the upper right-hand corner. There was distress in imperial England, and there were wars and rumors of wars in the air. There was not much to comfort the serious observer in 1887. The bright morning of the Forties had turned into an ominous twilight.

The murky atmosphere of this later time is faithfully reflected in Browning's last use of the Andromeda myth. In the *Parleying with Francis Furini* the maiden is once more chained to the rock amidst the dark waters. Here in the dusk she symbolizes the poet's faith in the destiny of man and the providence of God. There is an air of desperation in the scene, for as yet no God has come in thunder from the stars to effect a rescue, and the sea beast comes apace.

And Elizabeth Barrett Browning, dead now for twenty-six years, has become –

> Perhaps but a memory, after all!
> – Of what came once when a woman leant
> To feel for my brow where her kiss might fall.
> [*Dubiety*, 21–3][4]

NOTES

[1] [For another view of *Christmas-Eve and Easter-Day* see Badger, p. 83–7 above.]

[2] [See W. O. Raymond, 'Browning's *The Statue and the Bust*', *UTQ*, XXVIII (1959), pp. 233–49.]

[3] [On *The Ring and the Book* see: Chesterton, *Browning* (EML), Ch. VII, pp. 160–76; Langbaum, *Experience*, Ch. III, pp. 109–36; E. D. H. Johnson, 'Robert Browning's Pluralistic Universe: A Reading of *The Ring and the Book*', *UTQ*, XXXI (1961), pp. 20–41.]

[4] [For other accounts of Browning's imagery see: John K. Bonnell, 'Touch Images in the Poetry of Browning', *PMLA*, XXXVII (1922), pp. 574–98; C. Willard Smith, *Browning's Star-Imagery* (1941); Honan, *Characters*, Ch. VI, pp. 166–206; R. E. Hughes, 'Browning's *Childe Roland* and the Broken Taboo', *Literature and Psychology*, IX (1959), pp. 18–19; C. C. Watkins, 'The "Abstruser Themes" of Browning's *Fifine at the Fair*', *PMLA*, LXXIV (1959), pp. 426–37.]

WILLIAM O. RAYMOND

'THE JEWELLED BOW': A STUDY IN BROWNING'S IMAGERY AND HUMANISM

I N Browning's second letter to Elizabeth Barrett he uses the imagery
of 'white light' versus 'prismatic hues' to represent the contrast
between the full and direct reflection of her personality in lyric
utterance, and the partial and oblique refraction of his own personality
in the medium of the dramatic monologue. A little later, he reveals
his consciousness of the limitations of his poetry through a kindred
image: 'these scenes and song-scraps *are* such mere and very escapes
of my inner power, which lives in me like the light in those crazy
Mediterranean phares I have watched at sea, wherein the light is
ever revolving in a dark gallery, bright and alive, and only after a
weary interval leaps out, for a moment, from the one narrow chink,
and then goes on with the blind wall between it and you . . .'[1] In
response, Elizabeth Barrett, while deprecating the merit of her own
poetry and paying tribute to the worth of Browning's, acknowledges
the justice of his self-criticism: 'and in fact, you have not written the
R. B. poem yet – your rays fall obliquely rather than directly straight.
I see you only in your moon' (I, 22). In one of her letters, though
referring to 'the glory of dramatic art', she urges: 'Yet I am conscious of wishing you to take the other crown besides – and after
having made your own creatures speak in clear human voices, to
speak yourself out of that personality which God made, and with the
voice which he tuned into such power and sweetness of speech'
(II, 182).

When contrasting lyric and dramatic poetry, it was inevitable that

---

From *PMLA*, LXX (1955), pp. 115-31.

Browning should have in mind not only Elizabeth Barrett's verse, but also the art and personality of Shelley, whose influence upon him was so potent. It is probable that the imagery of 'white light' versus 'prismatic hues' was suggested by Shelley's lines in *Adonais*:

> Life, like a dome of many-coloured glass,
> Stains the white radiance of Eternity.

Previously, in *Pauline*, he had apostrophized Shelley as the 'Sun-treader'; and the metaphor of 'white light' is frequently introduced as representative of the aspiration, idealism, and spiritual quality of Shelley's life and poetry. In a more general sense, the imagery of 'white light' is used by Browning in many connotations as a symbol of spiritual verities which are absolute and ideal – the nature of God, Truth, Beauty, Goodness, Heaven, the Soul. In the initial reference from his correspondence I have cited, he identifies 'the pure white light' with truth. Truth, in its absoluteness, is regarded by him as a divine endowment of the soul, enshrined in the depths of personality. As he wrote in *Paracelsus*:

> There is an inmost centre in us all,
> Where truth abides in fulness . . . (I, 727–8)

> and to know
> Rather consists in opening out a way
> Whence the imprisoned splendour may escape,
> Than in effecting entry for a light
> Supposed to be without. (I, 732–6)

The symbolism of 'white light' and of 'prismatic hues' is, in the main, confined in Browning's letters to an illustration of the limitation of his poetic medium of expression, the dramatic monologue. This, however, is a pendant to the comprehensive use of this metaphor in his poetry. Its occurrence is so frequent, and its application so varied, that it may be regarded as not merely illustrative, but of structural value. Before referring further to its employment in connection with Browning's art, I shall consider its wider significance. This involves basic aspects of the poet's life and thought which are both subjective and objective in their nature. They include

III

two normative attitudes of mind or dispositions of spirit which, psychologically, have their sources in his individual personality. They also include two important environmental influences instrumental in moulding his philosophy of life. These are his artistic inheritance of the ideals of romanticism as represented by the poetry of Shelley, and his religious convictions as represented by evangelical Christianity. It is with these larger references in view that I have linked the imagery of the prism, the rainbow, the broken and deflected light, with the humanism of his poetry. While the 'white light' of Browning's transcendentalism is of import, it is, as I shall strive to show, secondary to the 'prismatic hues' of his humanism.

Although Browning for many years regarded himself as a disciple of Shelley, it is important to realize the basic differences between the two poets. Shelley's life and poetry are, in a sense, all of one piece. Browning's, on the other hand, are complex, motivated by his consciousness of the necessity of reconciling the absolute claims of the ideal with the concrete realities of man's existence on earth. 'I . . . fear the pure white light, even if it is in me,' Browning told Elizabeth Barrett. He was aware that one side of his nature was in kinship with Shelley. As a scion of the romantic era in English poetry he inherited its transcendental idealism. This dominant artistic influence was reinforced by psychical elements in his personality. In *Pauline*, as was noted by John Stuart Mill, the intense self-consciousness of the youthful poet is everywhere in evidence.[2] Conscious of the prodigality of his intellectual and spiritual powers and of the boundless capacities of the soul, he, like Shelley, felt the urge to transcend the limitations of the external world, the barriers imposed by sense and time:

> How should this earth's life prove my only sphere?
> Can I so narrow sense but that in life
> Soul still exceeds it?   (634–6)

The romantic aspiration to spurn the trammels of the finite in quest of the infinite, to seek 'the pure white light', to give free expression to the fulness of personality, to press on towards the Absolute and its spiritual radiance of Truth, Beauty, and Goodness – these typical impulses and motifs of Shelley have their reflection in Browning.

There is, however, a strong counter-current in his life and poetry which flows like a gulf between him and Shelley. While the aspiration of the soul is infinite and its destiny immortal, Browning holds that it must stoop to conquer. The core of his ethics is that the limitations of this finite world are a school of discipline intended to serve the end of spiritual growth. Hence it is imperative for men to to work within these, even though constantly striving to make reality conform more nearly to the standard of the ideal. Browning's philosophy of life, with its deep sense of human experience as poised between the absolute and the relative, is reinforced by his religious belief, the profound influence of the spirit and tenets of Christianity. His humanism is nowhere more in evidence than in the place given in his poetry to the Christian doctrine of the Incarnation. His interpretation of this is not a mere echo of the formal and traditional theology of English Puritanism. For him the Incarnation of Christ is not only a matter of historical record enshrined in a creed or a body of religious opinion. It is an eternal truth verified in his inner and personal experience, and made the subject of deep and individual reflection. In particular, it is inseparably linked with what has been called 'the richest vein of pure ore' in his poetry, his view of the nature and function of love. The divine condescension to human weakness and imperfection is conceived of by Browning as flowing from the very essence of God as a being of infinite love:

> The very God! think, Abib; dost thou think?
> So, the All-Great, were the All-Loving too –
> So, through the thunder comes a human voice
> Saying, 'O heart I made, a heart beats here!
> Face, my hands fashioned, see it in myself!
> Thou hast no power nor mayst conceive of mine,
> But love I gave thee, with myself to love,
> And thou must love me who have died for thee!'
> (*Epistle of Karshish*, 304–11)

It is in *Pauline*, *Paracelsus*, and *Sordello*, elaborate studies of soul-development, that the interplay between the transcendental and humanistic elements of Browning's philosophy of life is most strikingly in evidence. In them we may trace the tension and conflict between what I have called the two basic attitudes or dispositions of his mind and spirit, and their reconciliation through the sovereign virtue of love. All poetry, Browning once wrote to Ruskin, is the problem of 'putting the infinite within the finite'.[3] It is this crux, in the sphere of life as well as art, that is the central theme of his three early monodramas; and it is also the poet's personal problem. The heroes of these poems are unmistakably of the romantic type. They are all characterized by a restless and eager self-consciousness, indomitable aspiration, illimitable desires, and a passion for the absolute which impel them to reject or scorn the bounds and imperfections of the finite. Images of white light or of the star are often introduced to symbolize their aims and qualities. The speaker in *Pauline* refers to his pride 'in wandering o'er thought's world' to seek 'the White Way for a star' [cf. 401–3]. Paracelsus, in his vain attempt 'to contemplate undazzled some one truth', confesses 'what was a speck expands into a star . . . till I near craze' [I. 555–9]. His mind, like Aprile's, became 'dazzled by shapes that filled its length with light' [II, 574]. Aprile is described as 'the over-radiant star / Too mad to drink the life-springs' [V, 873–4]. Sordello, 'thrusting in time, eternity's concern,' [I, 567] aspires to –

> Compress the starriest into one star,
> And grasp the whole at once!   (I, 855–6)

Allusions to Shelley, the 'Sun-treader', occur in all three poems, and it is clear that their principal characters reflect, in varying degrees, that side of Browning's nature which is in kinship with the transcendental idealism of Shelley. Aprile, in particular, embodies that conception of love as a spiritual principle, a thirst for the absolute, the pursuit of an eternal and perfect archetypal loveliness which is in harmony with the romantic Neo-Platonism of Shelley. Such a love, though 'through the web of being blindly wove', can be but dimly foreshadowed in the perishable forms of earth. This concept of love strikes a responsive chord in Browning's being, and he has given it fine poetic expression in Part II of *Paracelsus*.[4] Yet the deeper significance of the poem is not fully revealed until Part V. In it Browning represents love not as an infinite aspiration in keeping with the romantic idealism of Shelley, but rather in the spirit of the Christian *Magnificat*. He visualizes it as a love that stoops to conquer, submits itself to the lowliness of human nature, and refuses to spurn the body or despise the world in the interests of an ascetic ideal of spirituality:

> love – not serenely pure,
> But strong from weakness, like a chance-sown plant –
> (V, 698–9)

> Love which endures and doubts and is oppressed
> And cherished, suffering much and much sustained,
> And blind, oft-failing, yet believing love,
> A half-enlightened, often chequered trust . . .
> (V, 702–5)

It is from the standpoint of the second disposition of his spirit that Browning is acutely conscious of the one-sidedness of the idealism of the romantic Titans he has portrayed in his monodramas. Blinded by a vision of the absolute, 'the pure white light', they refuse to stoop to life on earth. They fail, as is pointed out in *Paracelsus*, because they have never grasped the deeper meaning of love. A comprehension of this would have taught them to sympathize with the weakness and imperfection of human nature, and not to disdain to work within the sphere of man's finite existence. This conception of love has its supreme prototype in the person of Christ, the Divine Love that for man's sake became poor and of low estate.

> 'T is the weakness in strength, that I cry for! my flesh, that I seek
> In the Godhead!   (*Saul*, XVIII, 22–3)

Browning parts company with Shelley in the interests of a noble humanism, and in accordance with the deepest convictions of his religious faith.

Browning's humanism has many facets. Its most obvious illustration is the variety and scope of his dramatic portrayal of individual character in flashes of crucial experience. 'My Elixir of Life' was

Rossetti's enthusiastic tribute to the delineation of human nature in *Men and Women*, a phrase revealing his delight in its vivacity and realism. The title of this collection of poems might aptly be regarded as summing up the central interest of the whole of Browning's poetry. While as a follower of the Romantic era he inherits its love of nature, he rarely describes nature for her own sake. Though there is much fine landscape painting in his poems, this is the background rather than the foreground of his canvas. Nature is subordinated to man. His portrayal of her is selective, designed to illustrate and enhance, either by likeness or contrast, those human moods or states which are the dominating motifs of his poetry.

The title *Men and Women* is also indicative of the particular quality of Browning's humanism. His primary concern is with the individual rather than with the group. The broad conception of humanity, so dear to the hearts of the poets of romanticism, is but faintly reflected in his verse. Nor is he greatly moved by the ideals of liberty, equality, and fraternity, associated with this humanitarian impulse in the epoch of the French Revolution. It is true that in *Sordello*, a work composed when Shelley's influence upon him was still potent, he represents his hero as finally dedicating himself to liberty and the service of humanity. But this generalized devotion to the principle of liberty and to man as man finds but little echo in the body of his verse. In his mature work he pays scarcely more than lip service to these concepts.

Nor is there evidence that the groupings of men in communal institutions, of which the nation is an outstanding example, kindled Browning's poetic imagination. In an early play, *Strafford*, he reveals his sympathy with the Puritans and the ideal of liberty they champion. Yet, even here, the drama is focused in the character of Strafford rather than in a national cause. As S. R. Gardiner comments: 'from the beginning to the end of the play the personal relations between the actors are exaggerated at the expense of the political.'[5]

Through his residence in Florence, Browning was in close touch with the Italian struggle for independence; and it is this which comes closest to being an inspiring patriotic motif in his poetry. There is, however, a contrast between the ardour of Mrs Browning's devotion to the national aspirations of Italy and her husband's more tempered sympathy. In particular, he never shared her enthusiasm for Louis Napoleon as the prospective deliverer of Italy from the yoke of Austria. Browning is far from indifferent. In occasional poems, such as *Pippa Passes*, *The Italian in England*, and *Old Pictures in Florence*, his support of Italy's cause is manifest. Yet in these his interest is incidental, subordinate in the first two instances to the dramatic representation of individual character, and in the third to the main theme of the paintings of the early Italian masters.

In the dedicatory letter to his friend Milsand, prefixed to *Sordello* [1863 version], Browning wrote: 'The historical decoration was purposely of no more importance than a background requires; and my stress lay on the incidents in the development of a soul: little else is worth study.' This statement would not be applicable to the whole of Browning's poetry without qualification. In *Pauline* and *Paracelsus* the poet is absorbed in the description and analysis of inner states of consciousness. There is no historical background in *Pauline* and only a minimum of it in *Paracelsus*. In *Sordello*, however, it assumes greater importance; and, beginning with the *Dramatic Lyrics* of 1842, the historical setting is a vital element in Browning's poetry. The men and women of his poems are representative of their eras and reflect the milieu – political, artistic, and religious – of the times in which they live. His interest in all the works of man is unflagging, and the fecundity of his humanism is finely illustrated by his panoramic vistas of the exhibition of these on the stage of history. His characters are not conceived in abstraction from their environments, but are motivated by the currents of active life and thought of their epochs, which range from ancient Israel and Athens to contemporary Italy and England.

Yet, despite this wealth of historical background, the primary and pivotal inspiration of Browning's poetry lies in the delineation of the individual rather than the group, and in inward consciousness rather than external circumstance. The historical settings of his poems are means to an end, their function being to influence or illumine cruxes in the lives of the men and women whose soul-development or soul-atrophy is his central theme. Unlike Tennyson, Browning shows little interest in social progress, the evolution of the the race, laws and principles which have a general bearing on humanity as an entity. 'Nor does he', as Edmund Dowden writes, 'anywhere study political phenomena or events except as they throw light on an individual character.'[6] It is significant that the favourite historical background of his poems is the Renaissance, an age of humanistic individualism, in contrast with the other-worldliness and social conformity of the Middle Ages.

The initial and most striking evidence of Browning's distinction as a humanist is the scope and variety of his portrait gallery of men and women, a wealth of character painting unsurpassed in modern poetry. In this connection he may be fairly compared with Chaucer, Shakespeare, and Scott. A master in the vivid, impressionistic medium of the dramatic monologue, he has given us a comprehensive vista of all manner and conditions of people, in climes and ages far asunder, in circumstances and situations of the most diverse sort.

My purpose, however, is not to enlarge upon Browning's dramatic portrayal of men and women, but rather to consider the intrinsic qualities of his humanism. In dealing with the relation between God and man, his convictions are those of a Christian humanist. However intimate their communion, the poet's sense of the pricelessness of individual personality prevents him from accepting any theory which would regard man as destined, here or hereafter, to be merged or absorbed in the being of God. Browning is not amongst the mystics of English poetry, and pantheism is abhorrent to him. In connection with man's life on earth, he constantly stresses its relative independence. There is a line of demarcation between God and man which God himself has ordained as a pledge and seal of the moral dignity of human freedom and responsibility.

> But also, God, whose pleasure brought
> Man into being, stands away
> As it were a handbreadth off, to give
> Room for the newly-made to live,
> And look at him from a place apart,
> And use his gifts of brain and heart,

> Given indeed, but to keep for ever . . .
> Man, therefore, stands on his own stock
> Of love and power as a pin-point rock!
>   (*Christmas-Eve*, V, 27–33, 44–5)

This divorce of man's 'rock' from God's 'boundless continent' is restated, with variant imagery, in the parables of *Ferishtah's Fancies*[7] and elsewhere.

The humanism of Browning's ethics may justly be called the core of his philosophy of life. This pivots on the worth and paramount importance of the moral struggle in the life of the individual. For Browning, as for Keats, the world is the 'vale of Soul-making.' In the *Epilogue* to *Dramatis Personae* he pictures all the powers of nature flowing like the currents of ocean 'toward some elected point of central rock', the personality of the individual:

> As though the pageant's end were to enhance
> His worth, and – once the life, his product, gained –
> Roll away elsewhere, keep the strife sustained . . .
>   (89–91)

In *By the Fireside* he exclaims:

> How the world is made for each of us!
> How all we perceive and know in it
> Tends to some moment's product thus,
> When a soul declares itself – to wit,
> By its fruit, the thing it does! (XLIX)

Browning's acute consciousness that the central purpose of life on earth is the fashioning of individual character led him to stress its hazards and hardships. The world is ordained to be a moral battle ground, a sphere of trial, testing, and probation. The limitations, obstacles, hostile forces with which man must grapple are the stern but indispensable conditions of soul-development. In order to accentuate the poignancy and arduousness of this process, the poet dwells with unflinching realism on the grim potency of evil and suffering. His distrust of human reason causes him to add to these the weakness of intellectual nescience:

> Were knowledge all thy faculty, then God
> Must be ignored . . . (*A Pillar at Sebzevar*, 134–5)

Nevertheless in this moral warfare man does not fight unaided without the help of God. Browning's sceptical theory of knowledge never invalidates the evidence of his heart that God and man are in communion through the sovereign instrumentality of love. Yet it is characteristic of his humanism and his perception of the integrity of individuality that he never represents God as weakening man's moral fibre by impinging upon his freedom of choice in any moral crisis. God may even for a time seem to stand aloof in order that the will and resolution with which he has endowed his creature may be evoked and tested:

> God, ever‑mindful in all strife and strait,
> Who, for our own good, makes the need extreme,
> Till at the last He puts forth might and saves.
> (*The Ring and the Book*, VII, 1386–8)

This view of the relation between God and man is in keeping with Browning's emphasis on the distinction between the spheres of eternity and time. Were an unclouded vision of eternity vouchsafed to man it would thwart the moral purpose of his earthly life, the development of his soul in a finite world of travail and temptation. This is the central theme of *An Epistle of Karshish*. Lazarus, whom Christ raised from the dead, is an illustration of 'Heaven opened to a soul while yet on earth, / Earth forced on a soul's use while seeing heaven' (141–2). Having beheld the white light of eternity he is incapacitated for the purposes of earth, blinded by remembrance of 'a vast distracting orb of glory'.[8]

A kindred aspect of Browning's humanism is his interpretation of the significance of the Incarnation as a historical event. Under human conditions man is incapable of comprehending the absolute fulness of God's being. But through the manifestation of God's nature in flesh and blood, in the person of Christ, the white light of His being is deflected in the prismatic hues of a revelation that can be grasped by man on earth in his weakness and finitude. In *The Ring and the Book* the Pope uses the imagery of the 'spectrum' and the 'convex glass' to illustrate the media through which the white light of eternal truth must pass to reach man's mind and heart, and

in his meditation on the prismatic incarnation of God's nature in the
historic life of Christ he reflects:

> Clouds obscure –
> But for which obscuration all were bright?
> Too hastily concluded! Sun-suffused,
> A cloud may soothe the eye made blind by blaze, –
> Better the very clarity of heaven:
> The soft streaks are the beautiful and dear.
> What but the weakness in a faith supplies
> The incentive to humanity . . .
> And that which men think weakness within strength,
> But angels know for strength and stronger yet . . .
> The divine instance of self-sacrifice
> That never ends and aye begins for man?
> (X, 1643–50, 1653–4, 1657–8)

In *Parleyings with Certain People of Importance* Browning uses the
imagery of the Sun as representative of God's absolute being, and
the myth of Prometheus bringing fire from heaven in a hollow tube
as a symbol of a revelation of the Divine nature which is adapted to
the lowliness and imperfect faculties of man. It is true that the fire
thus won is 'glass-conglobed', and narrowed to 'a pin-point circle'.
Nevertheless it is 'the very Sun in little', sharing its elemental nature,

> Comprising the Sun's self, but Sun disrobed
> Of that else-unconceived essential flame
> Borne by no naked sight.
> (*Bernard de Mandeville*, 307–9)[9]

While Browning's ethics are a pendant to his religious faith, it is in
this sphere, as I have stated, that his humanism is most markedly in
evidence. Though man's finite experiences, 'this dance of plastic circumstance', are in their ultimate purpose 'machinery just meant', like
the potter's wheel, to shape the soul [*Rabbi Ben Ezra*, XXVIII], it is
clear that the poet attributes positive values to the material as well
as the spiritual aspects of man's twofold nature. Nothing is more
characteristic of his humanism than the importance he ascribes to
the body and the senses. While his belief in the supremacy of the soul
is unfaltering, he rejects any ascetic conception of man's nature.

Although the body and the senses are from one point of view limitations of man's spiritual insight, they are the necessary conditions of his moral probation, the working tools through which the soul's development on earth is achieved. Throughout life the spiritual is bound up with the material; the body and the senses, so far from being spurned, are meant to serve as stepping stones to a realization of the spirit which uses these as vehicles of its temporal manifestation:

> Let us not always say,
>   'Spite of this flesh today
> I strove, made head, gained ground upon the whole!'
>   As the bird wings and sings,
>   Let us cry, 'All good things
> Are ours, nor soul helps flesh more, now, than flesh helps soul!'
>   (*Rabbi Ben Ezra*, XII)

In *Fra Lippo Lippi* Browning reveals his sympathy with the humanism and realism of Renaissance art, its protest against the asceticism of the Middle Ages, its appreciation of 'the value and significance of flesh', its conviction that 'the world and life's too big to pass for a dream', its delight in earth's sensuous loveliness:

> – The beauty and the wonder and the power,
> The shapes of things, their colours, lights and shades,
> Changes, surprises, – and God made it all! (283–5)

In *Saul*, David exclaims:

> Oh, our manhood's prime vigour! No spirit feels waste,
> Not a muscle is stopped in its playing nor sinew unbraced.
> Oh, the wild joys of living!   (IX, 1–3)

Browning's ethical humanism has a further reach. Even the checks and obstacles, the evil and suffering that environ man on earth are the indispensable conditions of soul-development. Only through conflict with and victory over these can character be fashioned and God's purposes for man realized.

There is, consequently, a wide difference between the attitudes of Shelley and Browning to the whole range of human experience. For Shelley the limitations of man's life on earth, the finitude of his lot,

are 'stains'; they dim and obscure 'the white radiance of Eternity'.
For Browning they are material for transmutation and transfigura-
tion. So considered, the facets of man's chequered experiences in
this finite world of space and time may be not stains but jewels,
enriching the white light by mellowing and humanizing it into
prismatic hues:

> Only the prism's obstruction shows aright
> The secret of a sunbeam, breaks its light
> Into the jewelled bow from blankest white;
> So may a glory from defect arise:
> > (*Deaf and Dumb*, 1-4)

Browning makes frequent use of the imagery of the rainbow. In
Sordello he writes:

> light, thwarted, breaks
> A limpid purity to rainbow flakes,
> > (V, 605-6)

In *Christmas-Eve* there is a superb description of a moon rainbow,
and the poet reflects:

> Have I been sure, this Christmas-Eve,
> God's own hand did the rainbow weave,
> Whereby the truth from heaven slid
> Into my soul?   (XX, 46-9)

In *Numpholeptos* the symbolism of the rainbow pervades the entire poem.

Although this monologue of Browning's has been regarded by
critics as strange and bizarre, it is of special interest as providing a
link between the poet's ethical and artistic humanism and illustrating the likeness between them. The theme of this poem centers on a
contrast between a nymph and her lover. The nymph is endowed with
spiritual qualities of purity, goodness, and truth, absolute in their
essence, but antecedent to and divorced from human experience.
The imagery of the moon, of silver, of 'quintessential whiteness'
symbolizes the ideal but prenatal nature of her innocence. The lover
who aspires to reach her feet must, as a mortal, pursue his aim under
the conditions of life on earth. As he treads various paths to his goal,

he is coloured by the hues of his finite experiences in a world of trial, moral endeavour, and imperfection:

> Here I reek suffused
> With crocus, saffron, orange, as I used
> With scarlet, purple, every dye o' the bow
> Born of the storm-cloud.   (82–5)

He describes himself to the nymph as, 'Your pilgrim jewelled as with drops o' the urn / The rainbow paints from' (120–1). Browning emphasizes the disparity between the abstract idealism of the nymph and the humanism of her lover by making the colour contrasts bold and vivid. The whiteness linked with the nymph is pallid, even cold. The imagery is that of pale moonbeams, delicate silver, rather than brilliant sunshine. On the other hand, the colours associated with the man are strong, positive, even crude, such as crimson and sulphurous yellow. Although these have origin in white light, the 'blank pure soul' of the nymph is at once 'the source and tomb of that prismatic glow'. In the sequel the lover finds it impossible to satisfy the requirements of the nymph that he appear before her in a whiteness that corresponds with her abstract idealism, a state of being which is divorced from human struggle and achievement.

Betty Miller, in her recent work on Browning, has called *Numpholeptos* one of his autobiographical poems.[10] She compares its moon symbolism with that of *One Word More*, in which he apostrophizes his wife as 'my moon of poets' and refers to himself as a 'moonstruck mortal'. There is, I believe, a slight autobiographical element in *Numpholeptos*, although of an indirect and glancing nature. In commenting on the moon imagery in *Pan and Luna*, William C. DeVane writes: 'As we may see in *One Word More*, the *Epilogue* to *Ferishtah's Fancies*, the *Parleying With Daniel Bartoli* and elsewhere, the moon to Browning was always, after 1855, a symbol for his wife.'[11] This association of moon imagery with Mrs Browning suggests the likelihood of its presence in *Numpholeptos*. Yet it seems evident that the primary contrast Browning has in mind in this poem is a difference between feminine and masculine natures. He refers to the nymph as endowed with –

> that thrice-superfine
> Feminity of sense, with right divine
> To waive all process, take result stain-free
> From out the very muck. . . .   (144–7)

This abstract idealism, typically feminine, is set over against a masculine realism. The 'quintessential whiteness' of the nymph is in keeping with Browning's conception of a woman as intuitively in touch with spiritual verities in their absolute essence. The 'every dye o' the bow' in which the lover is garbed is symbolic of the fact that a man can only strive towards the white light of the ideal while following the paths of finite human experience and immersed in its variegated colours. Browning elsewhere, as has been noted, introduces the contrast between 'white light' and 'prismatic hues' to symbolize the difference between the undeflected spiritual idealism of his wife's lyric poetry and the trammelled humanism of his dramatic verse. This is an indication that in his comparison of feminine and masculine natures in *Numpholeptos* he has in the back of his mind a difference between Elizabeth Browning and himself. Yet this analogy is only secondary and indeterminate. It is absurd to regard *Numpholeptos* as in any sense literal autobiography, or representative of the psychological relations between Browning and his wife.

The allegorical significance of this poem, with its contrasts of colour symbolism, is linked with the sphere of ethics. Since, however, in his letters to Elizabeth Barrett, Browning uses kindred imagery to describe the contrast between her poetry and his own, *Numpholeptos* is illustrative of a parallelism between his ethical and artistic humanism, and may serve as a point of transition to my discussion of the latter.

It is of interest to note that while Browning refers to the prismatic hues of his dramatic monologues, he tells Elizabeth Barrett that there is white light in him, even though he fears it. This fear is indicative of an element of tension and conflict in his poetry. In his letter to Ruskin he reveals that the difficulty of 'putting the infinite within the finite' was the central problem of his art as well as of his philosophy of life.

There is indeed 'white light' in what may be called the Shelleyan side of Browning's complex nature. 'I am made up of an intensest life' [268], he wrote in *Pauline*, and he links with this 'a principle of restlessness' in his inner consciousness 'which would be all, have, see, know, taste, feel, all' [277–8]. A passion for the absolute, a desire to exhibit the fulness of personality, an urge to realize the boundless capacities of the soul, even in a finite world, is the noble ambition – yet the cardinal error – of the heroes of his early monodramas. They are all dazzled by the blinding vision of the white light of eternity while yet in the sphere of time.

The ethical problem of Browning's own life which is reflected in these monodramas has its aesthetic analogue. As a poet, the crux of the struggle was what seemed to him the almost insuperable task of subduing the wealth and prodigality of his spiritual powers – his imagination and intellect – to embodiment in the sensuous media of art. The infinite content of his thought continually out-paced and chafed against the confinement of it in finite form. He felt with peculiar poignancy the tension of

> Thoughts hardly to be packed
> Into a narrow act,
> Fancies that broke through language and escaped . . .
> (*Rabbi Ben Ezra*, XXV, 1–3)

This tension is at its height in Browning's early monodramas. In the attempt to chronicle not one but successive stages in the development of a soul, extending over a long period of time, the poet is lost in the mazes of his theme. 'What was a speck expands into a star,' as Paracelsus puts it [I, 557]. The myriad digressions, the tortuous convolutions, and complexity of *Sordello* are proverbial. Despite splendid lines and passages, the shower of sparks struck from 'the quick forge and working-house of thought' are not fused to a steady flame. The poem lacks artistic restraint and discipline.

In contrast with his earlier poetry, Browning's fine series of dramatic monologues, published between 1843 and 1864, are a triumph of his individuality and his humanism. In them he solves, in large measure, the problem of fitting to the finite his infinity. Through a wise economy he concentrates his psychological analysis on a single situation, a single moment of time, and often on a single character. Linked with these are the self-imposed bounds of his thought and imagination by focusing them in dramatic representation.

Yet, while the white light of the undeflected radiation of Browning's personality is subordinated in the dramatic monologues of 1842–64 to the prismatic hues of his portrayal of men and women, it is too vital an element of his nature to be suppressed. Only occasionally does he attain the complete objective humanism of Shakespeare. His is seldom the art of the great playwright who stands aloof, as it were, letting character wait upon event and evolve with an independence and integrity not infringed by the personality of the dramatist. Browning, on the other hand, is prone to make his characters voice his own ideas, to grant them only semi-independence, or even to reduce them to mouthpieces of his personality. This complexity is in keeping with the constant interplay in his poetry and philosophy of the two basic dispositions of his mind and spirit. The tension of antinomies – moral, spiritual, and aesthetic – is ever present in his consciousness. In Love alone he finds their resolution. Yet it seems evident that humanism rather than transcendence – the 'prismatic hues' rather than the 'white light' – is the dominating note and characteristic of Browning's life and poetry. His humanism is broadly rooted, and is nurtured by physical, psychical, and spiritual elements in his personality.

The intimate connection between Browning's humanism and his conviction of the worth and integrity of individuality may be illustrated in various ways. C. H. Herford has pointed out that this has a physical basis in the nature of the perceptions of his senses.[12] These fasten upon the differences and divergences between objects, which give them individual character, rather than likenesses blending them into a common unity. In his portrayal of Nature, Browning is more apt to dwell on the clear, definite outline of each separate feature in the scene he is describing than to subordinate these to the symmetry and harmony of the landscape as a whole. Often his demarcations are characterized by sharpness and abruptness. It is the line of cleavage between objects rather than the circle of inclusiveness, the edge, the angle, the salient, the roughness of texture – everything contributing to visual and tactile impressions of distinctness – which he stresses. It is the individuality of the multitudinous and intricate phenomena of Nature which Browning's acute and realistic sensibilities are quick to detect.

Physically and spiritually, the humanism of Browning's poetry is reflected in his life and personality. Despite the handicap of certain bodily ailments, such as frequent headaches and a nervous excitability of temperament, his constitution was, in the main, sound and vigorous. His son has stated that he can scarcely recall any time when his father spent a day in bed up till his last illness. Mrs Sutherland Orr writes: 'he was healthy, even strong, in many essential respects. Until past the age of seventy he could take long walks without fatigue, and endure an amount of social and physical strain which would have tried many younger men.'[13]

Psychologically, Browning had a robustness and geniality of spirit which led him not only to accept but to rejoice in the natural pleasures and wealth of human association available to man on earth. As he tells us, he was one who 'both lives and likes life's way' [Prologue to *Fifine at the Fair*, 38]. Since, in a recent biography of the poet, he has been pictured as inhibited by neurotic and pathological weaknesses, it is well to recall the testimony of his contemporaries to the sanity, balance, and humane qualities of his personality. Jowett described Browning as 'entirely free from enmity, jealousy, or any other littleness, and thinking no more of himself than if he were an ordinary man'.[14] Carlyle, in acknowledging his presentation copy of *Men and Women*, wrote to the poet: 'My approval was hearty and spontaneous. . . . I shall look far, I believe, to find such a pair of eyes as I see there busy inspecting human life this long while – fresh, valiant, manful character, equipped with rugged humour, just love, just contempt, well carried and bestowed.'[15] Such was the estimate of two noted men who cannot be accused of Victorian sentimentalism in their appraisal of character. The joy and tingle of Browning's contact with life in its sensuous as well as its spiritual aspects; his comprehensive and many-faceted vision of it as a theatre for the play of man's dual nature, both body and soul; the vitality and exuberance of his personality – overflowing in actuality the bounds of imaginative art – evince the generosity of his humanism.

'The soft streaks are the beautiful and dear.' It is 'the prismatic hues' of Browning's humanism which constitute his most important contribution to English poetry. To represent his fear of the 'white light' as an apostasy from the ideals of Shelley, a tame submission to convention, a recreancy of mind and heart, is to travesty the independence and originality of his thought, and his depth of human insight. 'So may a glory from defect arise' [*Deaf and Dumb*, 4]. It is Browning's consciousness that the development of a soul on earth can be achieved only by the fashioning of it in the warp and woof of the coloured strands of human experience which underlies his philosophy of life and imparts warmth and realism to his poetry.[16]

NOTES

[1] *Letters of Robert Browning and Elizabeth Barrett Barrett 1845–46* (1899), I, p. 17.

[2] [See pp. 176–7 below.]

[3] *The Works of John Ruskin*, ed. E. T. Cook and Alexander Wedderburn (London: 1909), XXXVI, xxxiv. [Letter of December 10, 1855.]

[4] See in this connection Ch. 9, 'Browning's Conception of Love as Represented in *Paracelsus*', in my book *The Infinite Moment*. [See also F. E. L. Priestley, 'The Ironic Pattern of Browning's *Paracelsus*', *UTQ*, XXXIV (1964), pp. 68–81.]

[5] See his Introduction in Miss E. H. Hickey's edition of *Strafford* (London: 1884).

[6] *The Life of Browning*, Everyman's Library ed. (London: 1915), p. 111.

[7] cf. lines 31–9 in *Plot-Culture*:
> 'Thou wouldst not stand
> Distinctly Man,' – Ferishtah made reply,
> 'Not the mere creature, – did no limit-line
> Round thee about, apportion thee thy place
> Clean-cut from out and off the illimitable, –
> Minuteness severed from immensity.
> All of thee for the Maker, – for thyself,
> Workings inside the circle that evolve
> Thine all, – the product of thy cultured plot.'

[8] A similar idea is expressed in lines 648–51 of *Bishop Blougram's Apology*:
> Naked belief in God the Omnipotent,
> Omniscient, Omnipresent, sears too much

The sense of conscious creatures to be borne.
It were the seeing him, no flesh shall dare.

[9] cf. the imagery of the use of 'an optic glass' in *A Death in the Desert*. This is symbolic of the way in which, through the Incarnation of Christ, the truth of God's nature is adapted to man's apprehension by being 'reduced to plain historic fact' and 'diminished into clearness'.

[10] *Portrait*, pp. 259–61. I agree that Browning's statement to Furnivall, 'I had no particular woman in mind', does not preclude an autobiographical element in *Numpholeptos*. The poet was frequently evasive in answering questions of members of the Browning Society, especially when they seemed to pry into the privacy of his personal life. Moreover, the autobiographical reference is, as I have said, indirect and glancing, confined to the point of contrast between the nymph's idealism and her lover's humanism.

[11] *Handbook*, p. 457.

[12] *Robert Browning* (Edinburgh and London: 1905).

[13] *Life and Letters of Robert Browning* (London: 1891), p. 20.

[14] Evelyn Abbott and Lewis Campbell, *Life of Jowett*, I, 400–1.

[15] Letter of April 25, 1856.

[16] [cf. Duckworth, *Background*, esp. Chs. VI and IX; Lionel Stevenson, 'Tennyson, Browning and a Romantic Fallacy', *UTQ*, XIII (1944), pp. 175–95.]

ROBERT LANGBAUM

THE DRAMATIC ELEMENT:
TRUTH AS PERSPECTIVE

To see life steadily and whole, as Arnold tells us Sophocles saw it, is to see life with its moral and emotional meaning inside it. It is to see Truth. But it is precisely the modern condition that there is no publicly accepted moral and emotional Truth, there are only perspectives toward it – those partial meanings which individuals may get a glimpse of at particular moments but which, formulated as ideas for other moments and people, become problematical. The empiricism of the dramatic monologue, as demonstrated by its disequilibrium between sympathy and judgment, is a sign that it imitates not life but a particular perspective toward life, somebody's experience of it.

The particular perspective is especially apparent in the dramatic monologue, where we clearly adopt the speaker's point of view, both visual and moral, as our entry into the poem – the resulting limitation and even distortion of the physical and moral truth being among the main pleasures of the form. Followed through consistently, the particular angle of vision gives an unfamiliar view of familiar things, opening us to an apprehension of their meaning at the same time that it reminds us of their physical reality; while the consistency of the distortion gives unity to the poem by establishing the singleness of the point of view. Most important, however, the particular perspective is the visual expression of the meaning and, in its departure from the ordinary view, the sign of the presence of the speaker and of the new

Reprinted from *The Poetry of Experience* (1957), in which it constitutes Ch. IV, pp. 137–59.

thing the poem is saying. By seeing what the speaker sees we are able to identify ourselves with him, stand in his position and thus inside the poem where meaning resides. Since the projective leap is more apparent the more different from our own the view we take, the communication is likely to be more emphatic, the more particular, the more extraordinary even, the perspective.

Thus, the dramatic monologue specializes in the reprehensible speaker because his moral perspective is extraordinary; and it specializes for the same reason in the extraordinary visual perspective as the objective counterpart of the extraordinary moral perspective. Tennyson's St Simeon Stylites views the world, visually and morally, from the top of a pillar; while Browning's Caliban views it, visually and morally, from the bottom of a swamp. In both poems we adopt a view of the world which breaks up our ordinary idea of it. St Simeon's view is distorted not only by his elevated position 'betwixt the meadow and the cloud', but also because he has grown 'half deaf' and 'almost blind',

> So that I scarce can hear the people hum
> About the column's base, . . .
> And scarce can recognize the fields I know;

all detail is blurred. Caliban, on the other hand, sees with an extraordinary sharpness of detail the mud-bound crawling side of nature we seldom notice:

> Yon otter, sleek-wet, black, lithe as a leech;
> Yon auk, one fire-eye in a ball of foam,
> That floats and feeds; a certain badger brown
> He hath watched hunt with that slant white-wedge eye
> By moonlight; and the pie with the long tongue
> That pricks deep into oakwarts for a worm,
> And says a plain word when she finds her prize,
> But will not eat the ants; the ants themselves
> That build a wall of seeds and settled stalks
> About their hole.   [*Caliban upon Setebos*, 46–55]

The unusual minuteness and precision of proximate detail is as much a sign of myopia as the blur of distant detail; and their myopia makes superb poets of both speakers, accounting for the extraordinary visual perception of which their thought is a consequence. It is the blur of physical detail that accounts for St Simeon's vivid perception of the angel who comes with a heavenly crown:

> What's here? a shape, a shade,
> A flash of light. Is that the angel there
> That holds a crown? Come, blessed brother, come!
> I know thy glittering face. I waited long;
> My brows are ready. What! deny it now?
> Nay, draw, draw, draw nigh. So I clutch it. Christ!
> 'Tis gone: 'tis here again; the crown! the crown!
> So now 'tis fitted on and grows to me,
> And from it melt the dews of Paradise,
> Sweet! sweet! spikenard, and balm, and frankincense . . .

while the concreteness of Caliban's perception accounts for his attributing to the god, Setebos, the moral and aesthetic standards of the swamp. He not only equates Setebos' creation with the swamp but considers Setebos less beautiful than the creatures of the swamp, whom He created to make what He 'would fain, in a manner, be'. It is to demonstrate His power over creatures whom He envies that Setebos torments or rewards them capriciously; just as Caliban, if out of a desire for wings he fashioned a bird of clay, would delight to remind himself that the bird is after all his creation to do with as he pleases. ' 'Thinketh,' says Caliban referring to himself with the third-person verb, perhaps as a sign of his rudimentary mind, but also I think to satirize his absurd attempt at objectivity:

> such shows nor right nor wrong in Him,
> Nor kind, nor cruel: He is strong and Lord.
> 'Am strong myself compared to yonder crabs
> That march now from the mountain to the sea;
> 'Let twenty pass, and stone the twenty-first,
> Loving not, hating not, just choosing so.
> 'Say, the first straggler that boasts purple spots
> Shall join the file, one pincer twisted off;
> 'Say, this bruised fellow shall receive a worm,
> And two worms he whose nippers end in red;
> As it likes me each time, I do: so He.[1]   [98–108]

Both poems are effective just because we do not direct our judgment merely against the speakers' ideas, which would be in themselves too arbitrary for judgment, but against a whole visual organization of the world in which we have participated with sympathy and enjoyment, thus allowing an adequate foil against which our adverse judgment can make an impact. For the speaker's point of view must be built up before it can be torn down, if there is to be an adequate tension between our enjoyment of the point of view for its own sake on empiric grounds, and our judgment of it on grounds of truth or morality. The particular perspective is the device by which this disequilibrium between sympathy and judgment is achieved, because it leads away from judgment, from general ideas, toward the intensest concreteness. It is the device by which life is projected into the facts, since the facts were after all originally looked at, limited and distorted by the view of a particular person in a particular time and place. To present in their original concreteness, to *evoke*, as we say, a person, idea or historical period, is the whole purpose of the dramatic monologue – of which purpose the particular perspective is the condition, and the disequilibrium between sympathy and judgment the consequence.

Disequilibrium and the particular perspective are criteria not necessarily of the poem's success but of its success as a dramatic monologue; they are more apparent the more the poem is generating the effect characteristic of the dramatic monologue. *Rabbi Ben Ezra* is a dramatic monologue by virtue of its title only, because there is no way of apprehending the poetic statement other than intellectually, there is no split between its validity as somebody's apprehension and its objective validity as an idea. The reason for the lack of disequilibrium is the lack of a particular perspective; the statement is not conditioned by a particular person in a particular time and place, the poem is not located or anything in it seen. 'Grow old along with me . . . Then, welcome each rebuff . . . So, take and use thy work . . . Let age approve of youth, and death complete the same' – these are maxims put forward as universally applicable and deriving validity from the logical connection between them. They do not differ from the statements of any sermon or of Pope's *Essay on Man*. Call Pope's poem *Bolingbroke* (from whom most of its ideas derive), and you have the same kind of poem as *Rabbi Ben Ezra*.

It would be a mistake, however, to suppose that *Rabbi Ben Ezra* is not a dramatic monologue because it deals with ideas. Dramatic monologues may, as we have seen, deal with the most abstract ideas, but they make the kind of statement not open to dispute because limited in application to the conditions of the poem. The general idea emerges as an inference only, and is never identical with what the speaker says. What poem could be more abstract in idea than Browning's *Abt Vogler*, where music is presented as an expression of the Absolute, as emanating from the soul's deepest wish and therefore from the Divine Will? Yet the poem is a dramatic monologue rather than a philosophical statement, just to the extent that the statement rises out of an illusion, out of a visual organization of the world limited in duration to the speaker's ecstatic moment of inspiration as he extemporizes on the organ.

Abt Vogler *sees*, as his music mounts to a climax, an accumulating vision of totality – first, as a palace reaching from sordid fact up toward sublimity, constructed by the ascending and descending genii called forth by his musical notes:

> And one would bury his brow with a blind plunge down to hell,
> Burrow awhile and build, broad on the roots of things,
> Then up again swim into sight, having based me my palace well,
> Founded it, fearless of flame, flat on the nether springs.
>
> And another would mount and march, like the excellent minion
> he was,
> Ay, another and yet another, one crowd but with many a crest,
> Raising my rampired walls of gold as transparent as glass, . . .
> Up, the pinnacled glory reached, and the pride of my soul was
> in sight

then as a whole cosmic union in which heaven and earth yearn toward each other:

> In sight? Not half! for it seemed, it was certain, to match man's
> birth,
> Nature in turn conceived, obeying an impulse as I;
> And the emulous heaven yearned down, made effort to reach the
> earth,
> As the earth had done her best, in my passion, to scale the sky:
> Novel splendours burst forth, grew familiar and dwelt with mine,

> Not a point nor peak but found and fixed its wandering star;
> Meteor-moons, balls of blaze: and they did not pale nor pine,
> For earth had attained to heaven, there was no more near nor
> far

a cosmic union in which not only space is annihilated, but time, too, so that spirits of the yet unborn and of the long since dead walk in this re-created universe where possibility and actuality are identical:

> What never had been, was now; what was, as it shall be anon;
> And what is, – shall I say, matched both? for I was made
> perfect too.

Abt Vogler recognizes his vision as Absolute reality, because he recognizes it as his soul's wish flowing 'visibly forth'; and because that wish is realized instantaneously and completely – without discernible 'cause' for the 'effect', without art – Abt Vogler recognizes his wish as an instrument of the Divine Will and his music as a materialization of the 'finger of God, a flash of the will that can'.

It is the transient irrecoverable quality of music, especially extemporized music, that gives it such high import. Painting and poetry (and presumably written music) remain in place to be analyzed, to be accounted for by laws of art, while the undivided absorption in the instant of Abt Vogler's music gives it the miraculous totality reflective of the Absolute. In the same way, it is the absorption in the instant of Abt Vogler's vision – its departure from those ordinary laws of experience which have been abstracted as a norm from a multiplicity of instants – that gives it its dramatic concreteness. We say of this poem that it *evokes* a musical rhapsody, by which we mean that it is just its most fantastic part we believe in, its vision within the ecstatic instant of a transformed universe; for the vision is the counterpart of the music, and therefore evokes it.

When the ecstatic instant is over ('Well, it is gone at last, the palace of music I reared'), Abt Vogler judges the vision to have been illusory, but re-establishes its validity with a moral sentiment – that the illusion was an image of bliss to come:

> On the earth the broken arcs; in the heaven, a perfect round.

> All we have willed or hoped or dreamed of good shall exist;
> Not its semblance, but itself.

The speaker has shifted to a more ordinary perspective, and concomitantly moved into a more ordinary instant. The vision which was building before our eyes now exists in the past, through recollection. Only its moral meaning, not its empiric actuality, can be generalized, carried over in the 'C Major of this life'; and its moral meaning is problematical. Yet even these final stanzas are conditioned by the speaker's emotional attachment to the vision ('Gone! and the good tears start, the praises that come too slow'), so that the moral meaning itself rises out of a new particular perspective and is dramatically concrete to the extent that we share the speaker's emotion.

What we have, in other words, is not a vision located in time, followed by a speculation unlocated in time; but rather the speculation is itself dramatized, conditioned by the nostalgic instant following the ecstasy. We have two particular perspectives and therefore two present tenses, the particular perspective being the visual sign of the present tense. We have really, to make the point clear, two dramatic monologues about the same event, each taking place at a temporally and psychologically separate instant. And, as in *The Ring and the Book*, we judge between the two points of view according to their relative intensity.

For the vision is the centre of certainty, the empiric fact out of which the whole poem rises. We are most closely identified with the speaker, accepting his point of view with least reservation, within the perspective of the ecstasy; while his shift to a more ordinary perspective opens the way for argument and speculation on our part as well as his. His final doubt of the vision's objective validity actually reinforces its validity as a fact of experience, since such a development imitates the structure of our own experience in which illuminations burn at the centre with certainty and then shade off into ambiguity and doubt. Abt Vogler's instant of doubt makes the ecstatic instant believable by providing it with a recognizable setting, at the same time that it sets off the ecstatic instant by showing its incompatibility with ordinary judgment. Far from weakening our confidence in the vision, the incompatibility throws us back upon the more intense instant as the primary certainty; while the judg-

ROBERT BROWNING

ment that proceeds from the less intense instant appears as a problematical speculation. Although the disequilibrium between sympathy and judgment is handled in *Abt Vogler* in three declining steps of intensity instead of the usual two, here as elsewhere the poetic statement is as much as is absorbed within a particular perspective – the more particular, the more extraordinary even the perspective, the more positive and convincing the statement; while we enter the realm of speculation and finally move beyond the poetic statement altogether, as the perspective approaches and finally reaches the ordinary and unparticularized.[2]

By moving away from the general truth toward the eccentric particular, the dramatic monologue communicates with precision and concreteness the most general and tenuous ideas – making tangible such intangibles as the 'spirit' of an age, of a work of art, of a world-view. Perhaps the best example of the evocative power of the particular perspective is Browning's *Master Hugues of Saxe-Gotha*, which evokes not only the musical but also the historical atmosphere of a dry, dusty and difficult old organ fugue. I say best example because the music is evoked not as in *Abt Vogler* by visualizing the invisible, so that the word *perspective* applies only figuratively, but by giving a particular and *less* than usually spiritual view of a church – so that perspective is used, as in an extreme angle-shot in photography, to derive unusual meaning from a usual scene by exaggerating its realistic or homely aspects.

It is after hours in the church and the sacristan is extinguishing the candles preparatory to locking up for the night, as we sit with the old organist in his organ-loft atop the 'rotten-runged rat-riddled stairs', below the cobweb-covered roof. From the organist's vantage, the church is 'our huge house of the sounds'; for the scene beyond his three claviers is dominated by 'yon forest of pipes', while the 'our' includes the composer, Master Hugues, the enigma of whose intricate organ fugues the organist has spent a lifetime trying to penetrate. The organist sees Master Hugues peeping in the shade of the forest of pipes, and sees his face in the bars and notes of his score. As the poem begins, the organist calls down to the sacristan for five minutes more of light, then starts to play again one of the master's

138

fugues imploring him to yield his meaning this time, 'Quick, ere my candle's a snuff.'

Both the quality of the fugue and the character of the organist are revealed simultaneously through the unusual details appropriate to a church attendant's view of a church and to the distorted view from the organ-loft. The details are all of obsolescence and neglect, of dust, rust, rats and spider-webs; while the view of the church as a place to play music in combines with a view of it as a place to sweep up. For the organist church life occurs after hours when only he and the sacristan are about, and he conceives the church as having a life of its own at night when no one is about. Then, the sculptured saints leave their pedestals and, 'with the moon to admire', go their rounds as superior church attendants, 'Put rats and mice to the rout',

> Order things back to their place,
> Have a sharp eye lest the candlesticks rust,
> Rub the church-plate, darn the sacrament-lace,
> Clear the desk-velvet of dust.

In spite of the homely details, such a vision shows large imagination – the same imagination that can sense life behind the outmoded aridities of Master Hugues' music. For the details of obsolescence and neglect apply at every point to the music, which is more than once compared to an intricate spider-web:

> So your fugue broadens and thickens,
> Greatens and deepens and lengthens,
> Till we exclaim – 'But where's music, the dickens?
> Blot ye the gold, while your spider-web strengthens
> – Blacked to the stoutest of tickens?'

The 'gold' is the meaning which lies obscured behind the formal structure of the music, as the gilt roof of the church is obscured by spider-webs. Just as the two shabby old men left behind in the neglected church melt into the spirit of the place; so forgotten himself, and left alone with his forgotten composer, the organist penetrates the composer's life. But though the organist believes that Master Hugues' music has meaning, he has never been able to make out what it is. He thinks he is coming upon it as he plays a fugue over again this time – coming upon the golden roof behind the spider-webs, as he puts it – when the sacristan extinguishes the last candle and the organist stops playing to grumble at him. You obviously want to find me, when you come to sweep up one morning, dead at the foot of your 'rotten-runged rat-riddled stairs'. By what light am I to get down? 'Do I carry,' he complains in the final line, 'the moon in my pocket?'

A superb question, for of course the organist does carry his own light with him. The sculptured saints and the music have come alive in the moonlight of his imagination. For all its homely detail, the organist's vision is objectively as questionable as Abt Vogler's. What is certain is the strength and consistency of the imagination, of the master passion or master illusion which the organist reveals all unconsciously through his absorption in his own particular perspective.[3]

It is this absorption in the particular perspective that makes the speaker's self-revelation incidental to his purpose; and it is the incidental nature of the self-revelation that distinguishes the dramatic monologue from the form which is most often confused with it, the soliloquy. The difference is that the soliloquist's subject is himself, while the speaker of the dramatic monologue directs his attention outward. Since talking about one's self necessarily involves an objective stance, the soliloquist must see himself from a general perspective. It is not enough for him to think his thoughts and feel his feelings, he must also describe them as an observer would; for he is trying to understand himself in the way that the reader understands him – rationally, by relating his thoughts and feelings to general truths.

That is why we get self-analysis and internal debate in the soliloquy but not in the dramatic monologue. The soliloquist is concerned with truth, he is trying to find the right point of view; while the speaker of the dramatic monologue starts with an established point of view, and is not concerned with its truth but with trying to impress it on the outside world. The meaning of the soliloquy is equivalent to what the soliloquist reveals and understands, the poetic statement being as much as he has been able to rationalize, to see in terms of the general perspective. But the meaning of the dramatic monologue is in disequilibrium with what the speaker reveals and understands. We understand the speaker's point of view not through his description of it but indirectly, through seeing what he sees while judging the limitations and distortions of what he sees. The result is that we understand, if not more, at least something other than the speaker understands, and the meaning is conveyed as much by what the speaker conceals and distorts as by what he reveals.

Pope's *Eloisa to Abelard* is a good case in point. Although it is often cited as a dramatic monologue and deals with the moral and emotional ambiguities appropriate to the dramatic monologue, it is essentially a soliloquy because written from a general perspective – or, as Professor Tillotson puts it, because Eloisa is 'the "artist" of emotion rather than the experiencer of it'.[4] Eloisa writes a letter from her convent to Abelard in his, imploring him to come and telling him how she is torn between love and religious duty. She tells how her sinful dreams at night reveal her true desires, and how Abelard's image steals even into her prayers to claim the devotion meant for God. Her very penances are suspect, for she wonders whether she sighs for her sins or her lost love:

> Assist me heav'n! but whence arose that pray'r?
> Sprung it from piety, or from despair?
> Ev'n here, where frozen chastity retires,
> Love finds an altar for forbidden fires.

She breaks the self-description at intervals to bid Abelard come to her for reasons that alternate along with her emotions. He is to come as lover to seduce her from her religious duty; ah no, he is to come to instruct her in her religious duty. She finally bids him come, at the moment when her penance is sincerest and grace is dawning in her soul, to snatch her from salvation. Then recoiling in horror from the blasphemous thought, she bids him fly her and renounce her for the sake of both their souls. The poem ends with Eloisa's reconciliation to her religious duty. She looks forward to her own and

Abelard's salvation and to their burial together in the Monastery of the Paraclete, where they will serve as a warning to future lovers and where sympathetic visitors may be moved to pity and forgive them. She also hopes that some future bard will be inspired by his own unhappy love to tell their story.

The poem is a soliloquy rather than a dramatic monologue to the extent that the paradox is in the moral problem rather than in the character of Eloisa, to the extent in other words that the paradox is stated rather than enacted.

> I ought to grieve, but cannot what I ought;
> I mourn the lover, not lament the fault

is not the language of a woman in the midst of internal conflict but of one who has clearly put the experience behind her, since she is able to analyse it into two neatly defined alternatives. The epigrammatic style does not in itself prove the poem to be no dramatic monologue; it merely confirms what we gather from the content as well – that Eloisa understands everything, even her own self-deceptions and submerged motives, that she understands herself as an observer would understand her. The fact that she can debate between love and religious duty means that she is not so committed to either alternative as to have her point of view conditioned by it, that she judges by a third principle, the general perspective.

She chooses religious duty in the end because it is identical with the general perspective. The sign of this is that the religious alternative has really had the victory from the start, as evidenced by the values assigned the alternatives. Love is always spoken of as sin and religion as virtue. Eloisa does, to be sure, speak of a time when she was willing to 'Curse on all laws but those which love has made'; and if the poem had taken place at that time, it might have been a dramatic monologue since love might then have arisen out of its own intellectual and moral view of the world. As it is, that time is spoken of through recollection and from the point of view of a quite alien law which has since been embraced. All of Eloisa's description of her emotional conflict is recollected, which is why she understands everything about it. For she is not, as she writes the letter, absorbed in her emotions; she is judging them from the *right* perspective. She is telling the *truth* about them.

This does not mean that dramatic monologues cannot discuss past action. But the utterance about the past must have a strategic significance within a present-tense situation. The utterance must be conditioned by the effect the speaker wants to create at the moment, so that its truth is of less concern than its success as strategy. The distortion or deviation from truth of the particular perspective is the sign of the speaker's absorption in his strategy, and therefore the sign that the utterance is, even if about the past, in the present tense.

Browning's Andrea del Sarto describes to his wife, Lucrezia, the long years of conflict between his artistic conscience and his love of her. But Andrea is using his account to make love to Lucrezia, to persuade her to spend the evening home with him rather than go out to meet the 'Cousin' who whistles for her in the street below. He is trying to impress her, on the one hand, with all that he has sacrificed for her in the way of artistic accomplishment; and on the other, with how important a painter he nevertheless is. We see of course that his musings on art and his self-pity do not interest the lady, that he is talking entirely too much about himself for successful love-making. He half-sees this too:

> You don't understand
> Nor care to understand about my art,

and he demonstrates his awareness of her purely pecuniary interest in his art, when he assures her that if she would sit thus by him every night,

> I should work better, do you comprehend?
> I mean that I should earn more, give you more.

What he does not see, however, is that he cares less to make love than to indulge in self-pity – that he enjoys degrading himself before his wife, enjoys making clear his awareness of the 'Cousin' below and his awareness that she stays with him only for the money he promises, money with which to pay for 'this same Cousin's freak'. He does not realize that he enjoys playing her victim since it means that he has resigned his will to her and can blame her for his moral failure in art. 'Had you not grown restless . . .' he suggests in a timid, unfinished sentence, he would not have left the protection of the French King Francis, where he had been doing his best work. And had she enjoined upon him 'the play, the insight and the stretch', which his work for all its technical perfection now lacks,

> Had you enjoined them on me, given me soul,
> We might have risen to Rafael, I and you!

Had she as his model, with all her physical perfections intact,

> but brought a mind!
> Some women do so. Had the mouth there urged
> 'God and the glory! never care for gain.
> The present by the future, what is that?
> Live for fame, side by side with Agnolo!
> Rafael is waiting: up to God, all three!'
> I might have done it for you.

He has not even the moral courage to make his accusation squarely, so as to antagonize her and cause her to defend herself. Each time he makes the accusation he withdraws it immediately, taking the blame upon himself but in such a way as not to invalidate the accusation and to make him feel considerate, self-castigating and infinitely injured. 'So it seems', he continues,

> Perhaps not. All is as God over-rules.
> Beside, incentives come from the soul's self;
> The rest avail not. Why do I need you?
> What wife had Rafael, or has Agnolo?

The question is ambiguous, with at least one meaning unfavourable to Lucrezia. It is this meaning that Andrea takes up again at the end, where he fancies himself competing in heaven against Leonard, Rafael and Agnolo:

> the three first without a wife,
> While I have mine! So – still they overcome
> Because there's still Lucrezia, – as I choose.

> Again the Cousin's whistle! Go, my Love.

He deceives himself by his acknowledgment of having chosen. For the pretence of self-understanding prevents him from seeing how much he has chosen – that he has chosen, indeed composed as for a painting, all the details of the poem. He starts by describing the poem's setting as he would paint it – as a 'twilight-piece' in which 'A common grayness silvers everything' and 'autumn grows, autumn in everything', while Lucrezia would figure as the moon, beautiful and cruelly unresponsive. But he does not see that he is a voluptuary creating the ideal conditions for his pleasure – that the hour, as he sees it, washes away with an enchanting vagueness all moral issues, while both season and hour stimulate soft regret and self-pity. In such a picture, the 'Cousin' as symbol of Andrea's degradation is by no means an unwelcome figure; and Andrea does not realize that he introduces and re-introduces the 'Cousin' deliberately, even using him in the final line as the final excruciating pleasure and to set the seal upon the special kind of victory he wins over Lucrezia in those last four lines.

Self-deception on this scale is not to be found in Pope's poem, and we must therefore read the two poems differently. We cannot understand Eloisa as we do Andrea, in a way other than she understands herself; for her self-description is true, it is expository. This is both the result and the sign of the fact that she does not use her self-description strategically to manipulate Abelard, as Andrea uses his to manipulate Lucrezia and secure his own gratification. The only passages in Pope's poem which correspond to Andrea's utterance are those in which Eloisa breaks her self-description to bid Abelard come to her. There, she is directing herself to a present-tense situation and is, significantly, for that space self-deceived. She bids Abelard come for a variety of reasons in each of which she believes while she is giving it, although we understand, as she for that space cannot, that her reasons are all rationalizations of the same sexual motive. When Eloisa says –

> Oh come! oh teach me nature to subdue,
> Renounce my love, my life, my self – and you.
> Fill my fond heart with God alone, for he
> Alone can rival, can succeed to thee

she supposes that she has broken through to the right reason, after having urged Abelard to come as her lover. But we see still the same reason, for we see that Abelard will be hardly her most effective teacher of renunciation.

The poem is in these few passages a dramatic monologue, and would be a dramatic monologue in its entirety if the strategy of these passages were reinforced, instead of counteracted, by the self-description. As it is, Eloisa shows in describing herself that she understands as much as we do about the self-deception in the above passage. It is she who has alerted us to it by telling us, in one epigram after another, how ubiquitous love usurps every time the emotion which starts out to be religious: 'Thy image steals between my God and me.'

Perhaps the major sign of Eloisa's incomplete commitment to her strategy – or in other words, her incomplete absorption in a particular perspective – is the fact that she changes her mind at the end of the poem. After temporizing in many ways with her desire to have Abelard come, she finally reverses the desire and bidding him fly her, renounce her, comes to the *right* conclusion. Now it is significant that the speakers of dramatic monologues never change their minds. Even when it looks as though they might, as in the case of Don Juan in *Fifine*, it is only a bluff to be followed by a more daring assertion than ever of their original position. This unlooked-for and almost superfluous self-assertion in the end replaces in the dramatic monologue the kind of climax supplied by the conversion in Pope's poem. Thus Don Juan proves to his wife, Elvire, that his flirtation with the gipsy-girl, Fifine, is not incompatible with his love for her. Then in a surprise ending, he returns for 'five minutes' to Fifine, even revealing that things between them had gone farther than we had supposed. There is no reversal in this, the surprise comes from an intensification of what we already knew, in that Don Juan is being even more himself than we had calculated.

When in the last two-and-a-half lines the duke of *My Last Duchess* makes his insolent, trivial, egotistical and hyperaesthetic pause before that bronze by Claus of Innsbruck, he manages to add a new shock to the shocks we have already endured. We have seen him as all these things, but not until now with such compression. Even in

Browning's *A Forgiveness*, where the betrayed husband forgives his wife after a long period of hatred, there is no reversal in his kind of forgiveness. The wife has to earn his forgiveness by letting the life blood flow out of her, so that his hate may be satisfied and pass away into love. And in telling the story, the husband shows himself to be the same vindictive person still: he tells it in the confessional, as we learn in the last stanza, to the monk whom he knows to have been his wife's lover, in order that the monk may not hope to elude 'My vengeance in the cloister's solitude'. Not even in the religious dramatic monologues do the speakers convert. The already uneasy paganism of Karshish and Cleon is simply made more uneasy by their exposure to Christianity; while the only effect on Tennyson's Rizpah of the evangelical lady's preaching is to confirm Rizpah's belief that her love for her son is more important than religion.

Andrea del Sarto makes clear from the beginning his expectation that Lucrezia will not spend the evening with him, and that in his internal conflict love will win again over the claims of artistic conscience. Both expectations are realized, yet the foreshadowed victory of Andrea's expectation does not have the same effect as the foreshadowed victory of the general perspective in *Eloisa to Abelard*. For there is no reversal in Browning's poem, and there is a reversal in Pope's. Although the general perspective establishes its judgment from the beginning of Pope's poem, Eloisa struggles against it until her final change of mind; whereas Browning's poem begins and ends with Andrea's perspective.

Andrea begins by surrendering to Lucrezia in the first line: 'But do not let us quarrel any more', blaming her for his loss of artistic integrity:

> I'll work then for your friend's friend, never fear,
> Treat his own subject after his own way,
> Fix his own time, accept too his own price,
> And shut the money into this small hand

and ends by conceding artistic defeat even in heaven, 'Because there's still Lucrezia – as I choose'. The development is one of simple intensification. The unlooked-for leap, which is the climax, is supplied by no change of direction but by a final revelation that brings into startling focus our accumulated suspicions, surprising us into certainty. Our sympathy for Andrea (self-pity is one of the best poles for sympathy, as witness the fondness for Werther, Childe Harold and Prufrock) suppresses our apprehension of his culpability until suddenly, in the end, he reveals flaws more definitely criminal than the mere weaknesses we have hitherto noted. He alludes to having swindled King Francis and allowed his parents to die of want. But even for these crimes he refuses to take moral responsibility: 'I regret little, I would change still less.' 'It is true,' he says of the wrong to Francis, and 'all is said' – as though acknowledgment were enough. And of the wrong to his parents, 'Some good son,' he says,

> Paint my two hundred pictures – let him try!
> No doubt, there's something strikes a balance.

The 'something' is not only his art. It takes on a new meaning in the next line where he justifies himself again, according to the pattern already established in the poem, by subtle transition to Lucrezia. 'Yes,' he says appearing to change the subject abruptly, 'You loved me quite enough, it seems tonight.' But the 'Yes', which stands alone between the two lines, serves double duty. He uses it to answer what is probably Lucrezia's impatient request to be gone. But he also uses it to confirm his own speculation, the 'no doubt' of the previous line, by relating it to Lucrezia and her request. 'Yes,' he says even as he gives her permission to betray him, she is the 'something' that 'strikes a balance', the price he pays for his sins.

When we see him shift to Lucrezia the blame not this time for his weaknesses but for his crimes, our suspicion hardens into certainty; we see clearly the use he has been making of her throughout the poem, as the penance offered in place of moral responsibility. Even in heaven, he goes on to say, I would choose Lucrezia; even in heaven I neither could, nor would I choose to take steps to save myself. Such a position is, after all, impregnable. There is in it a mixture of self-abasement and pride, of pride in self-abasement, which is the weak man's heroism. It explains the sense Andrea has of himself as both heroic and pathetic when he makes that final gesture of surrender: 'the Cousin's whistle! Go, my Love'. The gesture dramatizes the whole basis of his self-justification, the pretence of knowing the worst about himself. But intent as he is on his strategy of self-justification, and without introducing any other perspective – indeed, because he is so absorbed in his own perspective – he yet reveals himself as more contemptible and yes, as in a way more attractive too (his absorption is attractive, it is a pole for sympathy) than he is aware.

This kind of climax, through an intensified and succinctly dramatized restatement of what has already been said, is the most effective climax in dramatic monologues. That is because the dramatic monologue is organized around a single perspective and must therefore move in a single direction. The reversal, as we find it in Eloisa's change of mind, requires the introduction of another perspective by which the character judges his own and to which he eventually converts. The reversal brings about the *right* conclusion, and there can be no *right* conclusion where there is only the speaker's perspective. There can be only self-revelation climaxed by the self-revelation that strips the mask even from self-revelation, revealing its strategy and thus revealing character with a concreteness beyond what we had thought possible.

I have called *Eloisa to Abelard* a soliloquy rather than a dramatic monologue just because it has this *rightness*, this meaning independent of character by which character is judged. Character bears the same relation to meaning in Pope's poem that it would in a play, for Eloisa speaks only part of the time for herself and most of the time for the general perspective or meaning. She wants Abelard to come to her, but she must also make it clear that this is the wrong thing to want and that it will be a good thing when she finally changes her mind. The result is that Eloisa speaks more often like the soliloquy than like the dialogue of a play. She exposes the meaning more often than she pursues her own strategy. The final sign of this is in the ending, where Eloisa adopts the storyteller's hindsight as to the subsequent fame of the lovers – a perspective not *characteristically* hers.

The dramatic monologue, on the other hand, in spite of its obvious resemblance to the soliloquy, corresponds in its style of address to the dialogue, where each speaker is absorbed in his own strategy. In the most typical dialogues, of course, each speaker is counteracted by the other, so that no single perspective prevails as in the dramatic monologue. Nevertheless, the style of address is the same in that the speakers in dialogue and in the dramatic monologue communicate with the audience indirectly. They neither speak *to* the audience, nor are they concerned to describe themselves *truly*, that is for the benefit of the audience; they are concerned only to exert force on the scene around them. Yet the audience are not mere eavesdroppers, the speakers do address them in that they communicate to the audience something which is not quite the same as what they say in the dramatic scene. The speakers communicate to the audience in spite of their absorption; their absorption is, in its intensity and direction, among the things they communicate.

The style of address is much more complicated in the dialogue and dramatic monologue than in the soliloquy. For the soliloquist, like the speaker in the traditional lyric, follows the style of address of ordinary conversation. He turns to the audience when he wants to tell them something and, when he wants to describe himself, he stands outside himself and talks about himself. There is no disparity between what he says and what he intends to say. He is as much aware as we are of the meaning of his utterance, and his utterance can therefore be judged as true in the same way that we judge the statements of ordinary conversation.

There is a discernible shift in the style of address between those passages in which Eloisa speaks the truth about herself and those few passages beginning with 'Come!' in which she is so absorbed in her design upon Abelard that we understand her utterance as she cannot. But Andrea's style of address is consistent because he is absorbed at every instant in his design upon Lucrezia. Browning's *Soliloquy of the Spanish Cloister* is for the same reason not a soliloquy at all but a dramatic monologue. Although Brother Lawrence does not hear the imprecations directed against him, the speaker is entirely absorbed in them and manages to communicate about Brother Lawrence and himself something quite other than he intends. The utterance of Tennyson's St Simeon is also a dramatic monologue, though no one hears it; for it, too, is strategic (St Simeon is praying and arguing his way into heaven) and to be understood in a way other than he intends. The bias in the style of address corresponds to the particularity of the perspective. Both make clear that the utterance is to be understood not as true or false but as characteristic. And both make necessary our double apprehension within and without the bias or perspective, our apprehension through sympathy and judgment.

The style of address and the perspective both show the utterance as incomplete, and make it impossible for the dramatic monologue to achieve that logical completeness which we traditionally expect in dramatic poetry. Since the dramatic monologue is in its style of address really one voice of a dialogue, it lacks the logical completeness not only of the soliloquy but also of the dialogue. It lacks the conflicting voice of the dialogue and consequently the final judgment that resolves the conflict. The final judgment, which is impossible where there is only one voice of a dialogue, corresponds to the reversal, which is impossible where there is only a single perspective. Without reversal or final judgment there can be no logical completeness, no *right* conclusion.

When Eloisa finally changes her mind, she solves the problem of the poem; we feel that the problem will never occur again. But Andrea has talked this way before to Lucrezia, and will talk this way again with the same result. In the same way, the duke of *My Last Duchess* has been showing the duchess's portrait to visitors and will go on showing it, and the speaker of *The Spanish Cloister* has always growled at Brother Lawrence and will go on growling at him. If St Simeon Stylites does not go on pleading his case with God, and Browning's bishop does not go on ordering his tomb, it will be because they have died. The whole point of the dramatic monologue is to present not the Aristotelian complete action but habitual action.

This means that the dramatic monologue has no *necessary* beginning and end but only arbitrary limits, limits which do not cut the action off from the events that precede and follow but shade into those events, suggesting as much as possible of the speaker's whole life and experience. They are naturalistic limits, imposed not by logical necessity but by physical conditions such as location and perspective and ultimately by the physical limitations on life and experience. Since the speaker's death is the only ultimate conclusion of a dramatic monologue, the dramatic monologue must be read not as a definitive unit, a complete action, but as a characteristic and characterizing episode in the speaker's career.

The Ring and the Book, of course, and Tennyson's *Maud* tell a complete story. But they achieve completeness through devices outside the scope of the dramatic monologue. *Maud* comes to the *right* conclusion through a reversal; the speaker gives up brooding and goes to fight in the Crimean War. The conclusion would be absurd enough in a narrative or play, since it abandons the problem instead of solving it. But it represents a particular abandonment of the dramatic monologue, since the speaker abandons his character as well as the problem. The reversal does show that Tennyson could not have achieved a *right* conclusion with the dramatic monologue. Some external force, corresponding to the miracle of grace in Pope's poem, was necessary; for left to its own logic, the speaker's character could have led only to madness and suicide – a conclusion of sheer character revelation, proving nothing morally.

The Ring and the Book achieves completeness through juxtaposing dramatic monologues, creating a master context in which each dramatic monologue is to be read. But such a total organization works against the single perspective and thus against the organization of each dramatic monologue. For the juxtaposition of dramatic monologues turns them into dialogue; we can no longer give entire assent to any single perspective, but must adopt a general perspective by which to judge among the utterances. Browning helps to establish this general perspective by abandoning the dramatic monologue entirely – by speaking in his own voice in the first and last Books in order to establish the *right* judgments, and by bringing the poem to a *right* conclusion with the Pope's monologue which is, according to the distinction I have drawn, less a dramatic monologue than a soliloquy. Not only is the Pope addressing himself, but he is wrestling with the truth rather than pursuing a strategy. And his judgments, even about himself and his own motives, are clearly something more in the master context than one man's opinion; they are clearly *right* and therefore expository.

The Pope's monologue is a soliloquy to the extent that *The Ring and the Book* approaches the condition of drama in having a general perspective for which the Pope can speak and which gives his speech authority, making it not merely another point of view but the resolution of the poem. To the extent that the Pope does not, however, gain authority from an ethos to which we give assent for reasons outside the poem, to the extent that he has only as much authority as he has earned through superiority of mind and character, we would not consider the poem to be morally resolved and the Pope's speech would remain a dramatic monologue. The issue demonstrates again, as in *Maud*, that the dramatic monologue must at some point be abandoned where logical completeness is desired.

The issue also demonstrates that drama, in the old sense of the complete action, becomes impossible where we do not bring an effective ethos to the poem. It suggests that our ability to read dramatic monologues depends on the modern habit of allowing the literary work to establish its own moral judgments. The habit is, indeed, necessary for reading modern literature where we can never know what the moral judgments are going to be, but it would have surprised our ancestors who expected to find, at least in their dramatic literature, Truth rather than points of view. The complete structure of traditional drama is a sign that it imitates or illustrates a complete idea; whereas the incomplete structure of the dramatic monologue is a sign that it projects a partial and problematical idea, a point of view. It is significant that when we misread old plays it is usually because we have lost sight of the ethos out of which they were written, and that we almost always misread in the same way. Instead of subordinating the points of view of the characters to the general perspective and allowing the plot to determine our judgments, we allow the central character to have his way with us; we see the play through his point of view and as an episode in his career. We turn the complete drama into an incomplete one. We turn it into a dramatic monologue.[5]

NOTES

[1] [See E. K. Brown, 'The First Person in *Caliban upon Setebos*', *MLN*, LXVI (1951), pp. 392–5.]

[2] [For *Abt Vogler* cf. Benziger, *Images*, pp. 183–6; G. M. Ridenour, 'Browning's Music Poems: Fancy and Fact', *PMLA*, LXXVIII (1963), pp. 369–77.]

[3] [For *Master Hugues* cf. Ridenour as above.]

[4] Twickenham edition of Pope, Vol. II: *The Rape of the Lock and Other Poems*, ed. Geoffrey Tillotson (London: Methuen; New Haven: Yale University Press, 1954), p. 289.

[5] [cf. H. B. Forman, *Robert Browning and the Epic of Psychology* (1869), a review article on *The Ring and the Book* reprinted from *London Quarterly Review*, XXXII (1869), pp. 325–57; H. B. Forman's review of W. W. Story's poems in the *Fortnightly Review* (January 1869); Ina Beth Sessions, 'The Dramatic Monologue', *PMLA*, LXII (1947), pp. 503–16; Honan, *Characters*, pp. 104–65; J. H. Miller, *Disappearance of God*, pp. 124–33; William Cadbury, 'Lyric and Anti-Lyric Forms: A Method for Judging Browning', *UTQ*, XXXIV (1964), pp. 49–67; W. David Shaw, 'Character and Philosophy in *Fra Lippo Lippi*', *VP*, II (1964), pp. 127–32.]

III

STUDIES OF
SINGLE POEMS

ROBERT PREYER

ROBERT BROWNING: A READING
OF THE EARLY NARRATIVES

I

THE early poetry of Robert Browning is certainly interesting enough in its kind, and varied enough within its kind, to warrant a special approach. I want here to consider not only the nature of that kind but also Browning's approach to the making of it; and to explore a little the relations between this early work and the later dramatic monologue which came eventually to replace it. Commentators and biographers have noted that there was indeed a major shift of emphasis around 1840; some have called attention to the poet's efforts to discount the earlier productions. Yet the nature of that early work and the reason for abandoning it continue to perplex. A purely psychological explanation such as we find in Mrs Miller's biography of the poet sounds convincing until we recall that a similar shift occurs in the writing of Tennyson. And if we consider the blighted careers of poets who continued writing according to the idea of poetry with which Tennyson and Browning began – I refer to Beddoes, Darley, Clare, and the 'Spasmodic' group – then the shift begins to appear as a major cultural fact and no mere private idiosyncrasy. Something of importance was occurring to the mind of England in the interregnum period of the 'thirties, and as one might expect, it was taking a toll among those artists most exposed to the resulting conflicts.

The testimony of writers who live through such troubled periods is instructive. They insist that alterations introduced into style

Reprinted from *ELH*, XXVI (1959), pp. 531–48.

directly reflect alterations in the psyche. Or they claim that had they continued writing according to the traditions available to them in youth the result might have been both artistic and psychological disaster. (I am thinking especially of Wordsworth and Coleridge, Keats, Tennyson, and Yeats.) Browning certainly felt much the same; and he would doubtless subscribe to Yeats' well-known quatrain which reads,

> They that hold that I do wrong
> Whenever I remake a song
> Should recollect what is at stake:
> It is myself that I remake.

I dwell on this subject because it seemed of major importance to all the artists in the nineteenth century. To remake the style meant to remake the self; and woe to the artist who attempted to continue, in his life or work, as he began. Wordsworth warns:

> We Poets in our youth begin in gladness;
> But thereof come in the end despondency and madness.

Arnold's sage, the doomed Empedocles, knows what fate is awaiting the youthful Callicles: when young, he reflects,

> we receive the shock of mighty thoughts
> On simple minds with a pure natural joy!

but once past this youthful stage

> Joy and the outward world must die to him
> As they are dead to me. . . .

But Callicles will learn.

Yeats, with an even larger perspective of ruined poets behind him, declares that it is youth with its dreams which destroys the mature artist by preventing any further development of his powers:

> The best-endowed, the elect,
> All by their youth undone,
> All, all, by that inhuman
> Bitter glory wrecked.

His proud yet bitter cry of triumph is this: the child in him is no longer father of the man.

> But I have straightened out
> Ruin, wreck, and wrack;
> I toiled long years and at length
> Came to so deep a thought
> I can summon back
> All their unwholesome strength.

Neither Arnold nor Browning were able to make such a dazzling, if unclear claim – nor Wordsworth, with his

> We will grieve not, rather find
> Strength in what remains behind. . .
> In years that bring the philosophic mind.
> (*Intimations of Immortality*)

All these writers are plunged into dejection and despair or guilt and frustration when they summon back the 'unwholesome strength' of their youth. That is an experience from which few poets recover; they all try to fight clear of its potent spell and the debilitating sense of loss and nostalgia which recollection evokes.

This is especially the case with Browning who suffered intermittently all his life from the conviction that he had somehow sold his poetic birthright. 'You speak out', he wrote his wife, 'I never do!'[1] And in the introduction to his masterpiece *The Ring and the Book*, he is at pains to explain that he deliberately does *not* speak out. The implication seems to be that he writes under a self-imposed restriction. It is of course the figure of Shelley that looms large in his youthful dedication to art; and it was the Shelleyan mode of speaking out which he repressed. The 'inhuman bitter glory' of the Sun-treader both enthralled him and seemed to threaten his ruin. Browning was eventually to make a great symbolist poem out of the complex lure of his youthful ideal: *Childe Roland*. Consciously he determined not to be 'undone', as Childe Roland was, by the dream of his fervent youth. Yet the attraction remained; out of this tension was born the great symbolist poem.[2]

Browning seems to have arrived at this decision very early in his career. In *Paracelsus* (1835) and *Sordello* (1840) he is offering apologies for the 'misguided' hero who had set out on the quest for the ideal. Even in *Pauline* (1833) the strain is evident. It is to these works we must return if we want to understand the choice which Browning saw before him. I shall be arguing that one path led directly into symbolism and its obsessive subject-matter, a direction Browning tried to avoid. The other path led on to the remarkable discoveries in the handling of a wide range of subjects which we find in the dramatic monologues. The decision Browning made was crucial, for the man as well as the artist; and the fact that others made similar decisions in these decades proved decisive for the development of English poetry.

II

Around 1800 European literature had become preoccupied with the discrepancy between the relatively inexhaustible reservoir of potentiality within the individual psyche and the drastically reduced field of action in which it could be deployed. The aspiration toward individual self-realization had collided head on with the demands imposed by a reactionary and repressive social order.

It was the age of Werther, of the Byronic hero, and of Rousseau's *Confessions*; an age which recognized that the stress was falling most heavily on its youth. It was also an age which developed a remarkable genre, the spiritual confession or monodrama, to convey the acuteness of this stress. We may go to the Preface of Shelley's *Alastor, or the Spirit of Solitude* (1815) to get some idea of the area of experience governed by the form. This poem, Shelley tells us, is 'allegorical of one of the most interesting situations of the human mind. It represents a youth of uncorrupted feelings and adventurous genius led forth by an imagination inflamed and purified through familiarity with all that is excellent and majestic, to the contemplation of the universe. . . . So long as it is possible for his desires to point towards objects thus infinite and unmeasured, he is joyous, and tranquil, and self-possessed. But the period arrives when these objects cease to suffice. His mind is at length suddenly awakened and thirsts for intercourse with an intelligence similar to itself.' That 'intelligence' appears (in a dream) as a young lady and the poet pursues her through a magical landscape until he is exhausted and dies. Death takes place, appropriately, in a curious setting half-way between a blank heaven and an impersonal earth; a scene of total alienation. The argument in both poem and Preface is not well articulated but its direction is evident when we consider the curse Shelley calls down upon those who *deliberately* 'keep aloof from sympathies with their kind'. It is the presence of this stolid mass of people which makes it so difficult for the young idealist to feel at home in the world. As a consequence he is the predestined victim of 'illustrious superstition', develops 'too exquisite a perception' of the actuality of Platonic ideas, and ends his days pursuing a phantom of the imagination. The implication seems to be that in a better society 'the pure and tender-hearted' need not 'perish through the intensity of their search after . . . communities'. Or in terms of the narrative, a sympathetic young lady might have prevented the young man from pursuing a female phantasm, might conceivably have subdued what Shelley interestingly calls the 'sacred thirst for dubious knowledge'. (We shall have occasion, shortly, to pursue some of the implications of that 'sacred' yet 'dubious' thirst for knowledge.)

The Byronic version of dramatic confession does not, at first glance, resemble what we have found in *Alastor*. His hero is first seen, as a rule, in the guise of the pampered child of fortune, bored, disdainful, inactive. It is only the uncontrollable glint in his eye that marks him as melancholy's own, a guilty wanderer in the abyss of self. The protagonist may have had a stormy past – occasionally he is depicted as some giaour operating adventurously on the fringes of Europe – or he may have been stopped on the brink of action, having contracted a mysterious guilt in some unimagined, perhaps unimaginable past. Whatever the reason, he is excluded from normal occupations, normal activity. He exists in a social void. These heroes invariably possess superior talents, insight, or intensity – and the implication is there that these gifts are responsible for his being cut off from his fellows and from normal modes of experience. Frequently the 'conflict' in such a narrative commences when the hero begins to feel an attraction for a conventional pure young maid. She is the point of intersection between the subjective, daemonic world inhabited by the hero's feelings and the world of marriage, society and children.

Such a young lady cannot understand the nature of the threat she poses, even if it were possible for her to interrupt the prolonged declamations her presence seems to occasion. Will he cling to his gifts and to the more intense world of feeling he inhabits? If he accepts the obligations of normal love will he sink into the common herd? These and other questions are bruited about in a strenuous and often tiresome fashion. Meanwhile the young lady awaits the outcome of all this ranting in placid uncomprehending silence.[3]

It should be clear by now that Byron deals in the 'matter' of *Alastor* but in such a way that elements of probability tend to obscure the romantic and allegorical nature of the myth. The same thing seems to have happened in the narratives of the Spasmodic School. This had unfortunate consequences; it led readers to presume that all the characters were of the same degree of 'roundness'. Actually there is but one round character, the protagonist; all the others are something less than flat. As Robert Langbaum observed,[4] it would seriously distort the intention of *Faust* if the reader treated Gretchen as though she existed on the same level of actuality as the protagonist – and the same thing applies in Byron's work. Essentially, these authors were engaged in the production of *monodramas*. The focus is upon the developing soul of the protagonist; the other characters are there to show forth or articulate that development in all its particularlity.

According to Langbaum, minor characters in monodrama are sharply differentiated: black villains (often the devil himself), pure young maids and so on. What looks like melodrama is a convention of characterization designed to provide a rapid means of entry in the real subject of the narrative. The reader who accepts the convention will notice that subsidiary characters open up some possibility of action or aspect of mind which pertains to the protagonist. The plot then is not quite the silly business of a young man trying to decide whether to marry the pure maiden. It defines the mind's attempt to reconcile warring attitudes through a process of self-development. On this showing a pure maid may represent good instincts whereas the critical friend (Oswald in Wordsworth's *The Borderers* for instance) may be an incarnation of the devilish spirit of abstract thought. (The problem then might be how to keep one's friend and the girl as well.) The possibilities of the form are many, the opportunities for parody obviously rich. We may notice at this point a curious fact. The poet and the alchemist became almost interchangeable figures in the literature of spiritual confession. We have as protagonists in this form Faust, Paracelsus, the English necromancer Michael Scott (around whom Coleridge *planned* a stirring work) and a host of others. The presence of such figures should have removed some of the temptations to parody, if only by emphasizing anew the allegorizing tendency in the genre and its obsessive attention to a particular subject matter. Such figures, as Northrop Frye reminds us, have usually been treated as comic, their pretensions ridiculed as mere fraud. It was only with the honorific emphasis on 'becoming' and 'process' in the late eighteenth century that they recovered their dignity, becoming, in fact, emblematic of the aspiring soul of the poet.[5] In recent times Cassirer, Warburg, and Saxl have documented the analogy, arguing that pseudo-sciences like astrology provide a link between a mythical and a rational view of the world. If we translate this into the language of psychology, myth is seen as the product of emotion, reason as the product of the intellect. Poetry, as the romantics conceived it, had as one of its most urgent concerns the reforging of the links between these two areas of experience. The analogy between poet and alchemist is thus an exact one. Marcel Raymond has written that poetry in modern times tended to become 'some sort of irregular instrument of metaphysical knowledge' with the (largely unconscious) aim of 'reconquering man's irrational powers and transcending the dualism of the self and the universe'.[6] If we keep in mind that, for an Englishman, society makes up a large component of the 'universe', then this remark neatly defines the intention of the dramatic confessional.

It is easy enough to read works in this genre as incredibly crude examples of bourgeois tragedy or, for that matter, comedy of manners. But to do so is to miss the point. We will be equally wide of the mark if we read with the eyes of a pseudo-psychologist and dismiss these works because they enact attitudes and actions associated with adolescent daydreams. A clumsy parody like Prof. Aytoun's *Fir-*

milian: *A Spasmodic Tragedy* is preferable to the modern cant which damns this form as 'adolescent' or immature. (Let us hope that *Catcher in the Rye* marks the beginning of a renewed interest in the problematic quality of adolescent experience.) I am not arguing now, about the worth of individual works within the genre. I am simply saying that one must be clear about the intentions of the form, and its conventions. The form offers many intractable difficulties and we will speak of them in a moment. But it offers some unique opportunities as well, enabling a writer to penetrate quickly and effectively into the recesses of consciousness and define there the area of feeling which is being mutilated by the pressure of conventional social norms. When we replace these works in the explosive and frustrating milieu to which they are a response – the age of Metternich and Tory repression – their relevance is apparent. It is the lament of these 'unemployable' idealists that their potentialities can find no vent in creative social action. As Browning put it in *Pauline*, 'I have nursed up energies, they will prey on me.' Precisely: for that energy of spirit is internalized, goes rotten, and poisons not only the individual victim of the *malaise* but all those with whom he comes into contact. *Corruptio optimi pessima*. The old Latin tag takes us to the heart of the romantic dilemma.

I have said that the risk of failure in this genre seems inordinately great – just as the possibilities, if one succeeds, are remarkable. The trouble comes with the attempt to harmonize plot, character, and setting. If the projected feelings or aspects of mind are developed into believable or interesting characters, then the drama of reconciliation through self-development is lost sight of and the imaginary landscape seems a needless imposition. If, on the other hand, the personified feelings are not given enough substance or identity it is impossible to see the point of the episodes they act out – or at least it is impossible to interest oneself in them. *Sordello* is tiresome precisely because Browning's attempt to introduce historical characters, local color, and politics, makes a shambles of the 'drama of internal development' and a nuisance of the evocative landscapes. One feels that in the seven years of its composition (1833–40) Browning began to overlay the original mode with conventions borrowed from current theatrical productions – historical settings, the intrigue plot, full characterization of a half dozen protagonists and so on.[7] Enough of both intentions remained to baffle future readers and cause at least one contemporary to think he had lost his mind. There are no keys to this muddle – or rather there are too many keys that almost fit. In *Paracelsus* (1835) we have a more successful drama which suffers from the fact that the hero's identity is clearly meant to include that aspect of mind personified by the character Aprile but evidently does not include that of the two other leading characters, Festus and Michal. Mrs Miller surmises that these intrusive friends really represent the poet's mother and father. This seems likely enough. Whatever their source, they do not fit into a scheme which allows us to envisage characters as interacting aspects of a single consciousness. According to its Preface, *Strafford* (1837) was a play of 'Action in Character, rather than Character in Action'. Once more we wander between two sets of conventions not knowing which to apply at any given point. Browning's friend Milsand put his finger on the difficulty when he remarked that Browning was attempting, perhaps unconsciously, 'the fusion of two kinds of poetry into one', the dramatic and the lyrical.[8] The result, as might have been anticipated, was that his works became increasingly obscure – until the fusion was complete and a proper form discovered. *Pauline* (1833), the earliest of these works, is also the least troubled by the effort to reconcile and combine two sorts of poem. *Sordello* (1840) and *Strafford* (1837) are almost total failures, *Paracelsus* (1835) is somewhere in between. It is to *Pauline* therefore that we must turn if we want to see in its 'purest' state the sort of poem and poetic with which Browning began – and from which he struggled to free himself in the transitional works that followed. It is one of the best poems of its kind in English; and if we wish to explore the relations between the early work and the later dramatic monologues here is the obvious point of departure.

III

Pauline appears to be a variant on the genre we have been describing. (The subtitle reads, 'A Fragment of a Confession'.) As in *Paracelsus* the author set out to 'reverse the method usually adopted by writers whose aim is to set forth any phenomena of the mind or passions, by the operation of persons and events' and to 'display somewhat minutely the mood itself in its rise and progress. . . .' By presenting the feelings he hopes to compose in the reader's mind an image of the personality which is their ground of being. Prof. DeVane's words on *Paracelsus* apply here as well: 'the soul is the stage and moods and thoughts are the characters.'[9] What is behind this effort to construct a drama out of subjective feelings? Why does Browning want to exclude the subject matter dramatized by what he calls, in the Shelley essay, 'objective artists', namely actions that are 'substantive, projected from himself and distinct'? The reason seems to be that he is consciously modelling *Pauline* on the method of Shelley, whom he terms the greatest modern writer in the subjective tradition. A subjective poet, *because* he is excluded from action, is enabled to achieve a special form of cognition which amounts to a direct insight into the structure of reality. This is Browning's conviction, affirmed often in his youth, and formulated in these words in 1850:

Not what man sees, but what God sees – the *Ideas* of Plato, seeds of creation lying burningly on the Divine Hand – it is toward these that he [the subjective poet] struggles.

Browning glories in this exalted and comprehensive role assigned to the poet; he believes, further, that the subjective poet has a means, at once simple and profound, of attaining to such knowledge. It is the means employed in *Pauline* and described in the Shelley essay with these words:

Not with the combination of humanity in action, but with the primal elements of humanity he has to do; and he digs where he stands, – preferring to seek them in his own soul as the nearest reflex of that absolute Mind, according to the intuitions of which he desires to perceive and speak.[10]

The road to the absolute is through the subjective. A century later we find St J. Perse recommending the same procedure: 'French literature . . . is rediscovering its infinite in the very depths of the well of the human heart.'[11] The romantic (and symbolist) assumption behind both these statements seems to be this. Certain minds are so constituted they can respond to the 'summons from the deep', body forth as images a reality that cannot be transposed to the plan of discursive intelligence. Now this verges on magic; and I think that Browning was uneasily aware of the fact. We should take quite seriously the Latin quotation from Cornelius Agrippa which served as an admonitory preface to the first edition of *Pauline*. Agrippa is quoted as saying some will cry out 'that we are teaching forbidden things, are scattering the seeds of heresies. . . . To these I now give counsel not to read our book, neither to understand it nor remember it; for it is harmful, poisonous; the gate of Hell is in this book . . . FOR I DO NOT RECOMMEND THESE THINGS TO YOU: I MERELY TELL YOU OF THEM.' I submit that Browning, in appending that quotation had grounds other than a delight in mystification; that he had caught sight of a conflict between reason, the Revelation of Scripture, and the revelation offered by the vatic poet. 'I . . . consider Shelley's poetry as a sublime fragmentary essay towards a presentment of the correspondency of the universe to Deity, of the natural to the spiritual, and of the actual to the ideal', he was to declare. In other words, he attributed to Shelley a revelation of what Arthur Symons grandly called 'that central secret of the mystics, from Pythagoras onwards, the secret which the Smaragdine Tablet of Hermes betrays in its "As things are below, so they are above"; which Boehme had classed in his teaching of "signatures" and Swedenborg has systematized in his doctrine of "correspondences". . . .'[12] This revelation down through the centuries had been granted alike to Christian and non-Christian – that was one difficulty for Browning. But another difficulty was the irrational quality of this revelation. These were the dangers which led him to append the long warning from Cornelius Agrippa's *Concerning Occult Philosophy*: for some readers the gate of Hell might very well be in this book. As the despairing Paracelsus cries out,

> Ha, have I, after all
> Mistaken the wild nursling of my breast?
> Knowledge it seemed, and power, and recompense! . . .

M   167

God! Thou art mind! Unto the master-mind
Mind should be precious. Spare my mind alone!
(II, 221–3, 229–30)

If we look closely at *Pauline* I think we will begin to see how deeply
Browning had become immersed in such vatic revelations. As the
above quotation makes clear, Browning felt that Shelley elucidated a
system of 'vertical' correspondences, i.e. that he read appearances as
signs or symbols reflecting a supra-sensible world behind them.
This means that there exists an intermediate common language which
makes it possible for the actual and the ideal, both spiritual in their
essence, to reveal themselves and recognize each other. This is the
'language' of analogies and symbols, a musical, alogical discourse
relying on synaesthesia very heavily and syntax and the logical
rendering of sequential events as lightly as possible.

The effect of the discovery of such a language, and a good
account of its structure, is provided by a long passage in *Pauline*
beginning on line 411. Browning tells us he had begun to hear the
melodies of passion in which Shelley 'clothed' his aspirations. The
passage continues:

> such first
> Caught me and set me, slave of a sweet task,
> To disentangle, gather sense from song:
> Since, song-inwoven, lurked there words which seemed
> A key to a new world, the muttering
> Of angels, something yet unguessed by man.
> How my heart leapt as still I sought and found
> Much there, I felt my own soul had conceived,
> But there living and burning! Soon the orb
> Of his conceptions dawned on me . . .

I am not here concerned with the 'doctrine' but with Browning's
way of discovering it. These words, sounding here and there from
their lurking places in the 'song-inwoven' verses, seem to form among
themselves an esoteric order of meaning. We have, apparently, the
symbolist tendency to use words as if they were recurring *leit
motifs* in a musical structure – a structure that is superimposed upon
the narrative sequence and the normal sentence syntax which orders

it. The two kinds of meaning exist simultaneously and we must resort
to the spatial metaphor of two levels of meaning to describe them.
On one level a bait is provided to occupy the watchdog of the
intellect. On the other level, and as a consequence, the imagination is
freed to wander about in a sort of conceptual space, where all things
bear witness to a common kinship, words with emotions, thoughts
with sounds, images with feelings. The verse rhythms and the narrative satisfy the intellect and simultaneously awaken a sense of the
correspondency between words, thoughts, and feelings. Eventually
they point beyond this world to 'something yet unguessed by man'.

As befits one who believed significant actions can occur outside
the narrative dimension of time,

> I . . . who lived
> With Plato and who had the key to life   [*Pauline*, 435–6]

– Browning listens intently for the chimes of magical correspondence, for the 'song', 'passion's melodies', which provide a second
level of awareness for the initiate.

'Music', he had written, 'is earnest of a heaven, / Seeing we know
emotions strange by it, / Not else to be revealed' [*Pauline*, 365–7].
Yet Shelley had shown him that words and images could be used to
re-create the same effects – just as the 'song' in *Kubla Khan* enabled
the poet to 'see' a vision. Nor was that all. Browning was capable
himself of creating a verse which rendered these effects. Having said
that music was the sole means at our disposal for revealing a certain
order of emotional experience he goes on to manage an analogous
feat in words:

> For music . . . is like a voice,
> A low voice calling fancy, as a friend
> To the green woods in the gay summer time:
> And she fills all the way with dancing shapes
> Which have made painters pale, and they go on
> Till stars look at them and winds call to them
> As they leave life's path for the twilight world
> Where the dead gather.   [*Pauline*, 365–74]

This could easily be mistaken for the very best of the early Yeats –
the ending of *When You Are Old* for example, when we are told

> how love fled
> And paced upon the mountains overhead
> And hid his face amid a crowd of stars.

It is the evocative 'magic' of the romantic image, a poetry which aspires to the condition of music.[13]

No wonder we find him writing as one 'Created by some power whose reign is done, / Having no part in God and his bright world' [*Pauline*, 249–50]. He is deeply immersed in the underworld of feeling, a daemonic region well below the surface of normal everyday affairs. Nor is that all. Browning feels that he is trembling on the verge of some occult meaning which is 'revealed' in music (and the 'music' of verse) but is otherwise inexpressible. These arts revealed 'correspondences' between levels of existence rather than propositions that could be validated by analysis. Perhaps this was the form which thinking took in the golden age of the poets. At any event Browning thought of himself as living in some earlier age ('Created by some power whose reign is done') and spoke of the total identification he felt when reading the mythical literature of early Greece:

> And I myself went with the tale – a god
> Wandering after beauty, or a giant
> Standing vast in the sunset – an old hunter
> Talking with gods, or a high-crested chief
> Sailing with troops of friends to Tenedos.
> I tell you, nought has ever been so clear
> As the place, the time, the fashion of those lives:
>
> never morn broke clear as those
> On the dim clustered isles in the blue sea,
> The deep groves and white temples and wet caves:
> And nothing ever will surprise me now –
> Who stood beside the naked Swift-footed,
> Who bound my forehead with Proserpine's hair.
>   [*Pauline*, 321–7, 330–5]

The result of this –

> Was a vague sense of power though folded up –
> A sense that, though those shades and times were past,
> Their spirit dwelt in me, with them should rule.   [341–3]

Is it too far-fetched to suggest that he saw a connection between this second, alogical or musical mode of meaning in the arts and the mythical world he had delighted in as a boy? If so, it is but a step to the esoteric doctrines which Cornelius Agrippa retailed; and Browning lets us know that he was already deep in Neoplatonism. Here indeed was consolation (I had almost said fatal consolation) for the isolated artist – so much so that he can hardly find it in him to take Pauline and the problem she posed quite seriously.

> Thou art not more dear
> Than song was once to me. [76–7]

The excitements of the esoteric were beginning to carry him away from the serious social import of his narrative, namely the effects of isolation and self-centeredness on a young man whose potential has been ignored by society. Browning seems to be caught up in that lonely pride which led the youthful Yeats to confide exultantly, 'in the second part of *Oisin* under disguise of symbolism I have said several things to which only I have the key. The romance is for the readers. They must not even know there is a symbol anywhere.' His credentials as poet seem somehow bound up with his ability to sense the presence of some symbolic or occluded meaning:

> And, though this weak soul sink and darkness whelm
> Some little word shall light it, raise aloft,
> To where I clearlier see and better love,
> As I again go o'er the tracts of thought
> Like one who has a right, and I shall live
> With poets, calmer, purer still each time,
> And beauteous shapes will come for me to seize,
> And unknown secrets will be trusted me
> Which were denied the waverer once . . .
> [*Pauline*, 1010–18]

As the passage above indicates, Browning had moments when the whole elaborate structure seemed nonsense.

> 'Twas in my plan to look on real life,
> The life all new to me; my theories
> Were firm, so them I left, to look and learn
> Mankind, its cares, hopes, fears, its woes and joys; . . .

> And suddenly without heart-wreck I awoke
> As from a dream: I said "'Twas beautiful,
> Yet but a dream, and so adieu to it!'
> > [*Pauline*, 441–4, 448–50]

Nevertheless, when Browning wanted to indicate a revival of his poetic powers he commenced with an account of a magical landscape with obvious symbolic ramifications – as in lines 729 through 810. When these powers flag he is overwhelmed with symbolic nightmares,

> dreams in which
> I seemed the fate from which I fled; I felt
> A strange delight in causing my decay. [96–8]

Two marvelous dreams display guilt fixations centred upon the arrogance and self-preoccupation that seemed necessary to a poet intent upon reaching the absolute through the subjective (ll. 95–123). In this state he is prepared to 'give up all gained, as willingly / As one gives up a charm which shuts him out / From hope or part or care in human kind' [128–30]. He is appalled at the fate he has deliberately courted

> Sure I must own
> That I am fallen, having chosen gifts
> Distinct from theirs – that I am sad and fain
> Would give up all to be but where I was,
> Not high as I had been if faithful found,
> But low and weak yet full of hope . . .
>
> I would lose
> All this gay mastery of mind, to sit
> Once more with them, trusting in truth and love
> And with an aim – not being what I am. [79–88]

The poem wavers back and forth: one moment on fire with vatic ambitions, the next moment longing for release from these alienating dreams. As the quotations indicate, Browning can't decide what tenses to use in describing his state of mind. The muddled time sequences mime his state of mind:

> Sad confession first
> Remorse and pardon and old claims renewed,

Ere I can be – as I shall be no more.
I had been spared this shame if I had sat
By thee for ever from the first, in place
Of my wild dreams of beauty and of good,
Or with them, as an earnest of their truth: [25–31]

Eventually he was led to abandon the struggle, unable to sustain that 'reckless courage in entering into the abyss of himself'[14] which Yeats demanded of the symbolist poet. The poem concludes with a touching appeal: he hopes Shelley will understand why he must abandon these esoteric poetic excitements in favour of the life of morality and social commitment. The magic was dead or dying, the spell broken. It had been recognized by the young poet as a compensatory device for one who could not actively enter into the life about him. But was it only that?

To sum up: in the 1830s Browning felt all the attraction of the hero gifted above others in his power of experiencing and comprehending excellence. He could see that such a man, for the very reason that he was fated to experience an intenser range of emotional experiences, was subject to loneliness and misunderstanding. But he could not as yet see how to get beyond this static Gloomy Egotist stereotype without calling in some form of magic. The obsessive subject matter of his youth had become the self and its prehensions seen as other than or opposed to society and reason. But it was no easy problem (as Goethe had discovered before him) to drive beyond this 'subjectivity' and replace, at the centre of his art, the relations and interconnections between the self and society. That he did so is evident in the masterpieces of his maturity; but the effort cost him almost ten years of sustained effort and defeat.

One of the traditional functions of the artist has been to remind us of the enduring human needs and desires which must somehow be satisfied by any organization of society which seeks to be just and humane. At times he will envisage a paradisiacal society where the constructive powers of the psyche are placed under the least possible restraint and energy finds a release in 'toil that does not bruise the soul'. At other times he will count the cost, in broken or twisted lives, that a repressive society exacts – for sometimes society loses all sense of its humane goal. Now we have observed that there is a great hole in the middle of this romantic literature around 1800, a blank in that portion of the canvas usually given over to the celebration of 'works and days'. It is as though the authors have been stunned by the inhumanity of both tory repression and middle class industrialism. They can conceive of no joy or dignity or meaning in the toil such a society offered its victims. Hence they stand aloof, become revolutionary, or fill the void with some magical dream of poetry. A situation had arisen which, in the words of Marcel Raymond, 'aggravated to an almost intolerable degree the natural discordance between the total exigencies of the mind and the limited existence which is the lot of man'. The human demands that custom and religion had managed to exorcize or channel into acceptable forms of work were ignored in the new society. Hence there arose that longing for a happiness which the world of common experience made no pretense of satisfying, a disillusionment that sprang from the clash between the inner dream and the empty, hostile environment.

Browning was among the first to realize the extent of the cost of the romantic vision, the price that it exacted of its adherents. And he was also aware of the nobility of that dream. He knew that Romantic disillusionment, romantic contempt for normal living, could easily turn into something contemptible: an evasion of moral choices and a striking of attitudes. But he also knew that romantic disillusionment could spring from the conflict between impulses and emotions that were often sound and the prevailing middle class *bêtise* that corroded them. It was this double knowledge which came to expression, eventually, in the great gallery of criminals, quacks, poseurs, and artists who constitute the *dramatis personae* of the dramatic monologues.[15]

NOTES

[1] Quoted in B. Miller, *Portrait*, p. 14. The passage continues, 'I only make men and women speak – give . . . the truth broken into prismatic hues, *and fear the pure white light*' (my italics). [cf. W. O. Raymond, pp. 110–130 above.]

[2] *Childe Roland* was composed in Paris, January 2, 1852, at the height of the excitement over Napoleon's III's *coup d'état*. It was at this time also that the Shelley essay was written. The poem came to him 'in a sort of dream' he re-

ported, a final image of guilt, despair, and hopeless heroism. It seems to me that these emotions were appropriate to the occasion – an occasion which underscored the impossible grandeur of the Shelleyan quest for an ideal liberty.

[3] The notes J. S. Mill jotted down in a review copy of *Pauline* suggest that he was on the right track until sidetracked by moral considerations. 'If she *existed* and loved him, he treats her most ungenerously and unfeelingly', he wrote. Precisely: but as Mill knew, she did not exist as a character and therefore it was not a fault that 'all his aspirings and longings and regrets point to other things, never to her'. [For Mill's review see pp. 176–7 below.]

[4] Langbaum, *Experience*, pp. 63–4.

[5] Northrop Frye, *Anatomy of Criticism* (Princeton: 1957), p. 172.

[6] Marcel Raymond, *From Baudelaire to Symbolism* (London: 1957), pp. 5–6.

[7] DeVane, *Handbook*, distinguishes at least four poetic directions in *Sordello*.

[8] Quoted in Langbaum, *Experience*, p. 81.

[9] DeVane, *Handbook*, p. 55.

[10] [For a different interpretation see Philip Drew, 'Browning's *Essay on Shelley*', *VP*, I (1963), pp. 1–6.]

[11] St J. Perse, 'André Gide: 1909', tr. Mina Curtiss, *Sewanee Review*, LX, 4, p. 601.

[12] Quoted in Frank Kermode, *Romantic Image* (London: 1957), p. 111.

[13] Browning often attempted musical effects in verse and (more significantly) the effect of music on its listeners or on musicians: cf. *Abt Vogler*, *A Toccata of Galuppi's*, etc. Perhaps the most 'romantic' of all such passages occurs in *Pauline*:

> At first I sang as I in dream have seen
> Music wait on a lyrist for some thought
> Yet singing to herself until it came. [377–9.]

[See George M. Ridenour, 'Browning's Music Poems: Fancy and Fact', *PMLA*, LXXVIII (1963), pp. 369–77.]

[14] Quoted in Richard Ellman, *Yeats: The Man and the Masks* (New York: 1948).

[15] [cf. Lionel Stevenson, 'Tennyson, Browning and A Romantic Fallacy', *UTQ*, XIII (1943–4), pp. 175–95; Honan, *Characters* esp. Ch. I; Benziger, *Images*, Ch. VI, esp. pp. 164–79; F. E. L. Priestley, 'The Ironic Pattern of Browning's *Paracelsus*', *UTQ*, XXXIV (1964), pp. 68–81.]

JOHN STUART MILL

PAULINE

WITH considerable poetic powers, the writer seems to me possessed with a more intense and morbid self-consciousness than I ever knew in any sane human being. I should think it a sincere confession, though of a most unlovable state, if the 'Pauline' were not evidently a mere phantom. All about her is full of inconsistency – he neither loves her nor fancies he loves her, yet insists upon *talking* love to her. If she *existed* and loved him, he treats her most ungenerously and unfeelingly. All his aspirings and yearnings and regrets point to other things, never to her; then he *pays her off* toward the end by a piece of flummery, amounting to the modest request that she will love him and live with him and give herself up to him *without* his *loving her* – *moyennant quoi* he will think her and call her everything that is handsome, and he promises her that she shall find it mighty pleasant. Then he leaves off by saying he knows he shall have changed his mind by tomorrow, and despite 'these intents which seem so fair', but that having been thus visited once no doubt he will be again – and is therefore 'in perfect joy', bad luck to him! as the Irish say.[1] A cento of most beautiful passages might be made from this poem, and the psychological history of himself is powerful and truthful – *truth-like* certainly, all but the last stage. *That*, he evidently has not yet got into. The self-seeking and self-worshipping state is well described – beyond that, I should think the writer had made, as yet, only the next step, viz. into despising his own state. I even question whether part even of that self-disdain is not *assumed*. He is evidently *dissatisfied*, and feels

From Mill's notes for a review of the poem. See Introduction p. 4.

176

part of the badness of his state; he does not write as if it were purged out of him. If he once could muster a hearty hatred of his selfishness it would *go*; as it is, he feels only the *lack* of *good*, not the positive evil. He feels not remorse, but only disappointment; a mind in that state can only be regenerated by some new passion, and I know not what to wish for him but that he may meet with a *real* Pauline.

Meanwhile he should not attempt to show how a person may be *recovered* from this morbid state – for *he* is hardly convalescent, and 'what should we speak of but that which we know?'[2]

NOTES

[1] [Mill fails to notice that the poem is spoken by an assumed character who is on the point of death.]

[2] [See: W. L. Phelps, 'Notes on Browning's *Pauline*', *MLN*, XLVII (1932), pp. 292–9; L. F. Haines, 'Mill and *Pauline*: the "Review" that "Retarded" Browning's Fame', *MLN*, LIX (1944), pp. 410–2; C. N. Wenger, 'Sources of Mill's Criticism of *Pauline*', *MLN*, LX (1945), p. 338. For another version with slightly different readings see *Letters of Robert Browning* edited by T. L. Hood (1933), pp. 366–7.]

ELMER EDGAR STOLL

BROWNING'S *IN A BALCONY*

THERE is an interesting difference of opinion, of which I have only of late become aware, concerning the value of Browning's closet drama *In a Balcony* as well as the interpretation of it. In 1940 I had written of it as follows, at the conclusion of a discussion of the tragic situation, involving conventions or postulates, in both the *Oedipus Tyrannus* and *Othello*:

Browning the psychologist, the impressionist before his time, achieved what is perhaps his greatest situation, in *In a Balcony*, after a really similar fashion, at equal cost to probability, when Constance persuades her frank and noble lover Norbert, out of love for him and gratitude to the Queen, to declare to their mistress that all his service has been prompted by his love for her. The improbability lies not only in the success of the deception but also in the willingness of Constance and Norbert to take the risk; nor is it overcome by all Browning's careful preparation and motivation. The improbability, the deception, is, as in *Othello* (and indeed in the *Oedipus*), the price still necessarily paid for a superbly ironical *contretemps* such as that when the Queen, who, though married, has never known love, rushes to Constance, apparently for confirmation of the news, but really to tell her what love is like, bid her once the time comes give up everything for it, and, when Constance reminds her of obstacles in the way, cry out, as if not to her but to the stars,

> Hear her! There, there now – could she love like me? [539]

> Hear her! I thank you, sweet, for that surprise.
> You have the fair face: for the soul, see mine!
> I have the strong soul: let me teach you here. [551-3]

Reprinted from *From Shakespeare to Joyce* (1944), pp. 328–38, copyright 1944 by Elmer Edgar Stoll.

Les grands sujets de la tragédie, says Corneille, himself not always remembering it, *doivent toujours aller au delà du vraisemblable.*

Of the situation thus secured Mr Arthur Symons, as I then knew, had a high opinion, and as I have later found, Professor C. H. Herford. The former, writing in 1886 (revising in 1906), says of it: 'passionate and highly wrought, to a degree never before reached, except in the crowning scene of *Pippa Passes.*' And he thus condenses the latter part of the story:

His [Norbert's] aim, all the while, though unknown, as he thinks, to her, has been the hope of winning Constance, the Queen's cousin and dependant. He is now about to claim her as his recompense; but Constance, fearing for the result, persuades him, reluctant though he is, to ask in a roundabout way, so as to flatter or touch the Queen. He over-acts his part. The Queen, a heart-starved and now ageing woman, believes that he loves her, and responds to him with the passion of a long-thwarted nature. She announces the wonderful news, with more than the ecstasy of a girl, to Constance. Constance resolves to resign her lover, for his good and the Queen's, and, when he appears, she endeavours to make him understand and enter into her plot. But he cannot and will not see it. In the presence of the Queen he declares his love for Constance, and for her alone. The Queen goes out, in white silence. The lovers embrace in new knowledge and fervour of love. Measured steps are heard within, and we know that the guard is approaching.[1]

'Each of the characters', Symons continues, 'is admirably delineated;' Norbert, 'honest, straightforward, single-minded, passionate', presenting the strongest contrast to Constance's feminine over-subtlety. She is 'peculiarly wily for goodness, curiously rich in resource for unalloyed and inexperienced virtue'. Does then her proposal to relinquish Norbert in favour of the Queen show her to be lacking in love for him? Is she 'noble and magnanimous' or 'radically insincere and inconstant'?

Her love, we cannot doubt, was true and intense up to the measure of her capacity; but her nature was, instinctively, less outspoken and truthful, more subtle, more reasoning. At the critical moment she is seized by a whirl of emotions, and, with very feminine but singularly unloverlike instinct, she resolves, as she would phrase it, to sacrifice herself, not seeing that she is insulting her lover by the very notion of his accepting such a sacrifice. Her character has not the pure and steadfast nobility of Norbert's but . . . it is genuinely human.

In the matter of postulates or premises Professor Herford, in 1905, anticipates me, though his are not the same.

In its social presuppositions this community belongs to a world as visionary as the mystic dream-politics of M. Maeterlinck. But those pre-suppositions granted [that love is the absorbing preoccupation of this society and that for a brilliant young minister to fail to make love to his sovereign is a kind of high treason], everything has the uncompromising clearness and persuasive reality that Browning invariably communicates to his dreams. The three figures who in a few hours taste the height of ecstasy and then the bitterness of disillusion or severance, are drawn with remarkable psychologic force and truth. . . . One of them, the Queen, has hardly her like for pity and dread. A 'lavish soul' long starved, but kindling into the ecstasy of girlhood at the seeming touch of love; then, as her dream is shattered by the indignant honesty of Norbert, transmuted at once into the daemonic Gudrun or Brynhild glaring in speechless white-heat and implacable frenzy upon the man who has scorned her proffered heart and the hapless girl he has chosen.[2]

Concerning the artistic value of the Queen's character there seems to be little difference of opinion, but plenty of it concerning that of Constance, upon whom the situation depends. Of her, however, Herford thinks still more highly than Symons. 'Between these powerful, rigid, and simple natures stands Constance, ardent as they, but with the lithe and palpitating ardour of a flame. She is concentrated Romance' (p. 146).

A very different judgment is Mr Stopford Brooke's, in 1902.[3] He finds the 'lying' of Constance 'unendurable'; and her self-sacrifice, 'supposed by some to be noble, done in pity for the Queen', he takes to be not that but 'more like jealousy'.

No one, I suppose, believes her motive is wholly pity; it is, much more, love for Norbert, which stands steadfast when the Queen comes to her for confirmation; yet to this critic himself 'Constance, even as a study of jealousy', is quite unsatisfactory. 'The situations she causes are almost too ugly.' Her lying is to be explained or excused 'only by the madness of jealousy, and she, though jealous, not maddened enough by jealousy to excuse her lies'. And 'jealousy has,' he acknowledges, 'none of these labyrinthine methods; it goes straight with fiery passion to its end. . . . But it may be a study by Browning of what he thought in his intellect jealousy would be. At any rate Constance, as a study of self-sacrifice, is a miserable failure. Moreover, it does not make much matter whether she is a study of this or that, because she is eminently wrong-natured.' And presently he roundly declares her 'radically false', and though Norbert is 'radically true', is of the opinion that after their momentary outburst of love at the end 'nothing could be better for them both than death'.

In general, Brooke is not by any means the equal of Symons or of Herford as a critic; and at this point, where not only the others agree but also Browning himself, with whom, as Mr DeVane says, the poem was a favourite, Brooke might almost be ruled out of court. But in aesthetic matters, as not in the scientific, the opinion of the humblest (and Brooke is of course not that), if it is considered an honest opinion (and Brooke's is surely that), deserves attention. A poem, obviously, like any other work of art, depends for its value, as for its meaning, upon the purpose of the artist, but also, and as much, upon its effect. And that is not merely the effect produced in the highest circles.

Why, then, is not the word of Brooke, who is possibly nearer to the common man, for whom, as Wordsworth and other poets loyally say, the poet writes, as good as that of Symons and Herford? For several reasons it is not.

First and foremost, Brooke has not at the outset yielded himself frankly and freely to the spell, as the common man, reader or spectator, either, would do. *Laissons-nous aller de bonne foi*, Molière begs us, *aux choses qui nous prennent par les entrailles*. If the critic had responded generously and adequately to the situation between Constance and the Queen after the latter gets the news, he would have found the justifications for the violations of probability, the answers to his troubled questions.

Second, the critic does not realize, or else not remember, that not only here but in general, as in the *Oedipus* and *Othello*, improbability, at the outset, is the inescapable price of the supreme situation; that, as Corneille says, the great subjects go beyond the probable. This does not mean the mere 'marvelous' of the Renaissance critics – incidents or achievements that are beyond the range of experience – but passions that are. As I have said elsewhere, 'Even if life were different, and itself afforded such good situations as those of ancient myth or poetic invention, still it would not do. In great drama they would therefore have to be better, that is (again) improbable – though not *within* the drama, of course, even as such situations in great drama, are not now.'[4] If not big, and (though probably) improbable, who cares to see or read them?

Third, the critic does not sufficiently value the principle of Aristotle, fully confirmed by poetic practice, that plot or situation comes first in importance, not characterization – the play of passion on the stage or in the story, which rouses the emotions in the the audience, not truth to life in either character or circumstance, which satisfies their intellects.

That is, the critic is wrong not because he is wanting in delicacy of discernment but because he is confined within a formula – realistic, psychological, and moral. The improbable – the conventions or presuppositions – he fails to recognize as the price paid for a bigger, higher effect than the probable, as the approach made to a world of passions beyond the probable; and though with far less fidelity to the text, he, like Mr Arlo Bates,[5] who thinks Constance is learning a lesson in love, endeavors to do away with them, to psychologize them. He cannot then enter into the passions, for in his own person he has not paid the price and lacks the warrant. His expectations and prejudices interfere with the natural, emotional response to them, and he does not bear in mind the critical principles by which they would be neutralized. In fact, if he were not troubled by the expectations and prejudices, he would not have much need of the corrective principles, would readily grant the improbable presuppositions and take instinctively to the auspicious method of approach. 'Poetry,' the late illustrious W. P. Ker observed, and in an essay on this same poet, 'is its own interpretation.' 'The best one can do,' he adds, 'and it is no dishonourable office, is to get the right point of view, to praise in the right way.'[6]

Little praising, as is apparent above, has Brooke done here, whether rightly or wrongly; and as I cannot but think, he has not got the right point of view. He has not appreciated – that is, not responded to – the poetic or dramatic power brought to bear; nor has he comprehended the author's meaning or purpose. The tragic tension of the colloquy between Constance and the Queen and the exaltation of the lovers when their pretenses are abandoned and their fate is upon them, leave him cold; and the charming impulsiveness of Constance and the haggard passionateness of the Queen do not convince him of their reality. Instead of praising he has done what Molière thereupon begs us *not* to do: *ne cherchons point de raisonnements pour nous empêcher d'avoir du plaisir.* Indeed, revolted by the duplicity and moved to incredulity by the self-sacrifice, he does what no reader and still less any critic should do, goes behind the returns – questions the word of the author as if the characters were real people, not fiction – to discover a new motive, of which in the text, where alone their whole existence lies, there is not the slightest inkling. Bates has some basis for his theory: Constance has learned at least to know Norbert better when, near the end, she murmurs, half to herself,

> . . . as if you were a man.
> Tempting him with a crown! [912–13]

But it is contrary to all the evidence that she should have been sounding either him or the Queen. In which case her duplicity would be even greater, for then she would have been deceiving Norbert too! Generosity that really is jealousy? In life that is to be found, no doubt; but the fact does not now concern us unless this is of such sort here in the play. Brooke is yielding to the present-day critic's taste for the paradoxical, or else for the subconscious, whether it is in the play or not. And nevertheless, in vain! For from the above it is sufficiently apparent that with his hypothesis the critic is dissatisfied himself.

Not that the fragmentary tragedy under discussion keeps up, in between, to the high level of the Queen's colloquy with Constance and that of Constance with Norbert at the close. There is a further improbability (though a heightened tension) in Norbert's not realizing the situation – the peril – they are in when he re-enters; and there is too much philosophy or morality on his lips and too much ingenuity on hers, both before they kiss farewell (in which business they are caught by the Queen) and after. Nor is it that as a whole the little tragedy is quite popular, immediately effective, like Shakespeare in his own time, or is meant for the 'unaccommodated man', however 'common'. Browning is here, as elsewhere, now and then a little difficult or esoteric. The main trouble, to be sure, is that our spectators or readers are, like Brooke, so realistic and psychological in taste or bent that the ancient dramatic conventions of persuasion and deception are not now so acceptable as in Shakespeare's day; though this flattering sort, practised upon a love-hungry woman, is inherently much more plausible than that upon Othello. Even the 'presuppositions' that Mr Herford notices are not made so clear and conspicuous as some readers or spectators would require. That function of the courtier as lover, expounded in Castiglione, and that fiction of the statesman as in love with the Queen (marrying a substitute only by her permission), exemplified at the court of Elizabeth, are matters now more familiar to the learned. And so with the duplicity. It would offend others, no doubt, than Brooke (though perhaps less deeply); but not the readers of ancient, medieval, and Renaissance poetry, where love and pity, as here they do, conspire.

With many a reader, nevertheless, and far more with the spectator, love and pity, without any erudition, would suffice. To the spectator, yielding, as he should do, to the main dramatic current, to the charm to which Nobert himself here yields, even Constance's 'unloverlike' taking of such chances would not give offence. Considerations which are not suggested to the audience, says Mr Courtney of drama in general, are considerations which do not exist for them. Spectators live more in the moment, under the spell (if there is one) of the dramatist and the action, and, so far, are almost as frankly and unreservedly receptive as hearers or readers in medieval times, when in fiction such self-sacrifice by either sex was common. There is the story of the maiden who offered her life's blood to save the leper, finely dramatized since Browning's day by Hauptmann; there is the story of Gisippus in Boccaccio (as of Valentine in *The Two Gentle-*

men of Verona) who gives up his betrothed out of devotion to his friend.[7] All three are, like the patient Griselda story, examples of the medieval carrying of a virtue to extremes; but the invention is similar to that in the legend of Faustus or in ancient myths like those of Oedipus, Orestes, and Prometheus, producing material for drama, not for psychology. Here, to be sure, it is the men that, to us, upon reflection, seem unloverlike; but is not Norbert so as well, in taking up, however unwillingly, with Constance's proposal? And is not Der Arme Heinrich? His chief advantage with the spectator, like that of a Faust, or an Oedipus or a Phaedra, lies in the familiarity of the improbable story. Not to cavil or call in question would the audience, thus attracted, be sitting there.

Nor, even in this unfamiliar story, would the duplicity give the ordinary spectator offense. Indeed, on psychological grounds the dramatist has somewhat provided against that. Near the outset – the proper place – he has reinforced the presupposition that the minister may be serving the Queen for love of her by letting Constance insist upon a distinction between the sexes, founded in fact – 'women hate a debt as men a gift' – and upon the superior wisdom of the women. In other words, women hate to pay; they want to give. Men hate to receive; they want to earn, deserve. Women feel the debt, but would pay it without seeming to do so, generously, beyond the bond. 'I owe that withered woman everything,' Constance avers; yet, in the same breath, she would have it that the tactful way is the sole way not only to keep the Queen's favor but also to win her permission.

This proceeding, then, has some warrant both in nature and also in expediency, or enough for the premise to a play. In any case, this lying, tragic in outcome, is magnanimous, is meant to bring happiness – 'Love, she is generous!' Constance mistakenly cries – to all three concerned. 'Just', as a man is, she apparently does not think her; and this is to be a compliment – though regrettably similar to most of the compliments we give, if not receive. Constance herself has no qualms, nor has Norbert, despite his own truthfulness and straightforwardness. At no time has he such a feeling as Brooke, that life with such a woman would be impossible – 'a fatal split inevitable'. Her duplicity, like her unloverlike treatment of love, is, though more prominent than his, overshadowed by her daring, her gallantry beforehand and her gameness afterwards. And the spectators, swept on by the action, by the passion, would remember only – and not then halt like a Hegel, to weigh the value of them in the scale of eternal justice – the devotion and the pity, however mistaken. Her love, as Symons says, we cannot doubt. She is alive, and even for that reason also in her conduct convincing – alive by her perceptibly individual accent; and at no time is she so convincing as when she shows her love:

> Oh my heart's heart,
> How I do love you, Norbert! That is right:
> But listen, or I take my hands away!
> You say, 'Let it be now'; you would go now
> And tell the Queen, perhaps six steps from us,
> You love me – so you do, thank God! [42–7]

Thus, surely, our doubts should be forestalled; and if any arise out of the recklessness of the venture, by her ecstasy at the recovery of what has been abandoned – they are scattered. Now, as before this, with the Queen alone, she is no longer ingenious, but reduced to the simplicity of outcry and repetition.

CONSTANCE: Feel my heart; let it die against your own!
NORBERT:　　Against my own. Explain not; let this be.
　　　　　　This is life's height.
CONSTANCE:　　　Yours, yours, yours!
NORBERT:　　　　　You and I –
　　　　　　Why care by what meanders we are here
　　　　　　I' the centre of the labyrinth? Men have died
　　　　　　Trying to find this place, which we have found.
CONSTANCE: Found, found!　　　　　　　　　　[904–10]

For it is even to reach the labyrinth – to achieve the big situation, with its ironical contrasts and tumultuous passions – that the improbabilities are incurred; and it is by the preliminary impact of these, together with the convincing individuality and fascination of the characters, in their speech rather than in any psychology, that we are reconciled to them. And if, in this age of realism, the two great contemporaries, Dickens and Balzac, draw, as Saintsbury says,

'with unerring faithfulness' the characters which they have themselves created, not imitated, how much truer is that of their still
greater contemporary! For he has at command also another, a readier,
still more time-honoured, means of access to the passions, beyond
the *vraisemblable* – and what but poetry?

When that fails, the situation suffers. Yet no one, so far as I am
aware, has objected to the very last word of the play, on the lady's
lips:

> CONSTANCE: There's the music stopped.
> What measured heavy tread? It is one blaze
> About me and within me.
> NORBERT: Oh, some death
> Will run its sudden finger round this spark,
> And sever us from the rest!
> CONSTANCE: And so do well.
> Now the doors open –
> NORBERT: 'Tis the guard comes.
> CONSTANCE: Kiss!   [914–19]

In itself the word sounds flat and prosy; indeed, it is too much by
itself, alone. By the phrase 'And so do well' it is a little supported
and enriched; and no doubt Browning would have us now remember
that farewell kiss which betrayed them to (and saved them from) the
Queen. That meant separation; this means – no less! – reunion. My
ear, however, misses that meaning in its fullness, the appropriate
passionate, tragic depth of tone. Elsewhere, at the important
moments, it does not. For though a psychologist and (in goodly
measure) a realist, and also a forerunner of the verse of today,
Browning was decidedly something more and better. And 'all
poetry', he once wrote to Ruskin, is the problem of 'putting the
infinite into the finite'.[8] He certainly then had in mind details such
as are here in question; yet, pretty certainly, also larger matters, the
situation and the total structure. He must himself have known that
he began with an improbability, and (however little he may have
paused to consider the question) known why. For he was a poet, not
unlike the greatest. Far less than any novelist did he imitate, reproduce.[9]

187

NOTES

[1] *Introduction to Browning* (London: Dent, 1906), p. 133.

[2] *Robert Browning* (London: Blackwood, 1905), pp. 144-5.

[3] *Poetry of Robert Browning* (Crowell, N.Y.), pp. 340-3.

[4] *Art and Artifice in Shakespeare* (1938), p. 163.

[5] [See the Introduction to his edition of *A Blot in the 'Scutcheon, etc.* (1904), xxiv-xxxi.]

[6] *Collected Essays* (1925), i, pp. 277-8.

[7] cf. Professor W. W. Lawrence's *Shakespeare's Problem Comedies* [1931, 2nd ed., 1960,] pp. 23-4, etc.

[8] [Letter of December 10, 1855. See W. G. Collingwood, *Life and Work of Ruskin* (1893], I, p. 199.]

[9] [See Katharine Bronson, 'Browning in Venice', *Cornhill*, LXXXV (second new series XII) (1902), pp. 145-71, esp. p. 159. cf. Langbaum, *Experience*, pp. 160-81.]

ROMA A. KING, JR

BROWNING: 'MAGE' AND 'MAKER'–
A STUDY IN POETIC
PURPOSE AND METHOD

'**M**Y stress lay on the incidents in the development of a soul', Browning said of *Sordello*, in language heavy with Victorian and Platonic overtones. Browning had in mind, however, the whole inner life of a character, his interest being psychological rather than moral or philosophical. 'Little else', he continued, 'is worth study.' His exploration of states of consciousness and his attempt to render them emotionally and sensuously recall John Donne and anticipate Ezra Pound and the twentieth century. Like Donne and Pound, Browning carefully manipulated his material and structural devices to create the actual sense of an interior 'soul' – experience in the process of being shaped. His poetry is neither sensation, nor emotion, nor idea recollected in tranquility, but all these immediately, dramatically perceived.

In short, Browning *renders* rather than writes about a subject; he is maker, not philosopher. The speaker in the poem '*Transcendentalism*' echoes Browning's own preferences when he chooses the magician over the philosopher, saying,

> Then, who helps more, pray, to repair our loss –
> Another Boehme with a tougher book
> And subtler meanings of what roses say, –
> Or some stout Mage like him of Halberstadt,
> John, who made things Boehme wrote thoughts about?

Browning did not merely write thoughts about things; he *made*

From *Victorian Newsletter* No. 20 (Fall 1961), pp. 22–5.

things and his favourite material was the 'soul' – the whole psychic life – of a character.

We can go one step further and characterize the particular kind of 'soul' which most attracted him. Although his interests were diverse and his achievements relatively broad, he returned again and again to the subject of man's intellectual and moral limitations which, counterpointed against his aspirations, produced frustration and often despair. The speaker of *Two in the Campagna* speaks for a host of other frustrated men and women from Browning's poetic world:

> Only I discern –
> Infinite passion, and the pain
> Of finite hearts that yearn.

'Infinite passion' and 'finite hearts' – this is the pervasive theme of all Browning's poetry.

Browning illustrated repeatedly both these characteristics: his interest in rendering the whole psychic life of a character and his preoccupation with failure and frustration. Perhaps I can best make my point clear by discussing in detail a single, representative poem.

Cleon is characteristically illustrative, I believe. I should like to study the poem primarily to demonstrate Browning's distinguishing purpose and method as a poet and, secondarily, to throw light upon the poem itself.

Let us begin with the subject. What is Browning 'saying' in the poem? What is his 'message'? *Cleon* appears superficially to represent a clash between Greek humanism and Christianity. It has been so interpreted often. But it is not a philosophical or religious treatise. Herein lies one of the distinctive characteristics of the poem – and of Browning's poetry in general. Ideas here are means, not ends. Browning concerns himself with 'soul', leaving philosophizing to Boehme and his ilk. Christianity is really not the issue; Cleon would have rejected a revealed Zeus as readily as a revealed Christ. In fact, Browning might have had it that way without altering his real meaning. He distinguishes here, as in *The Statue and the Bust*, between moral and psychological concerns, indicating his greater interest in the latter.

Nor is the poem biographical. Rather it is about Cleon's frustrations resulting from unrelievable tensions, a paradox – the conflict between 'infinite passion' and 'finite hearts'. Cleon is torn between sensitiveness to beauty and awareness of its fragility; joy in the physical life and his increasing debility; respect for the mind and the discovery of its limitations; a desire to eternalize time and the sense of its transience; instinctive longings for a revealed religion and his inability to accept one. In short, the central concern of Browning is the psychological conflict in the character – something he once referred to as action in character rather than character in action.[1]

Cleon assumes contradictory roles: the rational, humanistic philosopher and the imaginative, intuitive poet; the decaying body and the aspiring spirit. Unable to eliminate either or to reconcile the two, he falls into despair, like so many other of Browning's characters, becoming incapable of saving action.

Browning's subject then is conflict in character and his purpose is to *render* the actual sense of frustration and despair. Let us observe now what it means structurally in a Browning poem for him to 'make', 'render', rather than to write thoughts about something.

We begin with the rhetorical structure of the poem. In itself it is meaningful. Browning states little explicitly. Rather he permits Cleon to be acted upon, drawn out, dramatically exposed by both the other characters in the poem and by his intellectual and cultural milieu. In short, the poem is dramatic rather than expository.

Yet it is drama of a kind almost peculiar to Browning. Cleon undergoes no change, experiences no deepening insights which lead to purgating action. The movement consists rather in the steady heightening of the reader's sense of Cleon's frustration, reaching peak intensity in Cleon's total incapacity for action.

Browning initiates this movement by placing Cleon against two other figures: the king and St Paul. Each interacts upon the other, rendering more nearly complete the portrait of Cleon. There is a constantly shifting perspective, a deepening of reader insight, a heightening of irony. In the first section (lines 1–42), Cleon is the poet-philosopher, and the king the generous giver. Greek civilization is idealized. In the central section (lines 43–335), the king becomes the seeker and Cleon the giver, who, in his exposition, betrays the decadence of Greek humanism. Finally (lines 336–53), St Paul assumes the role of giver, offering Christianity to both the king and Cleon.

Cleon is additionally drawn out by his intellectual and cultural surroundings. Idealized Greece is first juxtaposed against the decadent Greece of Cleon's day, and finally both are set against the new order which Christianity will bring.

The sub-title of the poem, 'As certain also of your own poets have said', recalls the intellectual and spiritual unrest described in the seventeenth chapter of the Acts of the Apostles. 'For all Athenians,' the account states, 'and strangers which were there, spent their time in nothing else, but to tell, or to hear some new thing.' This intellectual dalliance suggests the decadence of Greek philosophy and the spiritual hunger which prepared for the Christian triumph.

Cleon reminds us, in fact, of Matthew Arnold's portrait of Marcus Aurelius:

What an affinity for Christianity had this persecutor of the Christians! The effusion of Christianity, its relieving tears, its happy self-sacrifice, were the very element, one feels, for which his soul longed; they were near him, they brushed him, he touched them, he passed them by. . . . We see him wise, just, self-governed, tender, thankful, blameless; yet, with all this, agitated, stretching out his arms for something beyond, – *tendentemque manus ripae ulterioris amore.*

Or perhaps Cleon reminds us of Arnold himself, 'Wandering between two worlds, one dead / The other powerless to be born'. Here then as in so many other Browning poems, meaning is communicated through the rhetorical structure.

Let us now look at a related matter – the dialectical movement of the poem, noting how Browning turns what might be philosophical rumination into the rendition of a psychological state. In the first forty-three lines Cleon is depicted as the poet who, the king thinks, must have attained the 'very crown and proper end of life'. And he has attained something. Like Marcus Aurelius, Cleon has the depth and sensitivity that make his final negation tragic.

In the second section, however, he displays another – and in many respects a contradictory – side of his nature: that of the rationalistic philosopher. Unlike other animals, he states, man has the power of introspection and self-evaluation and should be able to appropriate life's joys; but such, he has discovered, is not the case. His faculties – and here Cleon is the perceptive analyst of his own condition – do not equal his vision. Art and learning cannot assure happiness because they can neither substitute for experience nor promise personal existence after death. Already experiencing physical decline and facing death, Cleon concludes that it would be better if he did not have the vision since, because of his inadequate faculties, perceptiveness only contributes to his greater unhappiness. His advice to the king is:

> Live long and happy, and in that thought die:
> Glad for what was!

But Cleon, dissatisfied with his own advice, faces a paradox. On the one hand, he has intimations of a spirit world; on the other, he is limited by his concept of man. He cultivates his mind and art but finds them ineffectual against old age and death. He advances a theory of progress only to realize 'Most progress is most failure. . . .' His conflict produces a disintegration fully dramatized in the last section. We see Cleon successively as poet, philosopher, and cynic. Actually he is all three, simultaneously rather than chronologically. The divisions within him create the tense dialectic of the poem – as do, indeed, those divisions within Browning's other characters: Andrea, Fra Lippo and Bishop Blougram, for example.

The final episode brings the whole man into focus. In a situation which makes new demands on him, he displays a proud, querulous, and provincial, if not petty, outlook. Of the new religion, he says, 'Their doctrine could be held by no sane man', failing to realize or refusing to admit the ironic similarity between that insanity and his own intuitive longings.

He does not suffer from satiety, for he is yet sensitive to physical pleasures ('Every day my sense of joy / Grows more acute'). He realizes his increasing incapacity to experience life ('while every day my hairs fall more and more. . . .'). Enthusiastic over the king's gift of the 'one white she-slave', he nevertheless despairs because –

> . . . she turns to that young man,
> The muscles all a-ripple on his back.
> [298–9]

Having failed in mind and body, he needs a new set of values. In spite of his self-knowledge, however, he lacks the power to act. He cannot, on the one hand, because of psychological and cultural barriers, and, on the other, because of intellectual and moral limitations – an inescapable part of the 'human condition' as Browning understands it. He *cannot* – the imperative constitutes Cleon's tragedy. Browning's achievement in Cleon is to communicate an immediate sense of this failure through the rhetorical organization and the dialectical movement of the poem.

Here, as elsewhere, Browning skilfully uses other devices – sentence structure, sound, rhythm, imagery – to render his subject with emotional and sensuous immediacy. On the surface, Cleon's discourse is rational and logical rather than imaginative and emotional; that of the philosopher. He states, elaborates, illustrates, and summarizes. Appropriately, his sentences are tightly and logically constructed, his syntax rarely admitting inversion or any other poetic dislocation. He avoids sudden shifts in thought, incoherences, asyntactical elements, ellipses, and exclamatory statements.

But against these prosaic elements, Browning juxtaposes others of sensuous and emotional import, particularly sound. Frequent repetition of long sustained vowels gives *Cleon* a limpid, flowing movement. The relaxed, sustained, basically passive quality and dirge-like tone of the long *i*, *o*, *a*, and *e* functions metaphorically to render Cleon's passivity: 'I know not, nor am troubled much to know.' Additionally, they slow the movement and heighten the effect of the deliberate, rationalistic argument. The lightness of stress, the frequency of shared stress, and the tonal and emotional unity of the line produce a free, forward, though unemphatic movement, which characterizes the major portion of the poem.

In the central section, however, something important happens –

materially and structurally. Cleon's idea is rationalistic in the beginning. The movement of the lines is relatively broken. But with the triumph of emotion over concept toward the conclusion of the section, the movement changes. Beginning with line 301, Cleon drops his argumentative tone and becomes intensely personal. The lines become more lyrical, regular, and precise:

> Say rather that my fate is deadlier still,
> In this, that every day my sense of joy
> Grows more acute, my soul (intensified
> By power and insight) more enlarged, more keen;
> While every day my hairs fall more and more,
> My hand shakes, and the heavy years increase –
> The horror quickening still from year to year,
> The consummation coming past escape
> When I shall know most, and yet least enjoy –
> When all my works wherein I prove my worth,
> Being present still to mock me in men's mouths,
> Alive still, in the praise of such as thou,
> I, I the feeling, thinking, acting man,
> The man who loved his life so over-much,
> Sleep in my urn.   [309–23]

The pattern here is closer to iambic pentameter than in the earlier part of the section. There are departures from the regular pattern but the irregularities are fewer and they serve emotional rather than conceptual ends. *Sleep*, for instance, is thrust into prominence by an unexpected emphasis, bringing the passage to a powerful climax.[2] The line which follows, 'It is so horrible . . .' is adequately introduced and proceeds effectively on a lower and quieter pitch. Clearly, manipulation of meaning, rhythm, and sound helps render an acute sense of the 'horrible' in this passage.

Here Cleon, for a moment, exposes a part of his nature he has previously suppressed. He is probably unaware of this self-betrayal, resulting from a temporary relaxation of his rational faculty, and in the last paragraph, the outburst having exhausted itself, he becomes once more the cultivated philosopher. With the resumption of his dominant role, the rhythm becomes again that of the main body of the poem.

We look for a poet's sensitivity especially in his imagery. Cleon's figurative bareness results from and produces the sense of his emotional and sensuous atrophy. His images are of two kinds: the short metaphors and similes and the extended comparisons. The first are decorative bits of stock rhetoric; they stand alone, rarely combining with each other to form either a conceptual or symbolic pattern. They betray the imprecision of Cleon's perception and his inability to treat experience imaginatively and synthetically. He uses his extended comparisons to clarify and heighten abstract generalizations. Primarily intellectual, they appeal only incidentally to the emotions and senses, representing the fragmentation of his personality, the triumph of his mind over his emotions, the suppression of his senses. Both the shorter and the extended figures are functional, however, illustrating, indeed rendering, Cleon's emotional and sensuous atrophy.[3]

Finally his suppressed emotions overpower him momentarily, and in the passage ending 'Sleep in my urn' he expresses unrelievable despair. His gloom is as profound as that of Arnold's Empedocles.[4] In contrast, however, Cleon is incapable of even suicidal action.

This is not the entire poem, for Browning characteristically takes an ambivalent attitude toward his materials. Against Cleon's despair, which might so easily become sentimental, Browning counterposes a dry, intellectual irony. More a pattern involving the entire poem than individual lines, the irony, nevertheless, works frequently on two levels simultaneously. The discrepancy between literal and ironic meaning is rarely that of complete opposites, the meaning fluctuating along a scale from absolute positive to absolute negative. Also characteristic is the fact that the total meaning is revealed progressively. Individual statements take on additional meaning as the poem develops, achieving completeness only after the entire poem is finished.

Irony takes many forms. Between Cleon's 'truth' and that perceived by the reader there is a discrepancy. His thinking has hardened into a system, and he accepts or rejects as absolutes things clearly capable of ambivalent meaning. Infrequently totally wrong, he is generally partial or inconclusive. Being right on one level and wrong in varying degrees on a more important one makes his position particularly ironic. The reader is constantly cutting back and forth between two possibilities.

The ironic elements are brought together and given final meaning by the last section of the poem. The dramatic quality of the poem is conceptual and emotional (psychical) rather than narrative (biographical); spatial rather than temporal. Step by step Cleon enumerates the characteristics of a religion which he thinks might give life the meaning which he wishes it had; he dismisses each as incompatible with reason. His intuition reaches in the direction of Christ only to be frustrated by conscious will:

> Long since, I imaged, wrote the fiction out,
> That he or other god descended here
> And, once for all, showed simultaneously
> What, in its nature, never can be shown,
> Piecemeal or in succession . . .

> And prove Zeus' self, the latent everywhere!

> It is so horrible,
> I dare at times imagine to my need
> Some future state revealed to us by Zeus . . .
> Zeus has not yet revealed it; and alas,
> He must have done so, were it possible!

These lines, preparatory to the final section, give the poem both formal and conceptual unity. They make possible also the emotional impact of Cleon's rejection. Lines and situation, which taken out of context seem sentimental, are preserved in the whole poem by the balance between concept and emotion which irony maintains. Irony, the only device strong enough to bring together the disparate elements, is the chief unifying force in the poem.

When we finish *Cleon* we know a great deal: specifically, the nature and cause of Cleon's frustration. If Browning's purpose were philosophical and moral, this might be enough. But it isn't. Because *Cleon* is a 'soul' study and a poem, we more than *learn about* – we are made to *experience* the despair itself. Browning has given us a sense of what it means for a man to be frustrated and paralyzed by his 'infinite passion' and his 'finite heart'.

By poetic use of all the material and structural devices available to him, Browning has rendered intellectually, emotionally, and sensuously the psychic life of one of his characteristic failures. He has demonstrated himself the Mage and the Maker. This is Browning's characteristic role.[5]

NOTES

[1] [In the preface to *Strafford* (1837). See DeVane, *Handbook*, p. 62.]

[2] Browning obviously intended this effect. The line just before is iambic pentameter. In the first edition of the poem, the last line read 'Shall sleep . . .', continuing the iambic movement. The change throws emphasis upon the word and gives it the effect which I have noted.

[3] It would further illustrate my point to observe that Browning uses an entirely different kind of imagery – stronger, more imaginative, more masculine – in *Fra Lippo Lippi*, where he is, of course, treating a different type of character.

[4] For the relation between *Cleon* and Arnold's *Empedocles* see A. W. Crawford, 'Browning's *Cleon*', *Journal of English and Germanic Philology*, XXVI (1927), pp. 485–90.

[5] [cf. W. C. DeVane, 'Browning and the Spirit of Greece', in *Nineteenth-century Studies* (Cornell, 1940), pp. 179–98; H. B. Charlton, 'Browning as Poet of Religion', *Bulletin of the John Rylands Library*, XXVII (1943), pp. 271–307, esp. pp. 282–90; William Irvine, 'Four Monologues in Browning's *Men and Women*' [*Fra Lippo Lippi*, *Bishop Blougram's Apology*, *An Epistle of Karshish*, and *Cleon*], *VP*, II (1964), pp. 155–64.]

RICHARD D. ALTICK

A GRAMMARIAN'S FUNERAL: BROWNING'S PRAISE OF FOLLY?

Is *A Grammarian's Funeral* what it has virtually always been said to be: a paean of praise for the dead gerund-grinder? In a fashion, yes; for such an interpretation can be bulwarked by citing parallel doctrine in other familiar Browning poems. For example, the grammarian did what he wanted to do, and we know that Browning heartily approved of a man's following the promptings of his instincts. Again, the grammarian left to God the task of making 'the heavenly period / Perfect the earthen', and we inevitably hear echoes of Andrea del Sarto's view of the function of heaven. The poem can be read as one more celebration of success in the midst of apparent failure. It is easy to regard the grammarian as a typical Browning hero, a Rabbi Ben Ezra of the verb-endings.

But our response cannot be merely one of placid assent to the attitude of the student-chorus. Today we are too much aware of Browning's personal ambivalences, which so often find reflection in his presentation of character, to accept unreservedly the traditional reading of the poem.[1] Seldom does Browning wholly condemn a character – even seemingly lost souls have a few redeeming features; but seldom, on the other hand, does he praise a character without qualification. Furthermore, the device of the dramatic mask enables him, as we learn from every fresh intensive study of his best monologues, to indulge his ambivalences by talking out of both sides of his mouth. And slowly we are coming to realize that his gift of satire was both more considerable and more cunning than either his

From *Studies in English Literature*, III (1963), pp. 449-60.

immediate audience or later critics knew. Such considerations necessarily complicate the reading of *A Grammarian's Funeral*, a poem
that is not as simple or transparent as has usually been thought.

The crucial point is that the ideas of the poem are uttered by
personae whose objectivity is gravely suspect. The chorus is composed of students who will become, for better or worse, the gram-
marians of the next generation. In their admiration for their deceased
master, they reveal themselves as pedants off the old block. Their
subscription to the grammarian's view of life defines their own
limitations. Heaven, and Robert Browning, forbid that we should
assent wholeheartedly to the assumptions that underlie their praise:

> He knew the signal, and stepped on with pride
> Over men's pity;
> Left play for work, and grappled with the world
> Bent on escaping:
> 'What's in the scroll,' quoth he, 'thou keepest furled?
> Show me their shaping,
> Theirs, who most studied man, the bard and sage, –
> Give!' – So he gowned him,
> Straight got by heart that book to its last page:
> Learned, we found him!   (43–52)

> Oh, such a life as he resolved to live,
> When he had learned it,
> When he had gathered all books had to give;
> Sooner, he spurned it!
> Image the whole, then execute the parts –
> Fancy the fabric
> Quite, ere you build, ere steel strike fire from quartz,
> Ere mortar dab brick!   (65–72)

> Yea, this in him was the peculiar grace
> (Hearten our chorus)
> Still before living he'd learn how to live –
> No end to learning.
> Earn the means first – God surely will contrive
> Use for our earning.   (75–80)

> Was it not great? did not he throw on God,
> (He loves the burthen) –

God's task to make the heavenly period
　　Perfect the earthen?
Did not he magnify the mind, shew clear
　　Just what it all meant?
He would not discount life, as fools do here,
　　Paid by instalment!
He ventured neck or nothing – heaven's success
　　Found, or earth's failure:
'Wilt thou trust death or not?' he answered 'Yes:
　　Hence with life's pale lure!'　　　　　(101–12)

The grammarian was the type of 'high man' who 'with a great thing to pursue, / Dies ere he knows it' (115–16); who, 'aiming at a million, / Misses an unit' (119–20); who 'throws himself on God, and unperplext / Seeking shall find Him' (123–4). 'This man', in sum, 'decided not to Live but Know' (139).

Beyond question the grammarian is the *students'* hero, but Browning scarcely means him to be ours – certainly not to the same uncritical degree. Far from following Browning's customary advice that man should live life to the utmost, he withdrew from life, preferring to read about it (and in the end not even doing that). To be sure, he aspired, was devoted to a cause. But one may question whether, in Browning's own terms, his special aspiration was praiseworthy, his particular cause worth the sacrifice of a whole lifetime. His goal, though superficially lofty, actually was low. And when he does go up the mountain, it is not under his own power, but as a corpse borne on the shoulders of his disciples.

The note of removal from common life is struck at once. The students bear the dead master away from 'the common crofts, the vulgar thorpes' (3), 'the unlettered plain' (13) – up a mountain 'cited to the top, / Crowded with culture' (15–16). 'Culture' may be interpreted as 'artificial, decadent, sophisticated life' – the sort of civilization Browning disparaged through the complacent figure of Cleon. The students thus are symbolically completing the process begun early in the grammarian's lifetime, of separating him from the human sources of strength. They are about to ensconce him in the sort of remote mausoleum from which the guilty Soul, in Tennyson's *The Palace of Art*, finally flees to seek renewal in 'a cottage in the vale'. As Lionel Stevenson has shown,[2] Browning, in his auto-biographically significant *Paracelsus* and *Sordello*, had moved steadily away from the romantic exaltation of self-sufficient egocentricity to the familiar Victorian position that art – and learning – must have social usefulness, that the artist and the scholar must maintain a vital contact with common life. Numerous passages of *Paracelsus*, indeed – far too many to list here – serve as illuminating glosses for *A Grammarian's Funeral*. The 'still voice', for instance, urges Paracelsus to 'know, not for knowing's sake, / But to become a star to men forever'; and Festus inquires of Paracelsus,

> How can that course be safe which from the first
> Produces carelessness to human love?
> It seems you have abjured the helps which men
> Who overpass their kind, as you would do,
> Have humbly sought. . . .   (I, 619–23)

Thus the grammarian's biography, as revealed by the students, is one of progressive detachment from life and increasing neglect of his duty to society at large: a course of which Browning, and not alone the youthful Browning of *Paracelsus*, could hardly have approved. Moreover, his choices involved denial of the ethical values that Browning himself most cherished. Born with the brightest conceivable prospects, the 'face and throat [of] lyric Apollo' (33–4), he failed utterly to realize his promise. Paracelsus accurately described, by anticipation, not only his own failure but the grammarian's as well:

> And men have oft grown old among their books
> To die case-hardened in their ignorance,
> Whose careless youth had promised what long years
> Of unremitted labour ne'er performed. (I, 745–8)

To have wasted God-given physical attributes, to have scorned the rich potentialities of youth and talent and preferred instead the dusty existence of a hermitic philosopher may be admirable in the eyes of the students, but not, one would suppose, in those of the poet who wrote *Fra Lippo Lippi*. The grammarian's youth, in any event, passed; spring turned at once to winter, without the normal intervention of the fruitful summer. Instead of living, he 'grappled with the world [which was] bent on escaping' (45–6) – not the world of direct personal experience, but life as reflected in books.[3] Nor were the books themselves the report of first-hand experience; instead they were the observations of 'the bard and sage': not men of action, but men who, like the grammarian, had studied or described life rather than participated in it – the poet, sculptor, and composer of *The Last Ride Together*, whom Browning chided for growing 'poor, sick, old ere your time' by devoting themselves to art instead of to life. Thus there is an extra irony: the grammarian is not one but two removes from actuality. And as his life wore on, he moved, like a crab, backward, ever farther from the (to Browning) precious realm of here-and-now existence.

From line 50 onward, the essence of the poem is contained in the ironic counterpoint of the words 'know', 'learn', and 'book', on the one hand, and 'life' and 'live' on the other. The grammarian grew 'learned', but his knowledge of life (symbolized as a 'book') was second- or third-hand, and it was completely uninspired, mechanical ('got by heart'). Urged to leave off learning and, before it is too late, live (note how in lines 55 and 57 the words 'taste' and 'actual' intensify the force of 'life'), he was scornful. 'Grant I have mastered learning's crabbed text, / Still, there's the comment' (59–60). And so, taking up the fine-print commentary, he moved even farther from actual life and devoted himself to books about books. In terms of what, in Browning's view, should have been his central concern – immediate, personal, intense experience of life – he steadily learned more and more about less and less. 'Let me know all,' he cried (61), but no amount of vicarious knowledge can atone for failure to live. The students praise their master's heroic passion for learning, but to Browning it is a misdirected passion in so far as it contravenes God's intention that life be used for living. The grammarian put the cart before the horse; while acknowledging the desirability of living, he pedantically chose to read all about it first. Nor, while at first glance it seems a praiseworthy ideal, was he right in his decision to 'image the whole, then execute the parts' (69). Browning, with his candid awareness of human limitations (as well as his presence in a Victorian culture which preferred systematic, cautious induction to the romantics' visionary aspiration toward the grand synthesis), probably was of two minds about it, as he seems to have been about other of the grammarian's alleged virtues. On the one hand, he would have applauded the heroism of the sentiment ('a man's reach . . .'); on the other, he would have deplored the grammarian's lack of realism. Aprile told Paracelsus:

> Knowing ourselves, our world, our task so great,
> Our time so brief, 'tis clear if we refuse
> The means so limited, the tools so rude
> To execute our purpose, life will fleet,
> And we shall fade, and leave our task undone.
> We will be wise in time: what though our work
> Be fashioned in despite of their ill-service,
> Be crippled every way? 'Twere little praise
> Did full resources wait on our goodwill
> At every turn.   (II, 497–506)

Knowledge of 'the whole' comes not in a single glorious vaulting of the mind but through a more prosaic fitting together of pieces. Only through viewing the prismatic colors, to recall an image of which Browning was fond, can one hope eventually to gain a vision of the white light into which they blend.[4]

To the others' urging, 'Live now or never,' the grammarian retorted, 'What's Time? leave Now for dogs and apes! / Man has Forever' (83–4).[5] Another fine sentiment, except that Browning elsewhere maintains that the Now must be taken full advantage of if man is to have the further benefit of Forever. Making the most of the possibilities that life offers is normally a prerequisite for more splendid opportunities in the hereafter. *Vivere est orare*: this, if anything, is the contention underlying Browning's recurrent attacks on asceticism – and the grammarian is as much of an ascetic as, say, Brother Lawrence's colleagues. The anti-procrastination parable of the unlit lamp and the ungirt loin is as apropos here as it is in *The Statue and the Bust*. The idealism described (97 ff.) in terms that to most interpreters have signified Browning's approval, is a perversion of what Browning seems, on the evidence of other poems, to have believed. It may be 'God's task to make the heavenly period / Perfect the earthen', but God cannot be relied on to do so without man's co-operation. To venture 'neck or nothing' is a fine histrionic sentiment, but confidence in eternity must be manifested by performance in time. Those who 'discount life ... Paid by instalment' are fools to the student-bearers, but Browning himself would not use so strong a term. Nor, certainly, would any true Browning hero put so meager a value on life as the grammarian does with his brusque 'Hence with life's pale lure!' (112).

The contrast, in lines 113–24, between the 'low man' and the 'high man', must be read against the narrow frame of reference the students have acquired from their teacher. The grammarian is a 'high man', and his purpose is 'great', only in their special scale of value. To understand the comparative aims of the two men one must remember that the grammarian's – to master the commentary on 'learning's crabbed text' – is far less exalted than the students admit. A man's reach should exceed his grasp, to be sure, but what is being reached for makes some difference. And even if we accept the students' standard of value, we return to the unblinkable fact that man's capacity for achievement is limited. The 'low man's' aim is more in accordance with the human being's powers. 'Success is nought, endeavour's all', Browning wrote later (*Red Cotton Night-Cap Country*, IV, 766), in one more statement of the conviction embodied in Andrea del Sarto's deathless rhetorical question; 'but,' he hastened to add,

> intellect adjusts the means to ends,
> Tries the low thing, and leaves it done, at least;
> No prejudice to high thing, intellect
> Would do and will do, only give the means.

'That low man seeks a little thing to do, / Sees it and does it': but doing it, however little, is something, as the Carlyle whose ideas Browning so often echoed had eloquently urged. 'This high man, with a great thing to pursue, / Dies ere he knows it': has he, in the end, won God's blessing? Full marks, no doubt, for selfless and total dedication, but certainly not for any reasonable view of what he can and cannot hope to accomplish as a mortal man. Ironically, his vocation was fulfilled solely in the achievement of a 'low man's' goal – something 'little', such as formulating the doctrine of the enclitic *De*, which *could* be done. And if his works are inadequate, when measured against his initial ambition, so too is his faith. The grammarian 'throws himself on God, and unperplext / Seeking shall find Him' (123-4): but, we learn in the lines immediately following, even while 'the throttling hands of Death' tightened about his throat – once that of lyric Apollo, now attacked by tussis – the 'seeking' took the form of still more obsessive grammar-grubbing. It is no more auspicious a deathbed than that of the Bishop of St Praxed's.

The grammarian's choice was, in effect, a denial of the very premise and spirit of Renaissance humanism, which Browning so much admired: the harmonious blending of living and learning, the study of the classics not as an end in itself but as a guide to a richer life. To the Renaissance humanist, settling *Hoti's* business and properly basing *Oun* were important pursuits, but only if viewed in ample perspective, as means to a higher end. As the years went by, the grammarian's vocation, originally lofty, degenerated into something perilously close to mere occupation: instead of keeping his eyes fixed on the sunlit mountain that was still to climb, he burrowed ever deeper into the dark mines. His energies were devoted to means, self-sufficient and picayune, which he increasingly mistook for ends. Browning's point is not far removed from Carlyle's and Matthew Arnold's criticism of 'machinery'.

Nor is it unconnected with the figure of Erasmus, who appeared, in the words of Browning's caption, 'shortly after the revival of learning in Europe', and indeed typified the noble strivings of humanism by his devotion to grammatical and related studies *as a means to an end*. The grammarian is a woefully incomplete Erasmus, a man whose scholarship deteriorates into mere pedantry for its own sake instead of serving as the necessary framework for momentous enterprises such as translating the New Testament. That Erasmus hovers somewhere in the background of *A Grammarian's Funeral* was suggested long ago,[6] but the implications of his possible presence have not been fully appreciated. They become clearer if we are aware of the resemblances Browning's poem bears to *The Praise of Folly*.

A Grammarian's Funeral, like *The Praise of Folly*, belongs to the species *encomium* of the rhetorical genus *oratio*. Both are delivered on an academic occasion (of sorts), and Browning's students, like Folly, may be presumed to be gowned. But *The Praise of Folly* is a *mock*-encomium; it is an adaptation and perversion, for satirical purposes, of the genuine article. And so too, I think, is *A Grammarian's Funeral*. The true encomium has the serious aim of eulogizing the generally acknowledged public accomplishments of a great and wise man. Erasmus's figure of Folly, on the other hand, praises – folly, the converse of wisdom. Browning's students praise a man whose public accomplishments have been nil, and of whose wisdom, in the world's eyes, there is grave doubt. Both Erasmus's prose work and Browning's poem are, in a way, exercises in self-praise on the part of the speaker: Folly lauds herself, and the students, in lauding their master, of whom they are younger replicas, flatter themselves, their ambitions, their limitations.

In the midst of a great deal of nonsense, of obvious non-wisdom, Erasmus manages to have Folly occasionally deviate into sense. The two passages in *The Praise of Folly* which most specifically link it with *A Grammarian's Funeral* associate compulsive pursuit of learning with folly. In one, which is said to describe Thomas Linacre, Erasmus, speaking through his mouthpiece, Folly, says:

I used to know a certain polymath versed in Greek, Latin, mathematics, philosophy, and medicine, and a master of them all, then some sixty years old; laying aside all the others, he vexed and tortured himself with grammar for more than twenty years, deeming that he would be happy if he were allowed to live until he had settled with certainty how the eight parts of speech are to be distinguished, a thing which none of the Greeks or Latins succeeded in doing definitively. It becomes a matter to be put to the test of battle, when someone makes a conjunction of a word which belongs in the bailiwick of the adverbs. . . . Do you prefer to call this madness or folly? It is no great matter to me; only confess that it is done with my assistance. . . .[7]

On an earlier page, Folly compares 'the lot of the wise man with that of the fool':

Fancy some pattern of wisdom to put up against him, a man who wore out his whole boyhood and youth in pursuing the learned disciplines. He wasted the pleasantest time of life in unintermitted watchings, cares, and studies; and through the remaining part of it he never tasted so much as a tittle of pleasure; always frugal, impecunious, sad, austere; unfair and strict toward himself, morose and unamiable to others; afflicted by pallor, leanness, invalidism, sore eyes, premature age and white hair; dying before his appointed day. By the way, what difference does it make when a man of that sort dies? He has never lived. There you have a clear picture of the wise man.[8]

The ironic inflection in Folly's voice is unmistakable: the 'wise man', the 'pattern of wisdom' is in truth a fool. That Folly here speaks for Erasmus is fairly clear. Admittedly, apart from the phrase 'morose and unamiable to others', the latter passage is, as the late Hoyt Hudson observed, 'an excellent self-portrait'. But only as far as it goes; for it omits those very qualities which Erasmus possessed and the grammarian lacked. 'The temper of Erasmus,' Professor Hudson continued, 'did not accord with that of Folly's despised scholar. A favorite word with him was *festivus* – festive, companionable. He refused to allow his scholarship to kill his humanity. And thus Folly's gird has point, even as used by her: the halfwit is understandably human, all too human, while the scholar may verge toward something inhuman or anti-human.'[9]

In both *The Praise of Folly* and (if I am right) *A Grammarian's Funeral* the *personae* express opinions which for the most part are not those of the respective authors. But the Erasmian strategy of occasionally allowing Folly to utter truth is, of course, a favourite with Browning as well. The difficulty in *A Grammarian's Funeral* is the same one presented, on a much more elaborate scale, by *Bishop Blougram's Apology*: exactly where, apart from those fragments of Browningian doctrine whose apparent intention turns out to be undercut by his satirical purpose, is Browning's own voice to be discerned?

Assuming that my somewhat heretical reading has validity, it is unlikely that he intended the poem to assert that by squandering, or, more precisely, failing to make use of the gift of life on earth, the grammarian forfeited his passport to heaven. On the contrary: the serious statement, embedded in the satire, may reside in the students' implicit confidence that God did, after all, smile on him. In this respect they are right, but for the wrong reasons. Neither by works nor by clear-eyed faith – *pace* the chorus – did the grammarian prove himself entitled to eternal life. But in Browning's moral universe justice is abundantly tempered by mercy, and the very disproportion between the grammarian's deserts and his reward is a measure of God's capacity to forgive. Read in this way, the poem acquires extra dramatic force: the effect of the satire is to lengthen the odds against the grammarian's winning heaven, and thus audaciously to heighten our final sense of God's boundless charity. Even those who do not earn salvation may find it, for God's will transcends whatever rules of the game man's ethical and religious thought, including Browning's own, may attribute to him. If *A Grammarian's Funeral* is, as is commonly held, a poem of praise, the praise is directed not toward the grammarian but toward an all-loving God who, it appears, will forgive men even for their folly.

If Browning's sanguine theology compelled him to imply a happy ending to the grammarian's story, his criticism of the grammarian's waste of his life is no less genuine, and it still constitutes, it seems to me, the central interest of the poem. The grammarian is not one of the poet's 'heroes' in the sense in which we ordinarily apply the word to his characters. Whatever posthumous salvage may be made of his career by the exercise of divine grace, the fact remains that he had the precious privilege of choice, and he chose wrongly. He grasped the stick of life by the wrong end. Instead of pursuing man's true goal, which is to extract meaning from life by living, he spent his years studying rather than being; he poured his energy into movement that carried him ever farther from fulfilment. For this not inconsiderable reason, Browning's verdict on him, as delivered through the inversion of satire, is severe. But beneath the satire lingers a poignant awareness of man's limitations: his myopic inability to comprehend, or in any event remain faithful to, the purpose implied in the gift of life, and, most tragic, the discrepancy between his desires and his powers. (Is it merely accidental that when it was first published, in *Men and Women*, this poem immediately followed *Two in the Campagna*, whose theme is embodied in its last lines, 'Infinite passion and the pain / Of finite hearts that yearn'?) Browning's condemnation thus is tempered by sympathy. The grammarian is an emblem of us all; while stubbornly refusing to concede that our ideal, however we may define it, is beyond attainment, we are in fact captives of the prison house of life and its treadmill. If Browning dissociates himself from the students' admiration of their hero, he is not lacking in compassion.[10]

NOTES

[1] One of the few annotators to question whether 'the poem illustrates Browning's characteristic philosophy of aspiration' is Walter E. Houghton, in the Spencer–Houghton–Barrows anthology, *British Literature* (Boston: 1952), II, p. 714. My own skepticism considerably antedates the publication of this provocative note.

[2] 'Tennyson, Browning, and a Romantic Fallacy', *UTQ*, XII (1944), pp. 175–95.

[3] Browning shared the strong and widespread Victorian preference for doing rather than thinking, for experience over learning. Compare such characteristic statements of the attitude as these, from Samuel Smiles's *Self-Help* (London: 1859): 'a man perfects himself by work much more than by reading . . . it is life rather than literature, action rather than study, and character rather than biography, that tends perpetually to renovate mankind' (p. 6), 'the experience gathered from books, though often valuable, is but of the nature of *learning*; whereas the experience gained from actual life is of the nature of wisdom; and a small store of the latter is worth vastly more than any stock of the former. . . . And it must be admitted that the chief object of culture is, not merely to fill the mind with other men's thoughts – and to be the passive recipients of their impressions of things – but to enlarge our individual intelligence . . .' (p. 258). 'It is not how much a man may know, that is of so much importance, as the end and purpose for which he knows it. . . . We must ourselves *be* and *do*, and not rest satisfied merely with reading and meditating over what other men have written and done. Our best light must be made life, and our best thought action' (p. 259).

That the grounds for the attitude toward the grammarian which I here ascribe to Browning were in harmony with prevailing Victorian values is further implied in Thackeray's comments (*Pendennis*, Ch. XXIX) on the relative worth of the lives led by his own version of the students' 'low man' and 'high man' – the two templars, Warrington, who takes the world as it comes, and the grimly studious Paley: 'The one could afford time to think, and the other never could. The one could have sympathies and do kindnesses; and the other must needs always be selfish. He could not cultivate a friendship or do a charity, or admire a work of genius, or kindle at the sight of beauty or the sound of a sweet song – he had no time, and no eyes for anything but his law-books. All was dark outside his reading-lamp. Love, and Nature, and Art (which is the expression of our praise and sense of the beautiful world of God), were shut out from him. And as he turned off his lonely lamp at night, he never thought but that he had spent the day profitably, and went to sleep alike thankless and remorseless.'

4 [See W. O. Raymond, "The Jewelled Bow', pp. 110–30 above.]

5 To the students' further plea that he at least 'take a little rest', he might have replied as did Antoine Arnauld, the seventeenth-century theologian, quoted by nineteenth-century English authors as diverse as Isaac Disraeli (*Curiosities of Literature*), Carlyle (*Sartor Resartus*), and Smiles (*Self-Help*): 'Rest? Rest? Shall I not have all eternity to rest in?'

6 First, apparently, by Joseph F. Payne in the introduction to his edition of Linacre's *Galen* (1881); see Sir John E. Sandys, *A History of Classical Scholarship* (Cambridge, 1903–8), II, p. 228. Payne, according to a correspondent in *Notes and Queries*, CXCIV (1949), p. 284, also put forward the idea in his Harveian Lecture of 1896 on *Harvey and Galen*. Mario Praz (*Times Literary Supplement*, December 6, 1957, p. 739), referring to the lines beginning 'So, with the throttling hands of death at strife, / Ground he at grammar', quoted Heinrich Strömer's letter to Johannes Cochleus on Erasmus's death: 'Totus erat, omnium vir doctissimus, in restituendo Graeco Origine; cui sic erat, iam iam morbi vi quam maxime urgente, addictus, ut ab illo non citius discesserit quam mors ipsa e manibus scribentis calamum extorserit.' A striking, though wholly accidental, demonstration of the 'peculiarly Erasmian' nature of Browning's religious ideas may be found in Wallace K. Ferguson's article, 'Renaissance Tendencies in the Religious Thought of Erasmus', *Journal of the History of Ideas*, XV (1954), pp. 499–508. Browning is nowhere mentioned; but the ease with which his name may be substituted for Erasmus's throughout the article suggests that the intellectual sympathies that bound him to the great humanist were numerous and strong.

7 The translation is by Hoyt Hudson (Princeton: 1941), p. 72.

8 *The Praise of Folly*, pp. 50–1.

9 *The Praise of Folly*, pp. xxxv–xxxvi.

10 [cf. C. C. Clarke, 'Humor and Wit in *Childe Roland*', *MLQ*, XXIII (1962), pp. 323–36, esp. pp. 324–5; William Cadbury, 'Lyric and Anti-Lyric Forms: A Method for Judging Browning', *UTQ*, XXXIV (1964), 49–67, esp. pp. 54–5.]

ISOBEL ARMSTRONG

BROWNING'S *MR SLUDGE,*
'THE MEDIUM'

WHEN *Mr Sludge, 'The Medium'* was first published in *Dramatis Personae* in 1864, the poem aroused some controversy. It was a provocative attack on spiritualism, and the portrait of Sludge was based on a living figure, the American medium, Daniel Home, who later attempted to defend his reputation.[1] Since this early controversy and for fairly obvious reasons, *Mr Sludge* has attracted little attention, and recent critics of Browning's dramatic monologues have not had much to say about the poem.[2] Because spiritualism is a dead issue, the subject of the poem seems recondite; the confession and self-justification of a quack medium suggest merely a study in eccentric psychology and an exercise in casuistry for its own sake. Even Browning's success in evoking the mean world of Sludge probably deters readers; the subterfuges of a trick séance, shoddy credulity and cynical suspicion, sentimentality, hysteria, prurience and eager self-titillation ('Let Sludge go on; we'll fancy it's in print!' [629]) appear gratuitously sordid.[3] But Browning seems to have seen in the subject an opportunity for writing more than a topical poem, which would expose spiritualist chicanery, and it is by looking at the way in which he exploited his dramatic situation – a medium on the defensive – that this can be understood. The strategy of the medium's defense gave him a unique way of exploring some arguments about the nature of truth, knowledge and the imagination, questions which recur in his poetry. In the course of the poem, these arguments develop startling implications, and

From *Victorian Poetry*, II (1964), pp. 1–9.

their force depends directly upon the dramatic context in which they are set. Very little of the detail is gratuitous. In *Mr Sludge* Browning chose a dramatic situation which would amplify the ideas he explored; which would, in fact, make it seem inevitable that they should be explored.

It is necessary, in the first place, to understand the importance of Sludge's position as a medium. Even though he has been caught in the act of cheating, Sludge maintains ultimately that he is the authentic agent of spiritual truth, 'seer of the supernatural' (875). There is some 'mode of intercourse / Between us men here' and the spiritual world, he claims (834–5). In effect, Sludge is making the same claims as other of Browning's visionaries. The speaker in *Christmas-Eve and Easter-Day* (1850), for instance, asserts that he has been granted insight into spiritual truth by special revelation. David, in *Saul* (in the final version in *Men and Women*, 1855), discovers that he is the chosen agent, or medium, of God's truth – 'Oh speak! through me now!' (299). In *Abt Vogler*, which appeared at the same time as *Mr Sludge* in *Dramatis Personae*, the musician attributes his imaginative vision also to special revelation – 'But God has a few of us whom he whispers in the ear' (XI). In the sense that special insight is granted to and interpreted by these visionaries, they are 'mediums'. Sludge, 'inspired', as he says, by the wine of his patron (Hiram E. Horsefall's champagne is a sophisticated variant of the traditional wine of inspiration, analogous with the 'soul-wine' which inspires David in *Saul*), is the degraded equivalent of these visionary prophets. In him the medium shifts from seer to charlatan, and expressions of the truth and authenticity of visionary experience are thus transposed, so as to appear as special pleading from the mouth of a quack. Inevitably they become suspect because the context of sham and shiftiness in which they are expressed undermines them. This sharply exposes the problems which the claim to authentic insight involves – the nature of truth, the limits of knowledge.

Besides presenting the idea of the medium in a pejorative rather than a praiseworthy way in *Mr Sludge*, Browning puts into Sludge's mouth arguments which often parallel those he himself had used apparently seriously, in other poems. Here, with slight shifts of emphasis and modification, they are parodied, and the arguments are used in such a way that they are discredited. At important points in his defense, which turns on the question of truth, Sludge illustrates his case by referring either to the workings of religious belief – a fairly obvious gambit for a spiritualist – or, a less obvious but important move, to the workings of the imagination. Sometimes he makes an analogy with religion or art, most frequently with literature, to support his case (thus contaminating both with the doubtful implications of the practices he tries to justify), and sometimes he uses arguments commonly used to defend the position of the religious believer or the artist, in support of his own position. At these points the arguments (which become suspect if they can be used in Sludge's defense at all) resemble those which Browning had used elsewhere in his poetry. This suggests that Browning may have found in *Mr Sludge* an opportunity for examining critically certain of his own assumptions. In outlining the manoeuvres by which Sludge defends himself, therefore, it will be instructive to concentrate upon those parts of the poem which parody the positions which Browning had taken up on previous occasions.[4]

There are three stages in Sludge's argument. The first stage of his defense occupies roughly the first half of the poem. Rather surprisingly, instead of pleading from the outset that he is a genuine medium, he offers to confess and tell the secret of his deceptions if his patron will agree to release him. In the extensive account of his trickery which follows, he seems to be conceding his guilt to his accuser, but the implicit object of his confession is to destroy confidence in the possibility of discovering truth empirically. His audience had felt certain of his authenticity because they had subjected him to what satisfied them as objective and empirical tests (see, for instance, ll. 488–94), and in this sense they believed in him on rational grounds. But he has deceived his audience with credible 'evidence', and if what seemed conclusively established was actually false, then the certainty of proof is undermined. By invalidating the notion of intellectual certainty, Sludge turns the obvious line of attack to his advantage. Empirical methods have exposed him, but before this they seemed to establish his authenticity, and are therefore unreliable; consequently, if we have no means of discovering whether somebody is telling the truth, we have no means of discovering whether he is lying. Instead of defending himself by an appeal to reason, he satirizes unsparingly those who purported to believe him on rational grounds. Rational men, he says, are 'eunuchs' playing coldly and impotently with superstition. He gives a ludicrous account of the pompous empiricist who dilates spiritualism at dinner parties and proves 'how much common sense he'll hack and hew / I' the critical minute 'twixt the soup and fish' (778-9). The associations of greed and coarseness which the dinner-party situation adds to the common metaphor of logic-chopping suggest the clumsy inadequateness of reason as a means of discovering the truth.

By undermining the notion of intellectual certainty, Sludge prepares the ground for the second part of his defense. When he has put the issue of truth outside the terms of reason, and suggested that the intellect cannot be a means to knowledge, he can safely make an appeal to uncertainty. It cannot be ascertained that he is authentic, but equally, it cannot be ascertained that he is not. Can his audience, can even Sludge himself, be quite sure that he is cheating? Sludge reaches the climax of his argument, justifying his mediumship by the very factors which should undermine it, asking audaciously,

'You've found me out in cheating!' That's enough
To make an apostle swear! Why, when I cheat,
Mean to cheat, do cheat, and am caught in the act,
Are you, or, rather, am I sure o' the fact? (1281-4)

It may be that his lies are 'genuine' and 'That every cheat's inspired, and every lie / Quick with a germ of truth' (1324-5).

Sludge's position is impregnable, but the implications of his argument are not reassuring. The cost of defending a position by making an appeal to uncertainty is that there are now no criteria for judging 'authenticity'. A philosophical deadlock is inevitable; in denying your adversary the means of proving you wrong, you also deprive yourself of the means of defending your position. What is the nature of the assumptions we make when we say we believe something to be true? Does the operation of belief differ from that of

P   215

credulity? from superstition? These are the questions raised by
Sludge's arguments. The charlatan as well as the seer appears to be
invulnerable. Paradoxically, he can only claim that he is in possession of the truth by undermining the validity of the ways in which it
might be ascertained. The word 'truth' is always on Sludge's lips,
but his arguments deprive it of meaning, and it is constantly de-
valued. The verbal metaphor here, for instance condemns his use of
the word. 'I can't help that / It's truth! I somehow vomit truth
today' (807–8).

This second stage of Sludge's argument marks the point at which
he turns from freely confessing to justifying his position. It is in this
part of the poem that the references to religion become frequent. 'As
for religion – why, I served it, sir!' he asserts.

> With my *phenomena*
> I laid the atheist sprawling on his back,
> Propped up Saint Paul, or, at least, Swedenborg!
> (665–7)

Sludge has already insinuated that in the sphere of the spiritual
and the supernatural our judgment is fallible and insecure; now, by
this explicit reference to religious belief, he shows that he and God
are in analogous positions. By transference, all that he has said of his
own case is applicable to belief in God. Doubt in his powers, doubt
in God (and the verb 'propped up' suggests that God's case is as
flimsy as his own), operate in exactly the same way. Conversely, we
can accept his authenticity on the same grounds as we accept the
existence of God. This enables Sludge to reinforce his appeal to
uncertainty by using arguments commonly used to support religious positions. For instance, it may no longer be possible to adhere
to a miraculous explanation of the universe, but he still believes in an
'unseen agency' which prompts and directs our actions (a parody of
the argument of the first cause), and he himself, tricks and all, might
well be the unconscious vehicle of divine purpose. Perversely
enough, religious belief supports his position and at the same time
the grounds for belief are made to seem ludicrous. Again, he asserts
his belief that God is immanent in creation. Just as the merest detail
of creation is significant of divine power, so for Sludge, supernatural

power is manifest in any trivial occurrence – 'the pure *obvious* super-natural' – and he simply interprets the divine immanence more liberally than most.

> What's a star?
> A world, or a world's sun: doesn't it serve
> As taper also, time-piece, weather-glass,
> And almanac? Are stars not set for signs
> When we should shear our sheep, sow corn, prune trees?
> The Bible says so. (914–19)

This absurdly trivial proposition contrasts ironically with the ecstatic celebration of this idea in *Saul*. David finds the whole universe significant of divine power. 'And the stars of night beat with emotion . . . the strong pain of pent knowledge' (319–20). In Sludge's terms it is impossible to distinguish between the two in-sights, the medium's or the seer's. It is impossible to 'distinguish between gift and gift, / Washington's oracle and Sludge's itch' (1179–80).

At the end of the poem, Sludge reverses his policy. In the third and last stage of his defense, he admits that he may well have been lying, but if this is the case, he will claim the same kind of 'truth' for his deceptions as that claimed by imaginative writers. His deceptions have performed the same function as the imagination because they have revitalized the lives of his audience – 'so, Sludge lies! / Why, he's at worst your poet' (1435–6). He has prepared the way for this discussion of the imagination by making seemingly casual references to the function of art in earlier parts of the poem, and again, because he can invoke art to his support, the function of the artist is called into question. In the first stage of his defense, for instance, while confessing to trickery, he attempts to minimize its importance by comparing his lies to the 'lies' of the artist, and raises directly the problem of the artist's 'truth'.

> Now mark! To be precise –
> Though I say, 'lies' all these, at this first stage,
> 'Tis just for science' sake: I call such grubs
> By the name of what they'll turn to, dragonflies.
> Strictly, it's what good people style untruth;

But yet, so far, not quite the full-grown thing:
It's fancying, fable-making, nonsense-work –
What never meant to be so very bad –
The knack of story-telling, brightening up
Each dull old bit of fact that drops its shine.
One does see somewhat when one shuts one's eyes,
If only spots and streaks.   (184–95)

This is an example of contaminating by analogy. Art is trivialized ('nonsense-work', 'story-telling') by being equated with trivial deception. The working of the imagination becomes a matter of slick manipulation, a shoddy knack which merely serves the function of 'brightening up' the world, and 'brightening up' carries with it the pejorative associations of surface-gilding, artificial veneer, synthetic restoration. There is no distinction here between 'fable-making' and deliberate falsification, so that art comes to be regarded as a sophisticated way of lying. The factitious accuracy of the distinction between 'lies' and 'untruths' and the spurious honesty with which Sludge points to the 'genuineness' of imaginative insight ('One does see somewhat when one shuts one's eyes . . .') only serves to enforce the equation of deception with art. Sludge exploits slippery language here, and his ingratiating showman's patter – hustling alliteration, deft, time-saving compounds alternating with sharp syllabic words, the persuasive repetition of synonymous phrases, rhetorical parentheses – hurries over distinctions. But his words counteract one another subtly. Browning allows the language to work in different directions. Lies, for instance, are likened in the first place to grubs, with the suggestion of a pun (insects, dirt), and, when telling a lie is compared a few lines later with the process of 'brightening up', the suggestion of dirt lends a suspect tawdriness to the brightening-up image, destroying the innocuousness which Sludge wishes to claim for his lies.

The connection of the imagination with the false and the trivial dirt, tawdry glitter and flimsy decoration is sustained in other references to art and the artist.[5] These culminate in the discussion of the imagination at the end of the poem, when Sludge abandons all pretensions to the truth. He holds at last that his real function is to renew hope in existence. Like the 'deceptions' of the work of imagination, his deceptions 'reanimate' the lives of those who believe him.

> Young, you've force
> Wasted like well-streams: old, – oh, then indeed,
> Behold a labyrinth of hydraulic pipes
> Through which you'd play off wondrous waterwork;
> Only, no water's left to feed their play.   (1367–70)

Only he can transform the aridity of life:

> There's your world!
>   Give it me! I slap it brisk
> With harlequin's pasteboard sceptre: what's it now?
> Changed like a rock-flat, rough with rusty weed,
> At first wash-over o' the returning wave!
> All the dry dead impracticable stuff
> Starts into life and light again; this world
> Pervaded by the influx from the next.
> I cheat, and what's the happy consequence?
> You find full justice straightway dealt you out,
> Each want supplied, each ignorance set at ease,
> Each folly fooled.   (1390–1400)

This imagery of machinery, water and conjuring trick closely parallels and parodies three metaphors used in a discussion of the function of the poet in Book Three of *Sordello* (1840). There, temporarily abandoning the method of impersonal narration, which he had followed up to this point, Browning describes the poet as the usurper of God. In syntax which suggests the wrenching effort of performing a superhuman act, he compares the poet to Moses, the bringer of water to the desert, miraculously life-giving and regenerating:

> – each dromedary lolls a tongue,
> Each camel churns a sick and frothy chap
>
> While awkwardly enough your Moses smites
> The rock, though he forego his Promised Land
> Thereby, have Satan claim his carcass, and
> Figure as Metaphysic Poet . . . ah
> Mark ye the first dim oozings?
>   (*Sordello*, III, 820–1, 826–30)

He describes a mode of existence which denies the power of the imagination as an arid and mechanistic condition of life, entirely encroached on by the devitalizing forces of rational and scientific thought, and presents an ironic picture of a dead, mechanistic universe, 'pray that I be not busy slitting steel / Or shredding brass ... before / I name a tithe o' the wheels I trust I do!' [III, 858–61]. Sludge's 'labyrinth of hydraulic pipes' corresponds with this image, but the transforming rod of Moses has become harlequin's gimcrack sceptre.

In perverting these images of regeneration, Sludge adds new force to the ancient charge that the work of imagination is no means to truth and knowledge because it deceives; all that he says of the imagination suggests that it is an insidiously debasing, corrupting agency. He describes the world he offers as a palace of art, enticing its inhabitants with a substitute world of enervating, solipsist fantasy:

> Thus it goes on, not quite like life perhaps,
> But so near, that the very difference piques
>
> And you arrive at the palace: all half real,
> And you, to suit it, less than real beside,
> In a dream, lethargic kind of death in life.
>
> (1410–11, 1415–17)

The image recalls the 'palace of music' which is created by Abt Vogler, and which signifies an ideal imaginative world of supreme and perfect order. But Sludge, who also pleads that he provides a 'Golden Age, old Paradise, / Or new Eutopia!' (1431–2), debases the concept of the poet's golden world. He ends his case by identifying the imagination straightforwardly with deception. It is strange, he suggests, that he should be accused of lying, while the writer who boasts, ' 'Tis fancy all; no particle of fact' (1464), merits the highest praise; he is compared with God. As he mimics the praise given to the artist, Sludge mimics the idea of the artist-God which was so important to Browning.

> '– Ah, the more wonderful the gift in you,
> The more creativeness and godlike craft!' (1468–9)

Sludge's patron lets him go instead of exposing him as he had threatened, and perhaps this testifies to the skill of his argument. Certainly, Browning spares nothing in exposing the religious and aesthetic problems arising from the medium's claim to authentic insight and spiritual vision. The poem puts to the test propositions about truth and belief and demonstrates their weaknesses. It challenges a consideration of the status of the untruths of the imagination. Sludge's nihilism may condemn itself, and his methods of persuasion – the alternation of extremes of arrogance with extremes of obsequiousness, calculated showmanship, inadvertent self-pity – may discredit him, but the problems he poses are genuine. In particular, there is the problem of the integrity of the creative imagination. Sludge, simultaneously quack and 'artist', has an affinity with a group of characters through whom Browning explored the theme of the artist whose powers carry with them an inherent possibility of corruption – the poets of *Pauline* (1833) and *Sordello* (1840), Aristophanes in *Aristophanes' Apology* (1875), for instance – and he demonstrates the problem in an acute form. Of course, in poems written both before and after *Mr Sludge*, Browning affirmed an optimistic belief in transcendental insight and the power of the imagination (*Christmas-Eve and Easter-Day* [1850], *Saul* [1855], *Abt Vogler* [1864]), but it would be difficult to see optimism in *Mr Sludge*, let alone the simple-minded optimism with which Browning is sometimes associated.[6]

NOTES

[1] Daniel Dunglas Home, *Incidents in My Life: Second Series* (London: 1872), pp. 95–111.

[2] The circumstances in which *Mr Sludge* was composed have been discussed by DeVane, *Handbook*, pp. 307–12; also by B. Miller, *Portrait*, pp. 191–9. The most notable discussion of the poem itself appeared over a decade ago. See Raymond, *Infinite Moment*, pp. 141–7.

[3] This and subsequent quotations from Browning's poetry are from *The Works of Robert Browning*, ed. Frederic George Kenyon, 10 vols. (London: 1912).

[4] An early critic of *Mr Sludge* noticed that Browning appeared to be parodying himself in the poem. But he concluded that Browning wished to show by this that even a depraved man gropes towards the truth, rather than suggesting that Browning may have wished to put certain of his own ideas to test. See Edwin

Johnson, 'On *Mr Sludge*, "*The Medium*"', *Browning Society Papers* (London: 1885–90), II, pp. 13–32.

[5] See, e.g. lines 252, 339–46, 427, 755–7.

[6] [See also Norton B. Crowell, *The Triple Soul: Browning's Theory of Knowledge* (U. of New Mexico, 1963), Ch. VI, esp. pp. 204–8.]

JOHN HOWARD

CALIBAN'S MIND

IN interpreting *Caliban upon Setebos*, critics since Browning's time have taken generally two distinct approaches, seeing the poem either as a satire or as a dramatization of a particular aspect of Browning's religious beliefs. Of the interpretations involving satire, C. R. Tracy has distinguished two groups: one interpreting the poem as an attack against the Darwinians and the followers of the Higher Criticism, another as a satire on such orthodox beliefs as Calvinism.[1] Tracy finds, however, that the poem is not a complete satire, but rather that '*Caliban* was written partly with the purpose of showing that religious faith can begin even far back in the evolutionary scale' (p. 489). Although Tracy's argument has been skilful enough to persuade DeVane, who gives it extended space in his treatment of *Caliban* in *A Browning Handbook*, this point of view needs more detail.

That *Caliban* is satire at all is, in the first place, questionable. The main argument for religious satire usually depends on Setebos' power and his lack of justice or feeling. ' 'Thinketh, such shows nor right nor wrong in Him, / Nor kind, nor cruel: He is strong and Lord' (98-9). Tracy points out that these lines are in a sense a parody of the Calvinist's conception of an amoral God; and certainly, while the poem contains no specific reference to Calvinism as such, one of the main tenets of Calvinistic thought, the sovereignty of God, might be read into this passage. Since one of Browning's major beliefs included the omnipotence of God, however, one must be careful not to confuse as satire a statement of belief by Caliban,

From *Victorian Poetry*, I (1963), pp. 249-57.

which Browning may have considered quite valid. One has only to remember Karshish's excited exclamation to his friend Abib: 'So, the All-Great, were the All-Loving too' [305] to see that Browning, far from denying the complete truth of Caliban's belief, would consider it only a limited segment of knowledge.

For evidence of satire on the growth of scientific doubt of the time, one might conjure up some connection between the fossilized newt that Caliban finds and such current thought as that attacked by Philip H. Gosse, who argued that God had 'before his mind a projection of the whole life-history of the globe . . . [and determined] to call this idea into actual existence'. Thus man appeared precisely as he 'would have appeared had he lived so many years'.[2] But that single detail of the poem hardly justifies the stretch of the imagination necessary to accept the argument that the poem is on the side of the Gosses of the world.

Some critics have attempted to broaden the object of the supposed satire of the poem. Hugh A. Clark said that the poem is an attack 'against the tendency in all religions to formulate the conception of God from man's own consciousness'.[3] C. G. Ames suggested that the poem is 'a satire upon all religious theories which construct a divinity out of the imperfections of humanity'.[4] DeVane (*Handbook*, p. 301) claims that it satirizes all those who think they have found the ultimate nature of God. Is one to believe that the poem is a satire on all these? The generalization of the object of satire, evident in DeVane's, Ames's, and Clark's interpretation, is a result of the attempt to include every *possible* object that the poem, by unintentional inference, *may* touch upon. Is it really possible to continue thinking a poem to be a satire when nothing specific can be found as the object of satire? The subject of the poem is clearly religious, but the intent can hardly be said, with adequate justification, to be satirical.

Rather it can be shown that Browning endeavoured to capture the limitations of the subhuman mind when confronted with religious speculation. The meaning of Caliban, as Robert Langbaum suggests, 'is the life-persistence, the biological vitality and cunning which Caliban finds in the swamp world and in what he deduces from the swamp world about the nature of the god, Setebos. The meaning is Caliban as he stands revealed in what he sees and thinks.'[5] In short, the poet's extreme care in handling even the small details of characterization gives a clear picture of Caliban as a primitive subhuman who contemplates God in the only way that he can.

To understand Browning's Caliban it is necessary first to investigate those characteristics of Caliban which Browning might have found in his source. Surprisingly enough there are many. From *The Tempest* Browning got the basic characters: Prospero, Miranda, Caliban's dam, Ariel, and of course Setebos. Caliban's reference to Miranda, the 'four legged serpent' who is his mock wife, is understandable only if the reader is aware of Shakespeare's Caliban and his desire for Miranda. Caliban's knowledge of the natural world, his use of animal comparison ('snaky sea', 'lithe as a leech', 'as a cuttlefish'), his possible source of the urchin-squirrel comparison, his basic need to jibe, and his tendency to fall down flat when confronted with danger, can also be traced to hints taken from a few lines from *The Tempest*. In Act II, scene ii, Caliban, burdened with a load of wood, enters, invoking sickness on Prospero. Although he knows he will be detected, he 'needs must curse' (4). He knows he will be frightened with 'urchin-shows' (5). Prospero's spirits will set upon him 'like apes' (9) or 'like hedgehogs' (10). When Trinculo enters, Caliban mistakes him for a spirit, and his immediate reaction is to prostrate himself. He says, 'I'll fall flat' (16). Sources can also be found for Caliban's mention of liquor (II, ii, 121), the raven of Setebos (I, ii, 321-2), his mess of whelks (II, ii, 176), his toothsome apples (II, ii, 171), and his song (II, ii, 184-9). Even the time setting of the poem is suggested by *The Tempest*. Shakespeare's Caliban is drudging when he meets Stephano and soon afterwards tells him that it is Prospero's custom to sleep in the afternoon (III, ii, 95-7). One notices that Browning's Caliban is sprawling in the heat of the day, the early afternoon when he should be drudging. Still another aspect of Caliban can be found in *The Tempest*. Browning's Caliban allies Setebos with the moon, and despite one critic's explanation of the history of early moon worship,[6] a closer source for this alliance can be found in Shakespeare's dialogue between Caliban and

Stephano. Moreover, the device of using Caliban as a theologian might well have been suggested by Shakespeare's Caliban, who is certainly preoccupied with finding a God (see II, ii, 121; V, i, 296; II, ii, 140–52). But the most important characteristic of Shakespeare's Caliban, at least for our purpose, is that Caliban is basically a sub-human, incapable of improvement. He is naturally depraved. Prospero says of him:

> But thy vile race,
> Though thou didst learn, had that in 't which good natures
> Could not abide to be with.   (I, ii, 358–60)

Caliban's nature in Shakespeare is the kind that is murderous, cruel, selfish; even in his desire to be rubbed and petted and made much of, he is nothing more than a beast. Browning certainly continues this characterization in Caliban. But the redeeming qualities Shakespeare gave to his monster have disappeared in Browning's Caliban, who is as cruel as nature itself.

Thus, although DeVane (*Handbook*, pp. 299–300) handles Browning's debt to Shakespeare as if it were for no more than a name and general conception,[7] we find that Browning has made more than token use of Shakespeare's Caliban; in fact, in a letter to Furnivall, Browning was at pains to justify the similarities of his Caliban to Shakespeare's. Moreover, in an illuminating comment in the same letter, he had said:

I don't see that, because a clown's conception of the laws of the Heavenly bodies is grotesque and impossible, that of Newton must be necessarily as absurd, or that the writer of *La Saisiaz* must see through such horny eyes as those of Caliban.[8]

By denying the need for finding any parallel to Caliban, Browning here seems to be denying that he had any satirical intention. Moreover, it is clear that his interest lay rather in the creation of a character (it would be most enlightening to have Furnivall's letter too). For in the letter Browning calls Caliban a fool and a clown; he says that Caliban's conceptions are grotesque and impossible; and, most enlightening of all, he says, 'my Caliban indulges his fancies long before even that beginning' (meaning the beginning of the play). In this statement he thus indicates that he has created a character who represents something early and undeveloped, something which is far back in the evolutionary scale, something belonging to the swamp world. A look at some of the qualities of the poem itself will reveal just how interested Browning was in pointing out Caliban's primitive character.

Although the first twenty-four lines of the poem are enclosed in brackets, as if they were not spoken by Caliban, we would be mistaken to assume some other speaker, for clearly the lines represent Caliban's thought. The speech depends on vague evaluative adjectives (italics mine): 'day is *best*' (1); 'pit's *much* mire' (2); '*great* fish' (14); 'It is *good* to cheat' (22). These contrast with very concrete physical details: 'fruit to *snap* at, *catch* and *crunch*' (11); 'Flat on his *belly*' (2); 'a *pompion-plant*, / Coating the cave top as a *brow* its eye' (7–8), a contrast that indicates the point of view of a perceptive but uncultivated mind. There is also a hint of the morbid bent of the mind in that it sees the sunbeams as a spider web. Further, the dramatic context of the line, 'Because to talk about him, vexes – ha, / Could He but know!' (17–18) indicates Caliban's pleased self-satisfaction.[9]

One has only to contrast the mesh-of-fire image used by Caliban with the complicated and metaphysical sphere image used in *Cleon* to realize that Browning intends the metaphors of the poem to reflect the actual kind of mind he is trying to portray. Caliban's mind sees the sunbeams cross and recross. If the reader attempts to visualize this picture from a scientific notion of sunlight, he will be unsuccessful; however, if he realizes that to Caliban the sunbeam is not a ray of light but the actual reflection of the early afternoon sun on the ocean (which does in fact make the ocean appear as a mesh of fire), he will see that the point of view is again that of a perceptive but unscientific mind.

The point of view of the uncultivated savage is seen throughout the poem in the imagery of Caliban's speech. The metaphors and similes that he uses are those which would be appropriate to the most acutely observant but uneducated speaker. The stream flowing into the sea has a visual and tactile appeal for him. It is a 'crystal spike 'twixt two warm walls of wave' (37). The otter is as 'lithe as a leech' (46). Since he has no word for drunkenness, he can only say 'maggots scamper through my brain' (72). Reflected in this line are not only Caliban's mode of expressing subjects which he has experienced yet never learned to discuss on an abstract level, but also his mind's sensibility, which seems to find comparisons of maggots not at all unsavoury; with great relish Caliban makes the comparison which, suggesting, as it does, decayed flesh, tends to orient his sensibility in the savage natural world of decay and primitive survival.

We have merely to count the number of various animals and plants (forty-seven different animals and thirteen plants or fruits) to realize that Browning intended to characterize Caliban's sensibility, formed by his own experience, as it appears in his talk. Caliban knows about grubs, efts, spiders, snakes, leeches, worms, ants, crabs, flies, beetles, crickets and grigs; and these unsavoury animals all reflect the focus of his interest. His reference to the grigs (grasshoppers) is again instructive. He wants his clay bird to 'nip' the 'horns / Of grigs high up that make the merry din' (82–83). In his speech he does not use a scientific term such as 'antennae', but the metaphoric term 'horn', a usage which again reflects the primitive nature of his mind. Frontal growths to him are the same on grasshoppers as goats – they are horns. He does not live in a world of biological distinctions.

Caliban's mind is able to see only parallel relationships. He sees the universe as a hierarchy of similar structures, something like a Chinese box. He sees a 'real' (147) world belonging to the Quiet and another world which he calls the 'bauble-world' (147) of Setebos, a world of change and vexation. Caliban himself has created his own bauble-world for 'solace' and 'sport' (149). In this bauble-world Prospero is parallel to the Quiet; Caliban himself is a sort of Prospero imagining that his pet ounce is Miranda, that a crane is Ariel, and that a 'lumpish' (163) sea beast is himself, Caliban. This bauble-world is a result of a mind limited in its ability to make distinctions. Despite its playful and sometimes cruel nature (he splits the sea beast's toes, blinds it, makes the ounce cower and snarl, forces the crane to disgorge), it does perceive parallel relationships, a characteristic of a rudimentary intelligence.

It is just this sort of mental sensibility that comes into play when he constructs his Deity. Perhaps the most abstract terms in which he can comprehend the cruelties of Setebos are those of marriage, a simple combination of opposites for the sake of pleasure or comfort. Setebos is ill at ease in his cold, and Caliban says that he dwells in the cold of the moon. Associated in Caliban's mind with the sun are warmth and safety – the ocean is 'Green-dense and dim-delicious, bred o' the sun' (40) – while the moon represents cold, ache, and general unpleasantness. It is the marriage between these two opposites that Caliban sees as Setebos' motive. Setebos made the sun to 'match' (26) the cold of the moon. Since he could not make something like himself, thinks Caliban, he must have made his opposite. 'He could not, Himself, make a second self / To be His mate; as well have made Himself' (57–8). When Caliban is less abstract, Setebos is a grub to turn into a butterfly. Caliban's over-god, the Quiet, is scarcely less concrete than Setebos. Again Caliban has only simple words to express this idea: the Quiet itself is as abstract a term as Caliban can command, and he must make his idea concrete by giving it an outpost in the stars, and like an animal, the Quiet may 'catch' (281) Setebos someday.

Of course, Caliban's two deities are colored by his own characteristics, and, by putting the passage from the fiftieth Psalm at the head of the poem, Browning makes sure that we realize as much. We ought not be surprised if we see Setebos as a cruel devil whose major motive seems to be spite. Nor should we be surprised that the Quiet, which has happy life, must also be feared – 'the worse for those / It works on!' (140–1). For the cruelty of Caliban is derived from the rude forces of the nature that he inhabits. Nor should we shudder at Caliban's own cruelties, for with close attention we see that Caliban is little different from the surrounding animals. The 'little birds that hate the jay / Flock' (120–1) to see if the jay is hurt, and are glad. The fierce orc waits for Caliban's tame beast 'to taste' (274). Most obvious is the long catalogue of life in the poem's beginning. The badger, the pie, the auk, the ants are all in the stark act of hunting for food. Of this sort of existence Caliban, a part of this fierce world, is acutely aware; and the deities that he can comprehend are a reflection of his only means of awareness, which is shaped by the world that surrounds him.

But as shocking as Caliban's cruelty may be there is nevertheless a quality of *naïveté*, or childishness, about him that is quite as strong as his cruelty. As he spins his thoughts in the first hundred lines, groping to find the right word ('that is it' (65), he says, when he finds it), slowly repeating the name of Setebos almost as if he were making a test to see if Setebos were listening, he is carried away at least twice with his ideas and reacts emotionally to his reflections. As he builds the clay bird in his mind, he is actually making one, perhaps out of the clay in his miry pit (italics mine): 'And *there*, a sting to do his foes offence, / *There*, and I will' (80-1). The *there* is a reflection of his satisfaction at his childish creation. Again, his sudden anger at his imaginary pipe reflects his naïve but engrossing imaginative ability.

In summary, it seems that Browning was trying to create a character who was to be associated with a primitive state of existence in which he was less capable of abstract knowledge than the fully developed human. Caliban reflects that state not only in his primitiveness, but in his very cruelty and childishness. His insight into his gods reflects his own mental abilities as well as the sort of existence that surrounds him.

It is Caliban's primitive mind that must be considered before it can be decided that Browning's intent was satirical. The apparent satire which causes such trouble because of its grotesque concepts of God is really quite understandable if we recognize that Browning's theories of religion are involved. Tracy has shown how, 'after making allowances for differences in evolutionary scale, Caliban's pair of deities represent a dual notion of divinity similar to Browning's. The Quiet is the result of Caliban's intuitive search for abstract truth, and like Browning's notion of the Godhead, it is remote from all human concerns' (p. 489). However, Caliban's two deities lack the essential element of love, for Setebos' cruelty is no worse than the Quiet's who must be feared. To Browning all nature was fitted to comprehend the deity. In *The Ring and the Book*, the Pope, in his apostrophe to God, says:

Here, as a whole proportioned to our sense, –
There, (which is nowhere, speech must babble thus!)
In the absolute immensity, the whole
Appreciable solely by Thyself, –
Here, by the little mind of man, reduced
To littleness that suits his faculty,
In the degree appreciable too;
Between Thee and ourselves – nay even, again,
Below us, to the extreme of the minute,
Appreciable by how many and what diverse
Modes of the life Thou madest be! (Why live
Except for love, – how love unless they know?)
Each of them, only filling to the edge,
Insect or angel, his just length and breadth,
Due facet of reflection, – full, no less,
Angel or insect, as Thou framedst things.

(X, 1317–32)

Thus Caliban, whom Browning takes pains to fix somewhere below man in this grand hierarchy (as Browning has borrowed him from Shakespeare), appreciates his conception of the Deity 'to the edge' of his limit. A metaphysician's struggle for knowledge is limited by his own sensibility; hence, his concept must inevitably reflect his own defects. Browning explicitly states this concept of the relativity of knowledge in the scale of development. The Pope again says:

Absolute, abstract, independent truth,
Historic, not reduced to suit man's mind, –
Or only truth reverberate, changed, made pass
A spectrum into mind, the narrow eye, –
The same and not the same, else unconceived –
Though quite conceivable to the next grade
Above it in intelligence, – as truth
Easy to man were blindness to the beast
By parity of procedure, – the same truth
In a new form, but changed in either case:
What matter so intelligence be filled?
To a child, the sea is angry, for it roars:
Frost bites, else why the tooth-like fret on face?
Man makes acoustics deal with the sea's wrath.

(X, 1389–1402)

Browning used the child's way of understanding to illustrate the importance of the form of a truth to its beholder. Caliban holds 'the same truth' in a much different form. Like the child, he reads direct cause into the effects, thus inferring the nature of the creator in the only way he can understand Him. Like the child he sees simple, direct relationships not scientific distinctions. Browning used the same metaphor in *Development* to illustrate the truth it embodies. A child understands by simple analogy, as does Caliban. To Browning it would be worse to 'leave weak eyes to grow sand-blind, / Content with darkness and vacuity' (22–3). Thus Caliban's gropings, no matter how limited, are good.

The one essential element which Caliban cannot deduce about God is his loving nature. Setebos and the Quiet are decidedly not loving – they are pointedly the opposite. Again in the Pope's monologue we find Browning's ideas stated:

> soar the conceivable height,
> Find cause to match the effect in evidence,
> The work i' the world, not man's but God's; leave man!
> Conjecture of the worker by the work:
> Is there strength there? – enough: intelligence?
> Ample: but goodness in a like degree?
> Not to the human eye in the present state,
> An isoscele deficient in the base.   (X, 1359–66)

Caliban has clearly found the power and intelligence of crafty Setebos, by looking at the 'work i' the world', but he cannot find the good. Revelation is necessary for that, and Caliban, being something primitive and below humanity, cannot receive it. It is David in *Saul* who has a vision of God the good, and he sees a likeness in God to himself in that he sees flesh in the Godhead. He sees a face. Caliban sees the Quiet who has to be feared. He sees Setebos as a vexer, even as he is.

Thus the poem, far from being a satire, is a picture of the belief of a creature, lower than man, understanding the Deity as best he can understand it. One interesting fact about the poem, which no one seems to have noted, is that the reader, despite the knowledge that for him there is no Setebos, comes to think of Setebos as real,

JOHN HOWARD

plaguing Caliban, with whom the reader eventually tends to sympathize. Browning's note from the fiftieth Psalm is therefore important as a counterbalance to the tendency of his artistic creation to convince too well. Without the constant thought that Caliban is limited in his concepts, we would become involved in the description of Setebos, thinking him merely a devilish deity. But the poem is part of Browning's way of showing that God reveals to each creature only what he is capable of understanding. In a creature like Caliban, who can only appreciate spite, envy, vexing and propitiation, there is little light. The question which Browning apparently never successfully answered was why the evil in such a creature as Caliban should exist.[10]

NOTES

[1] 'Caliban upon Setebos', *Studies in Philology*, XXXV (1938), p. 488.

[2] *Omphalos* (London: 1857), pp. 352–3.

[3] 'Caliban', *Poet-Lore*, III (May 1891), p. 293.

[4] *The Boston Browning Society Papers* (London: 1897), p. 70.

[5] Langbaum, *Experience*, p. 207.

[6] O. L. Triggs, 'In Re Caliban', *Poet-Lore*, XVII (1906), pp. 477–9.

[7] DeVane says that Browning, stimulated by the missing link controversy, 'leapt to the literary anticipation of such a creature – the figure of Caliban. . . . Being Browning he gave Caliban an interest in theology.' I think rather that Browning, stirred by Shakespeare's Caliban, attempted to go further into the sort of thought that Shakespeare's Caliban was capable of.

[8] *Letters of Robert Browning Collected by Thomas J. Wise*, ed. Thurman L. Hood (London: 1933), p. 228 [letter of April 25, 1884].

[9] Caliban's speech in the third person has excited many varied comments. Mrs Sutherland Orr, *A Handbook to the Works of Robert Browning* (London: 1910), p. 195, connects the speech with childishness. S. S. Curry, 'Browning's Caliban and Saul', *Arena*, XL (July 1908), p. 48, says that 'Caliban's degraded nature is indicated by the fact that he does not rise to the dignity of the pronoun "I".' More recently E. K. Brown, 'The First Person in *Caliban upon Setebos*', *MLN*, LXVI (1951), pp. 392–5, attempts to find a dramatic expression in the change of person throughout the poem that indicates Caliban's fear of Setebos. There the matter rests.

[10] [cf. Laurence Perrine, 'Browning's *Caliban upon Setebos*: A Reply', *VP*, II (1964), pp. 124–7.]

WATSON KIRKCONNELL

THE *EPILOGUE* TO *DRAMATIS PERSONAE*

THE *Epilogue* to *Dramatis Personae* is a brief deliverance of Browning's mature beliefs in religion and philosophy. The volume to which it forms a pendant was published in 1864, when the poet was in his fifty-third year and at the height of his powers. He had given the world no poetry for nearly ten years, and this decade of silence had witnessed a growth and conflict of human philosophies that had stirred the spiritual life of England to its depths. Moreover, Mrs Browning had died in 1861, and a man of Browning's temperament must have been driven by this bereavement to a profound scrutiny of the fundamental facts of life. In every way we are led to expect in *Dramatis Personae* a serious exposition of his ultimate philosophy, and in the *Epilogue* a cogent recapitulation of that faith.

To appreciate fully, however, the point and application of his teaching, we must examine for a moment the chief currents of thought in the years during which this volume was being written. There was first of all the steady advance of scientific thought which culminated in Charles Darwin's *Origin of Species* in 1859. Four years later, in 1863, *The Geological Evidence of the Antiquity of Man* came from the pen of Sir Charles Lyell, the greatest geologist of the century. These books established, once for all, the continuity of man with the lower animals, and many years passed before scandalized ecclesiastics ceased to fight against facts and proceeded to raise religion to a higher and more inspiring plane by the adoption and

From *Modern Language Notes*, XLI (1926), pp. 213–19.

sublimation of the principle of evolution. This duty is almost immediately, in *Dramatis Personae*, performed by Browning in no unsuccessful manner.

Another feature of the times was the great Oxford Movement inaugurated by those Anglicans who sought to preserve and intensify aspects of religion most typical of the Church of Rome. These Tractarians held that the Church of England was part of the visible Holy Catholic Church and could, through the uninterrupted personal delegation of sanctified authority from bishop to bishop through eighteen centuries, claim, unbroken and undiminished, the prerogatives of the primitive church, conceived of as sacerdotal authority divinely bestowed. Many of the Tractarians, including John Henry Newman, went over to Rome; but many others remained technically in the Anglican Church. These latter formed in 1860 the 'English Church Union' with the avowed purpose of upholding the use of eucharistic vestments, elaborate ritual, incense, and other perquisites of the Roman Church. Public feeling ran high and in 1860 and 1861 violent riots broke out in London against the ritualist party. Some measure of justification for this popular outburst came in 1864, when the Pope issued a Syllabus declaring that no man is free to adopt and profess the religion he considers true according to the light of reason; that the Church has the right to employ force in order to impose its doctrines; that metaphysics cannot and ought not to be pursued without reference to ecclesiastical authority; that Catholic states are wrong to allow foreign immigrants to exercise their own religion in public; and that the Pope expressly refused to make terms with progress, liberalism, and modern civilization.

The extremes of the religious reactionaries strengthened the hands of the Broad Church party (best represented by Dr Jowett), which was interested in German criticism and the scientific philosophy of the day. The year 1860 had been marked by the death of Baur, the head of the Tübingen school, whose *History of the Church* had been an epoch-making work. In that same year appeared a volume of *Essays and Reviews* by seven English writers, of whom six were clergymen. The view advocated in these essays seem mild enough today, and many of them would be accepted by most well-educated clergymen but at the time they produced a very painful impression. The whole spirit of the volume is perhaps expressed in the observation that

If any one perceives to how great an extent the origin itself of Christianity rests upon probable evidence, his principle will relieve him from many difficulties which might otherwise be very disturbing. For relations which may repose on doubtful grounds as matters of history, and, as history, be incapable of verification, may yet be equally suggestive of true ideas with facts absolutely certain –

that is, they may have a spiritual significance although they are historically false.

In 1863, John Colenso, Bishop of Natal, was deposed and ex-communicated by his fellow bishops of the Anglican Church for certain critical studies of the Pentateuch. The most notable book of this year was a *Life of Christ* by the profound French scholar, Ernest Renan, which maintained a rigid exclusion of all supernatural factors.

Another disturbing factor of the times, and one which menaced Christianity far more closely, was the growing interest in psychical research and the attempt to prove scientifically that the 'spirits' of dead people exist. D. D. Home, an American medium, was one of the leading exponents of spiritism in Browning's day, and won full credence from Mrs Browning, to her husband's unbounded disgust.

As might have been expected, *Dramatis Personae*, published in 1864, is colored through and through with these contemporary conceptions and speculations, yet the point of view is typically Browning's own, from which he scans out and considers the thought of the day.

Three short poems, *Prospice*, *May and Death*, and *A Face*, seem to spring directly from the death of his wife, and have no intentional further application.

Six others, which form the body of the volume, set forth his philosophical views at great length. *Gold Hair* is a frank counterblast to *Essays and Reviews*. In it, he tries to support the idea of Original Sin by recounting a story of secret covetousness in a Breton saint. *Mr Sludge, 'The Medium'*, explains the trickery and warped psychology of professional spiritists, illustrating at once the credulity of the public and the self-deception of the medium. In *Caliban upon Setebos*, Browning, pursuant on the doctrine of evolution, represents an undeveloped savage mind ruminating on the nature of God, and even, in his crude way, reaching out after higher conceptions. In *Abt Vogler* and *Rabbi Ben Ezra*, he places in the mouths of a German composer and of a famous Jewish scholar his favourite conception of man, the finite, developing steadily towards his full realization in the infinite. *A Death in the Desert* represents the last words of the Apostle John, in which he maintains the essential truth of Christianity underneath the change of superficial aspects which the progressive development of man's spiritual life makes necessary.

A second group of six poems deals with the principle of Love, on which the whole of his moral and religious doctrine rests. Love, for him, not only constitutes the nature of God and the moral ideal of man, but is also the purpose and essence of all created being. Three poems, *James Lee's Wife*, *The Worst of It*, and *Confessions*, set forth the supreme value of love even in the face of estrangement, infidelity, and impending death respectively. Three others, *Youth and Art*, *Dîs Aliter Visum*, and *Too Late*, arraign the sin of suppressing love through cowardice or calculating worldy wisdom, and so blighting the development of the soul.

The *Epilogue* sums up the volume. In it, Browning sets forth in dramatic monologues two of the outstanding faiths of the day and then answers them in thirty-six short lines which contain the master-arguments of his philosophy.

The first speaker is given as David. The scene pictured is the dedication of Solomon's temple in Second Chronicles, chapter 5:

The Levites, being arrayed in white linen, stood at the east end of the altar, and with them an hundred and twenty priests; and it came to pass, as the trumpeters and singers were as one, to make one sound to be heard in praising and thanking the Lord; and when they lifted up their voice with the trumpets and praised the Lord, saying, For he is good; for his mercy endureth for ever; that then the house was filled with a cloud, even the house of the Lord; so that the priests could not stand to minister by reason of the cloud: for the glory of the Lord had filled the house of God.

The very few critics, such as Berdoe and Mrs Orr, who have commented on the poem, take this first monologue literally. It represents, they say, the conception of God as the Old Testament David had it, as a terrible, all-glorious Deity who revealed Himself to His chosen people on certain extraordinary occasions as a cloud or a pillar of fire. But there are certain difficulties in the way of this interpretation. At the time of the dedication of the temple, here depicted, King David had been seventeen years dead. Browning, too, often enunciates the gradual development of man's religious conceptions as a perfectly natural process, in which the highest conceptions of any age are right for that age. David's views present the highest point reached by the purest Theism of the Hebrew people, yet Browning, in the third section of the *Epilogue*, rebukes him as '*witless alike of will and way divine*'. The poet would hardly waste time in 1864 A.D. condemning David for holding in 1000 B.C. views which he himself had often declared to be justified in that day. A further complication arises from the fact that in the poem *Saul*, published in 1855, he had already bestowed on David the views of the *third* speaker of the *Epilogue*.

There seems no doubt to my mind that in this first section of the *Epilogue* Browning has set forth, symbolically, a point of view which was finding acute expression in England at the time he wrote this poem, namely, the intense sacerdotalism of the Oxford Movement and the Church of Rome. To such superlatively orthodox Christians, our knowledge of the Divine is gained through special revelation; God's will is manifested in His church; and in the 'sacred' edifices, with their priestly services and sanctified ceremonial, we come into the Holy of Holies, into the presence of the glory of the Lord.

As the first speaker expresses the faith of reactionary orthodoxy, so the second speaker gives us the conclusions of despairing scepticism to which a frank recognition of modern advances in knowledge seemed to drive the sincere but broadminded Christians of the day. The spokesman here is Renan, perhaps France's greatest scholar during the century, whose rationalistic *La Vie de Jésus* had caused a tremendous stir at its publication in 1863.

Renan did not seek to overthrow Christianity. He attempted rather 'to serve religion by trying to carry it into the region of the unassailable, beyond particular dogmas and supernatural beliefs'. The general conclusions to which he was driven, however, were those of a grave Stoic pessimism, and are so represented by Browning in the second section of the *Epilogue*. His speech there may be roughly paraphrased as follows: Christ, here symbolized by the Biblical Star of Bethlehem, came to man as a new conception full of infinite hope and promise. There was no longer a great gulf fixed between the nature of man and the nature of God, for here the Divine seemed to stoop and touch the human and to thrill to the fervent love of man's heart. But man fails to preserve this fervour and this vision. His conception of the personal, loving nature of God in Christ changes to that of a Divine Being, distant and omnipotent, unmoved by any feeling for our natures and infirmities. The next natural step, on the extension of our knowledge of the infinity of the universe, is the denial of even this superhuman deity. Man is left alone, a spiritual orphan. There are many lights in the world which he may study, many phases of scientific truth. But how shall Science take the place of the incarnate God who came to earth? With the death of Christianity and the dethronement of the Deity, man finds himself the highest form of life in the world; but the greatest thinkers, on realizing this, are appalled, for man instinctively wants something to which he can look up. Hence even the highest types of mankind find this abolition of the Divine repugnant and hateful.

Renan thus shows disillusionment as to special revelation, along with regret for the lost ideal. He assumes that in years to come men will resign themselves to uncertainty and at last will confront the eternal problems of religion with scarcely an effort for their solution. It is the modern savant's despair of discovering the truth about the spiritual world. Religious aspiration and emotion are all that can be ours, and all effort after a systematic knowledge of the unseen world must be abandoned in despair.

Such, then, are the two typical views set forth: David's representing that of the orthodox reactionaries who embraced revealed religion and the Church without any concern for truth, and Renan's that of the baffled liberal Christian who has sought to reconcile reason and religion.

To both of these speakers Browning delivers a sweeping rebuke. 'Friends,' he says, 'you are blankly ignorant of God's will and God's ways. I have heard your views. Now listen to my explanation of it all.'

'Heaven's high,' he proceeds, 'does intertwine with earth's low.' The life of the universe is a manifestation of God, slowly expressing itself under aspects that press back towards the Divine. God is immanent in man and is likewise the character towards which he strives in his age-long process of development. It is not to abstract mankind in general that we must turn to realize this, but to the individual. Every man, even the humblest and most insignificant, has his unique personality, differing from every other, in which this spiritual principle is working itself out. As, in legends, Arctic currents gathered around some point of rock, giving it momentary importance, and then swept over it and on to another, so the forces of the world, evil and good, gather round each man, shaping by their influence the development of the spiritual essence within him, until *'the life, his product'* is *'gained'*. This sustained strife of spiritual forces goes forward incessantly, evolving the nature of God in mankind; yet it is not a vast impersonal process, a great chemical action in which men are only inert molecules, for the individual lives with their distinct individual characters and experiences are the medium through which the evolution goes on.

Thus Browning declares to the Churchman that God's presence is not limited to the buildings of brick and stone within which man has tried to confine Him; nor is His worship peculiarly served by ritual and ceremony. For God is actually present in His universe; He is the principle that gives it life and meaning; and the strenuous moral activity and spiritual growth of man are the highest forms of worship, for thereby comes the progressive realization of potential divinity.

And to the sceptic liberal, he declares that a calm survey of the universe does not wipe out the conception of God given us by Christ. For God is incarnate, potentially, in all mankind, and as man develops, the nature of God, the ideal towards which he strives, becomes more and more evident through the evolving nature of

humanity. The incomplete knowledge and faltering love of mankind
are revelations of the complete knowledge and perfect love of God:

> That one Face, far from vanish, rather grows,
> Or decomposes but to recompose,
> Become my universe that feels and knows.[1]

NOTE

[1] [See also Raymond, *Infinite Moment*, pp. 49–50. For Browning's religious views see works cited in footnotes to Badger, pp. 92–95, esp. Benziger, *Images*, pp. 192–7, and J. H. Miller, *Disappearance of God*, pp. 155–6. For Browning's views on Renan see his letter to Isa Blagden of November 19, 1863, *Dearest Isa*, ed. E. C. McAleer (1951), p. 180.]

F. E. L. PRIESTLEY

A READING OF *LA SAISIAZ*

OR readers of Browning's poetry, *La Saisiaz* must always hold a special interest as one of the poet's most extensive personal utterances. It is seldom, even in lyrics, that he writes a poem so directly occasional, and so immediate in form. Here his more usual techniques of indirection, of speaking through a *persona*, of substituting for the personal situation a devised dramatic one, are abandoned; the reticence suggested by the separation of *House* and *Shop* is here pushed aside by the urgent compulsion of the poet's emotion. The occasion of the poem, the sudden and shockingly unexpected death of his dear friend Anne Egerton Smith, is close in time to the composition; the poet's emotion is fresh and near to him; it is neither recollected in tranquillity nor distanced by his normal aesthetic devices. There is consequently behind the poem a sense of private urgency, a sense of emotional excitement straining against Browning's habit of control. The dualism so well described by F. R. G. Duckworth, the tension between 'speaking out' and preserving privacy, here takes on what is perhaps its most complex form.[1]

In its general pattern, the poem moves towards a tightening of control; that is, towards reticence. It moves from direct expression of emotion towards a suppression of it, from the personal to the impersonal, and one gets the impression that the real theme is contained precisely in this movement, that the poem records Browning's *katharsis*, his successful emergence from shock.

The first section (ll. 1–139) presents, as if by way of introduction, the direct experience in which the poem originates. The poet has

From *University of Toronto Quarterly*, XXV (1955), pp. 47–59.

climbed alone to the summit of Mt Salève, overlooking the village
of Collonge where Miss Smith is buried. It is only five days since
her death. On that morning they were to have climbed Salève together, when Browning, looking for her to start the ascent, learned
to his horror that she was unconscious and dying. As he now completes the climb alone, it becomes for him a symbolic act: the movement upward, each part of which reveals new scenes, new vistas,
new perspectives, suggests the journey of life; the poet at the summit
has 'dared and done', as his companion has 'dared and done' with
life. The abyss between the summit and Collonge suggests the
barrier separating living and dead:

Oh the barrier! yon Profound
Shrinks beside it, proves a pin-point: barrier this, without a bound!
Boundless though it be, I reach you: somehow seem to have you here
– Who are there. . . .
. . . Howe'er disjoints
Past from present, no less certain you are here, not there: have dared,
Done the feat of mountain-climbing. . . .   [19–26]

The recollection of the gay planning of the climb together, of the
casual, affectionate goodnight, of the dreadful morning discovery,
forms a narrative counterpointed by descriptions of the mountain
scenes. A final recollection of Miss Smith's shy, diffident, affectionate
nature completes the introduction by modulating to the main theme:

You supposed that few or none had known and loved you in the world:
May be! flower that's full-blown tempts the butterfly, not flower
    that's furled.
But more learned sense unlocked you, loosed the sheath and let expand
Bud to bell and outspread flower-shape at the least warm touch of hand
– Maybe, throb of heart, beneath which, – quickening farther
    than it knew, –
Treasure oft was disembosomed, scent all strange and unguessed hue.
Disembosomed, re-embosomed, – must one memory suffice,
Prove I knew an Alpine-rose which all beside named Edelweiss?
                                                              [123–30]

Her rich and charming spirit, known truly to few, can hope for no
long survival in living memories; can it hope for other survival?

            Dared and done today
        Climbing, – here I stand: but you – where? [138–9]

243

The elaboration of this question forms the second movement of the poem (140–216): 'Does the soul survive the body? Is there God's self, no or yes?' In shaping the question, the poet begins with two provisos: he will not shrink from the truth, 'come in whatsoe'er uncouth / Shape it should, nay, formidable'. For he has no pretence (and this is the second proviso) to 'pass off human lisp as echo of the sphere-song out of reach'. His is 'but man's truest answer', proceeding from weakness by weakness questioned; the truth he arrives at will be limited by man's finitude; it will be truth, for 'truth is truth in each degree', but it will not be ultimate truth as God sees it. It cannot hold the terror of ultimate truth, nor the splendour.

With these provisos, important for the further development of the theme, the poet turns to the problem. He recalls that only a week ago, he and Miss Smith had been discussing the Symposium, appearing in the *Nineteenth Century*, 'On the Soul and Future Life'. Their discussion last week had been gaily academic, objectively appreciative of 'parried thrust, subtle stroke'. The subject of the Symposium has suddenly ceased to be academic, the fence-play no longer play. The insistence by Frederic Harrison in the Symposium on a mere earthly immortality of reputation, a survival in mortal memory, as the only reality of 'future life', seems now (as it had seemed in *Saul*) the offer of a poor substitute. Nor does the thought of a possible richer earthly existence for future generations give much comfort. As Huxley said, it would be little comfort to the extinct Eohippus to know that his descendant would win the Derby; Browning points out that even if such knowledge would be a comfort, it is denied him. According to the Positivists,

There is but left for comfort, when the last spark proves extinct,
This – that somewhere new existence led by men and women new
Possibly attains perfection coveted by me and you;
While ourselves, the only witness to what work our life evolved,
Only to ourselves proposing problems proper to be solved
By ourselves alone, – who working ne'er shall know if work bear fruit
Others reap and garner, heedless how produced by stalk and root, –
. . . we, creative thought, must cease
In created word, thought's echo, due to impulse long since sped!
[185–95]

Nevertheless, repugnant as these conceptions are, the important question is whether they are true. 'Truth is truth howe'er it strike', and the poet resolves to have an answer. It is important to note his words:

> I will ask and have an answer, – with no favour, with no fear, –
> From myself. How much, how little, do I inwardly believe
> True that controverted doctrine? Is it fact to which I cleave,
> Is it fancy I but cherish, when I take upon my lips
> Phrase the solemn Tuscan fashioned, and declare the soul's eclipse
> Not the soul's extinction? take his 'I believe and I declare –
> Certain am I – from this life I pass into a better, there
> Where that lady lives of whom enamoured was my soul' – where this
> Other lady, my companion dear and true, she also is? [208–16]

Three things at least are significant in the passage quoted: the poet will have an answer 'from himself'. He speaks of one answer but is asking two questions: how much he inwardly believes the doctrine? whether the doctrine is fact or fancy? And lastly, he puts the doctrine, not in plain terms as before, but in the moving and favourite passage from Dante which expresses his deepest feeling for his dead wife, whom he now links with his lately dead friend. With the question put in these terms, and with his proviso about the nature of truth in mind, the procedure of the rest of the poem becomes clear. The main section (217–548) presents the answer.

Again Browning begins with provisos. The first (217–64) has to do with knowledge, and thus elaborates and extends the earlier one. It also begins the specific answer to the question about fact or fancy. The very terms of the original question presuppose

> that the thing itself which questions . . . *is*, it knows;
> As it also knows the thing perceived outside itself, – a force
> Actual ere its own beginning, operative through its course,
> Unaffected by its end, – that this thing likewise needs must be;
> Call this – God then, call that – soul. [218–22]

Immediate knowledge of Self and Not-self, and of the independence of Not-self, are the presuppositions of knowledge. As presuppositions, they are unproveable. These are the original 'facts', 'the only facts for me'. 'That they o'erpass my power of proving, proves them such.' All else follows from these facts; all else is construction of man's mind, efforts to deduce cause and effect. To these constructions, commonly thought of as the work of reason, and as knowledge, Browning gives the names of 'fancy' and 'surmise', illustrating by a series of contradictory arguments familiar to readers of theodicies, each argument calling up an equally plausible counter. These 'old sad contentions' have brought to some 'a half-escape:/ "We believe" is sighed'.

> I take the cup of comfort proffered thus,
> Taste and try each soft ingredient, sweet infusion, and discuss
> What their blending may accomplish for the cure of doubt, till – slow,
> Sorrowful, but how decided! needs must I o'erturn it – so!
>
> (251–4)

All that can be certainly known is one's own experience:

> Cause before, effect behind me – blanks! The midway point I am,
> Caused, itself – itself efficient. . . . (255–6)

> Things may be as I behold,
> Or may not be, but, without me and above me, things there are;
> I myself am what I know not – ignorance which proves no bar
> To the knowledge that I am, and, since I am, can recognize
> What to me is pain and pleasure: this is sure, the rest – surmise.
>
> (258–62)

This position leads to the next (265–92): as the poet surveys his own experience, he is forced to the conclusion that it can exhibit no coherence unless this life can be viewed as probationary:

> There is no reconciling wisdom with a world distraught,
> Goodness with triumphant evil, power with failure in the aim,
> If – (to my own sense, remember! though none other feel
>   the same!) –
> If you bar me from assuming earth to be a pupil's place. . . .
>
> (266–9)

Again he emphasizes the proviso in the parentheses: 'Knowledge stands on my experience' . . .

Here's my neighbour colour-blind,
Eyes like mine to all appearance: 'green as grass' do I affirm?
'Red as grass' he contradicts me – which employs the proper term?
Were we two the earth's sole tenants, with no third for referee,
How should I distinguish? Just so, God must judge 'twixt man and me.
[274–8]

It is important to note the referee; while each man must seek the truth of his own experience, attempt to create his own system of coherence, this does not imply that truth is relative. It will be recalled that in *Christmas-Eve* the speaker reaches a point of 'mild indifferentism', ready to view all faiths as equally good, and that at this point the hem of Christ's vestment is withdrawn from him; he then realizes that he has been passing a judgment appropriate to God, not to man:

> Needs must there be one way, our chief
> Best way of worship: let me strive
> To find it, and when found, contrive
> My fellows also take their share!
> This constitutes my earthly care:
> God's is above it and distinct.
> . . . I exult
> That God, by God's own ways occult,
> May – doth, I will believe – bring back
> All wanderers to a single track.
> Meantime, I can but testify
> God's care for me – no more, can I –
> It is but for myself I know. . . . [XX, 13–18, 23–9]

In *La Saisiaz* too man's task is to learn as best he can 'what is beauteous and what ugly, right to strive for, right to shun, / Fit to help and fit to hinder', to 'understand so much as may be understood'.

When now the poet turns to the task of judging the world of his own experience (293–348) he finds it incoherent and irrational, filled with the paradoxes that disturbed the rational deists: is God deficient in power, that his created world is so imperfect? or in will? The deistic attempts at theodicy offer no solution to Browning:

> Must the rose sigh 'Pluck – I perish!' must the eve weep
>   'Gaze – I fade!'
> – Every sweet warn "Ware my bitter!' every shine bid 'Wait
>   my shade'?
> Can we love but on condition, that the thing we love must die?
> Needs there groan a world in anguish just to teach us sympathy?
> [309-12]

If this life is all, Browning is forced to the conclusion that its sorrows outweigh its joys – still, of course, speaking for himself alone.

> Only my own joys and sorrows now to reckon real instead, –
> I must say – or choke in silence – 'Howsoever came my fate,
> Sorrow did and joy did nowise, – life well weighed, – preponderate.'
> [332-4]

(This is not as unusual a conclusion as some might think; it does not mark a temporary abandonment by Browning of his 'optimism'. Throughout his poetry, from *Paracelsus* on, runs the theme that this life receives its value not from itself alone, but from its significant relation to the eternal.) If the general unsatisfactoriness of life were ordained by necessity, it could be endured; but the suggestion that it represents all that 'a cause all-good, all-wise, all-potent' ordains is one that 'reason most revolts at'. The only condition that could reconcile the poet to the imperfections, sorrows, and frustrations of this life would be that it is prelude to something more perfect (349–90):

> Only grant a second life, I acquiesce
> In this present life as failure, count misfortune's worst assaults
> Triumph, not defeat, assured that loss so much the more exalts
> Gain about to be. . . .
>
> While for love – Oh how but, losing love, does whoso loves succeed
> By the death-pang to the birth-throe – learning what is love indeed?
> [358-61, 365-6]

If it were so,

> – Worst were best, defeat were triumph, utter loss were utmost gain.
> Can it be, and must, and will it? [389-90]

So far, the poet has worked to his original question: 'How much, how little, do I inwardly believe / True that controverted doctrine? Is it fact to which I cleave, / Is it fancy I but cherish . . .?' But in the process he has clarified what 'inwardly believe true' means to him, and has cast some doubts upon the simple opposition of 'fact' and 'fancy' as categories. As he now rephrases the question, he shifts the emphasis by substituting for references to himself (I believe, I cleave, I cherish) references to what would seem to be an external reality (can it be, and must, and will it?). The reader will, however, remember the limitations Browning has set upon our knowledge of the external; the shift is rather from the poet's feeling to his thought; from his desires, to his attempt to see 'his world' as coherent.

To the question thus posed, 'fact' offers no answer; 'surmise' alone is prepared 'to mutter hope, and also fear' and to dispute 'Fact's inexorable ruling "Outside fact, surmise be mute!"' The principle that surmise should be mute (a popular version of *Hypotheses non fingo*) is well, indeed best, in those areas where fact itself can speak:

> Ay, well and best, if fact's self I may force the answer from!
> 'Tis surmise I stop the mouth of. [393–4]

But what of those areas where fact itself is dumb? To the poet's urgent question, the world of fact returns no answer:

> Not above in yonder dome
> All a rapture with its rose-glow, . . . not beneath, where crickets creak,
> Birds assemble for their bed-time, soft the tree-top swell subsides, –
> No, nor yet within my deepest sentient self the knowledge hides.
> [394–8]

Yet the question demands an answer, and the poet calls upon Fancy and Reason to wage 'amicable war' and 'play the foe' as his soul stands umpire. Browning's phrasing here is again significant. In *The Ring and the Book* he had taken the popular opposition of 'fact' and 'fancy' and ironically juggled the terms: 'Fancy with fact is just one fact the more' [I, 464]. 'Fancy', the poetic imagination, reaches to the truth beyond the facts, seizes on dead fact and makes it live. So again here he selects the vulgar (and empiricist) opposition of Reason and Fancy (vulgarly concerned with 'truth' and 'fiction',

'fact' and 'surmise'); his own view is indicated by his terms 'amicable'
and 'play the foe' – Reason and Fancy in actuality co-operate in the
search for truth, as the dialogue that follows suggests.

Fancy starts the dialogue by conceding 'the thing refused', the
'mere surmise that after body dies soul lives again'.

> Two, the only facts acknowledged late, are now increased to three –
> God is, and the soul is, and, as certain, after death shall be.
> Put this third to use in life, the time for using fact!   [407–9]

Once again we have moved back to an earlier part of the poem, this
time to the establishing of the two 'facts' or primary certainties
beyond which all else is surmise (l. 223 following). To these Fancy
has added a 'surmise' which, conceded, becomes 'one fact the more'.
The last line quoted just above suggests what Browning here
means – 'fact' is for use in life. The purpose of life is action; action
depends upon a degree of coherence in one's view of the meaning of
life. (One recalls Bishop Blougram's cabin analogy, Gigadibs' aimless incoherence and his final resolution.) Our knowledge being
limited, we must supplement it, or indeed arrange its fragments,
with the help of postulates which 'go beyond the facts'. Since these
postulates are a vital part of the system of relations which turns
'facts' into 'knowledge', they can be properly considered themselves
'facts' in the popular sense (which equates facts with knowledge).

This I think explains why Browning has Reason readily accede to
Fancy's suggestion on the ground that 'it promises advantage'. From
this point on in the dialogue, Reason suggests to Fancy what further
postulates are necessary, approving each as offered. The bare notion
of a life to come better than the present one naturally invites an immediate exchange of this life for that; it must be that there is a compulsion to live out this life, and one's state in the future life must
depend upon conduct in this. Nor must this life be spent passively, or
again it becomes meaningless. Finally, the guide to proper conduct,
the moral law, must be sufficiently discernible to allow the exercise
of judgment, but not so unmistakable as to preclude will and choice.
Natural laws 'enforce themselves': 'to hear means to obey'; the moral
law, no less powerful, is not compulsive: a man may see and praise

the best yet follow the worst, 'since he disbelieves / In the heart of him that edict which for truth his head receives'.

All these postulates or 'surmises', granted as 'facts', make human life intelligible; they represent, in short, what Browning finds a coherent explanation, based on his own experience and guided by his reason and fancy, of the meaning of life. Each item is necessary to the explanation; apart from the first two 'facts' the rest depend on each other. Break the structure, and –

>   all is empty air – no sward
> Firm like my first fact to stand on 'God there is and soul there is,'
> And soul's earthly life-allotment: wherein, by hypothesis,
> Soul is bound to pass probation, prove its powers, and exercise
> Sense and thought on fact, and then, from fact educing fit surmise,
> Ask itself, and of itself have solely answer, 'Does the scope
> Earth affords of fact to judge by warrant future fear or hope?'
> [518–24]

As the poet notes, we are back at the original question:

> Thus have we come back full circle: fancy's footsteps one by one
> Go their round conducting reason to the point where they begun. . . .
> [525–6]

But the answer has really been given. Can the answer be *proved*? Can the first 'facts' be proved? 'That they o'erpass my power of proving, proves them such.' Certainty of the kind associated with physical fact would not make the scheme of life more significant, but less so; for Lazarus, in *An Epistle . . . of Karshish*, certainty has deprived this life of meaning – he is entirely passive; deprived of real choice, seeing things no longer in human perspective but *sub specie aeternitatis*, he is no longer strictly human.

>   Assurance may not be
> If, supplanting hope, assurance needs must change this life to me.
> So, I hope – no more than hope, but hope – no less than hope. . . .
> [533–5]

In the strictly human state, with life and laws judged as well as man may, 'Hope the arrowy, just as constant', comes to pierce the gloom,

compelled
By a power and by a purpose which, if no one else beheld,
I behold in life, so – hope!   [543–5]

The force of this passage, the conclusion to the main part of the
poem, derives from the modest 'no more than hope' followed at once
by the emphatic 'no less than hope', and the rising sweep of the lines
to the trumpeted final 'hope!' A double purpose is served by the
proviso 'if no one else beheld' – it creates a suspension to precede the
blunt 'I behold', and consequently adds to the rhetorical power; and
it reminds the reader of an important element in the theme throughout: 'His own world for every mortal.'

It is this element which leads into the *coda*. The poet becomes, as
it were, aware of his audience; he imagines their comment:

Sad summing-up of all to say!
Athanasius contra mundum, why should he hope more than they?
                    [545–6]

He recognizes that some or many will read his poem for its
'message', will look to it to influence their own passive natures:

So are men made notwithstanding, such magnetic virtue darts
From each head their fancy haloes to their unresisting hearts!
                    [547–8]

From the height of the mountain he can look down to the very
places where Rousseau and Byron walked; he finds in their influence examples of this 'magnetic virtue.' What their haloed heads
darted to mankind, their 'gospel-news,' was a message of despair:
Rousseau's,

'All that's good is gone and past;
Bad and worse still grows the present, and the worst of all comes last:
Which believe – for I believe it. . . .'   [561–3]

Byron's,

'Dying day with dolphin-hues!
. . . Ye mounts
Where I climb to 'scape my fellow, and thou sea wherein he counts
Not one inch of vile dominion! What were your especial worth

252

Failed ye to enforce the maxim "Of all objects found on earth
Man is meanest. . . ."
Which believe – for I believe it!'   [564–71]

Such is the comfort man received, sadly but perforce, from these.
Perforce for why? 'The famous bard believed!'

The contempt in the lines is unmistakable enough, even to a
reader who failed to remember Browning's persistent belief that each
man must hammer out his own faith and philosophy, not adopt it
passively because of the fame of an advocate. For Browning, belief
'perforce' is no faith: compare his explanation in *A Death in the
Desert* that miracles soon become void 'because too much: they would
compel, not help'. Remembering 'so are men made notwithstanding',
Browning is moved to an ironic revelation: if only he could have for a
moment the fame of a Rousseau or a Byron, could wave his giant
torch on high, what great message would he now give the passive
listeners to store up in 'their unresisting hearts'? Those who 'find
significance in fireworks' may, by the poet's help,

Confidently lay to heart and lock in head their life long – this:
'He there with the brand flamboyant, broad o'er night's forlorn abyss,
Crowned by prose and verse; and wielding, with Wit's bauble,
    Learning's rod . . .
Well? Why, he at least believed in Soul, was very sure of God.'
                                                                      [601–4]

The message he gives them is knowledge of the two first 'facts',
the two immediate certainties which all men have, the two from
which he himself started and upon which he built his 'super-
structure'. Let each man go and do likewise. Browning's faith is
hammered out from his own experience; it represents what the
world looks like to him; he does not expect it to fit other experiences,
or particularly wish it to. He finds the meaning of life in the task of
solving the problem: 'From thine apprehended scheme of things,
deduce / Praise or blame of its contriver. . . .' The meaning is not
to be found in an attempt to look up the answer in Browning's book.

After this ironic glance to the reader, the poet turns back to a
short *envoi*. In it he describes the poem as a chain of thoughts, and
what he says about the chain is highly suggestive:

Not so loosely thoughts were linked,
Six weeks since as I, descending in the sunset from Salève,
Found the chain, I seemed to forge there, flawless till it reached your
grave, –
Not so filmy was the texture, but I bore it in my breast
Safe thus far. And since I found a something in me would not rest
Till I, link by link, unravelled any tangle of the chain,
– Here it lies, for much or little! I have lived all o'er again
That last pregnant hour: I saved it, just as I could save a root
Disinterred for re-interment when the time best helps to shoot.
Life is stocked with germs of torpid life; but may I never wake
Those of mine whose resurrection could not be without earthquake!
Rest all such, unraised for ever! Be this, sad yet sweet, the sole
Memory evoked from slumber! Least part this: then what the whole?
[606–18]

The poem has, up to this last paragraph, tended to move away from the strongly personal and emotional tone of its opening; the problem has been strenuously forced into an intellectual pattern, and although the straining undercurrent of feeling has at times pushed through, the general movement has been towards a distancing, and a reining in of emotion, until in the *coda* Browning has, to use his own *House* and *Shop* analogy, closed the door to his living-quarters. Now, in the *envoi*, he returns to the immediate experience from which the poem started, but with his instinct for concealment active, as the obliqueness of the lines shows. Why were the thoughts less loosely linked as he descended Mt Salève than now, six weeks later, as he writes the poem? When he says that then he found the chain flawless till it reached Miss Smith's grave, does he mean that it was flawless to that point but not beyond? that the chain broke at the grave? or that the chain firmly joined himself and the grave? Why does he speak of the chain 'I *seemed* to forge there'? Does 'Not so filmy was the texture, but I bore it . . . safe thus far' mean, following 'not so loose', that the texture then was firmer? or merely that the chain was strong enough to bear away? What are the tangles that needed unravelling? If the chain was less loosely linked and not so filmy then, why was it tangled? And finally, what is the significance of the root symbol which replaces that of the chain?

It is easier to ask these questions than to answer them, although I

have no doubt other readers of the poem more perceptive than I have
found less difficulty here. My own consideration of these lines, in
relation to the rest of the poem, suggests an analogy which I offer
with all due diffidence. The analogy is with Bishop Blougram. It is
well known that the Bishop shares some of his author's qualities, and
I would suggest that one of them is a reluctance to reveal the inner
springs of his being. In his argument with Gigadibs, he proceeds
from the journalist's premises, and weaves a chain of argument
strong enough for his purpose and valid enough as far as it goes,
but based very little upon the genuine depths of his convictions. At
the end of the argument, he reviews it:

> 'On the whole,' he thought, 'I justify myself
> On every point where cavillers like this
> Oppugn my life: he tries one kind of fence,
> I close, he's worsted, that's enough for him.
> He's on the ground: if ground should break away
> I take my stand on, there's a firmer yet
> Beneath it, both of us may sink and reach.'
> [996–1002]

In part, his procedure is a matter of tactics, but also in part a result
of reticence (genuine and deeper feeling emerges from time to time),
a reluctance to 'unlock his heart,' particularly to Gigadibs.[2]

In *La Saisiaz*, as Professor DeVane has pointed out, Browning
argues from the premises of the contributors to the Modern Symposium, or perhaps more strictly, from premises acceptable to
Frederic Harrison. As Professor DeVane puts it, '*La Saisiaz* may be
said to be Browning's contribution to this debate' (*Handbook* p. 422).[3]
But since the poem was not actually contributed to the Symposium,
there is really no necessity for Browning to confine himself to these
terms, particularly since he represents himself in the poem as seeking
from himself the fullest, most honest and most urgent answer to the
question:

> Much less have I heart to palter when the matter to decide
> Now becomes 'Was ending ending once and always, when you died?'
> [171–2]

It is hard to believe that tactical considerations, or terms of debate, had a major influence on his procedure. It is, I think, much more understandable that Blougram's other motive, reticence, is operating here in Browning. Many other poems, including the Blougram, suggest much deeper grounds for the poet's faith than the 'chain' which occupies the main part of *La Saisiaz*. I would suggest that his real thoughts on Mt Salève included many of these deeper elements; the chain was not the loose and simple chain the poem presents, with its successive links of postulates conceded; but was stronger, more tangled, and included very different sorts of links, particularly where it reached the grave. Some hints appear in the poem of these other links: the quotation from Dante (213 ff.) momentarily draws aside a curtain; so does the passage (527 ff.),

> When, half a week
> Since, we walked and talked and thus I told you, how suffused a cheek
> You had turned me had I sudden brought the blush into the smile
> By some word like 'Idly argued! you know better all the while!'

Blougram, as he fenced with Gigadibs, knew better all the while; Browning and Miss Smith, as they discussed the 'fence-play' of the Symposium, also had deeper grounds of faith. But Browning's deeper grounds are bound up with his own personal tragedies – not only with the loss of his friend, but with that of his wife. To resurrect the buried roots of his faith 'could not be without earthquake'. The 'last pregnant hour', which he has re-lived in the poem, is now re-interred; the love and sorrow which it recalls, along with the living hope, will become a fruitful part of the poet's inner life. What he reveals in the poem, a true part of his thought, a true part of his emotion, gives some suggestion of the real depths; the most eloquent witness of the depth of his love and faith comes in the last line: 'Least part this: then what the whole?'[4]

NOTES

[1] [See Duckworth, *Background*, esp. Chapters VI and IX.]

[2] [See Rupert E. Palmer, Jr., 'The Uses of Character in *Bishop Blougram's Apology*', *Modern Philology*, LVIII (1960), pp. 108–18.]

[3] [See Hoxie N. Fairchild, '*La Saisiaz* and *The Nineteenth Century*', *Modern Philology*, XLVIII (1950), pp. 104–11.]

[4] [See Norton B. Crowell, *The Triple Soul: Browning's Theory of Knowledge* (U. of New Mexico, 1963), Ch. II, esp. pp. 69–77.]

TAILPIECE

FREDERICK PAGE

BROWNING: A CONVERSATION

Scene: SIBYLLA'S *drawing-room, December* 31, 1889

(ATTICUS *is in town for a few days.* FRANCES *and* COLIN *have dropped in to tea. Two Professors are coming on from the Funeral at the Abbey.*)

SIBYLLA: We are to have Mr Saintsbury and Mr Ker with us this afternoon, Atticus.

ATTICUS (*resignedly*): Ah, yes?

SIBYLLA: Oh, no! You mustn't say it like that. I want you not to be chilly with them.

ATTICUS: Am I not the most amiable of old gentlemen?

SIBYLLA: Not always. And you mustn't be perverse if the talk turns on Mr Browning, as it inevitably will. Frances and Colin, here, are Browning's devotees, and your disciples.

ATTICUS: I am glad that they discriminate.

FRANCES: We don't set you so far apart as perhaps you might expect.

(*But here the Professors arrive.* SIBYLLA *pours out tea,* COLIN *hands the cups and the cakes. The ceremony at the Abbey is discussed, and the crowd is mentioned.*)

SIBYLLA: Yes, "Mr Browning's public is now great and various. One cannot ignore that it is not limited to the lovers of poetry purely."

From *Essays mainly on the Nineteenth Century presented to Sir Humphrey Milford* (Oxford: 1948), pp. 14–28. Frederick Page explains: 'The words between "double quotes" are throughout those of my originals. Nothing else is historical, and anachronisms abound.'

ATTICUS: I would like you to convince me that Browning has any great quantity of what is purely poetry.

SIBYLLA: True it is that "his work may undergo division, selection, and rejection, and suffer no loss".

SAINTSBURY: We should all agree with each other's inclusions, and disagree with the exclusions!

SIBYLLA: We should have to take some notice of the charge of obscurity. I think that "no author should be blamed for obscurity provided that he has done his best to be intelligible, nor should any pains be grudged in the effort to understand him. Difficulty of thought is the very heart of poetry."

ATTICUS: Not the logician's or the metaphysician's difficult thought! But of course you don't mean that.

SIBYLLA: No. Dante's, or Wordsworth's.

ATTICUS: Browning's argufying?

SIBYLLA: "His thought is knotted – is as knotty indeed as a fugue. But no one who has not followed him through his labours of analysis, can understand the pleasure of the more studious reader" – forgive me, Atticus; *your* studies have lain elsewhere – "one's pleasure at hearing Mr Browning's cool, strong, argumentative voice break in the rare note of emotion, caused by his sudden rise to a higher moral and mental beauty. When this happens, not the feeling only, but the verse, softens and relaxes. When that higher fresher thought comes, it brings with it its own inevitable music."

COLIN: Its music! But Atticus has said that one "stumbles over the hillocks of potsherds and broken brickbats" of Browning's rhythm and diction.

W. P. KER: Why, certainly there is something in Browning that makes that description as plausible as it is witty.

SAINTSBURY: I think we shall not find that 'something' very easy to locate in the rhythm. "Browning, though an audacious, is almost invariably a correct prosodist – he goes often to the very edge, but hardly ever over it."

KER: Without o'erflowing, full.

SAINTSBURY: And "when he chooses (which is not so extremely seldom) he can be as smooth as smooth". I can concede just half a point to Atticus, that "not very seldom, likewise, he set his affected eccentricity of tongue against his native justness of ear. But even then the ear generally won."

COLIN: I am glad, Sir, you speak of his justness of ear, for that is what has been most borne in upon me, in my recent re-readings.

KER: But Atticus has asked how he is to disinter the soft pearl of distinction from the – well, you *did* say it, Sir – from the heaped potsherd and broken brickbats of a violent and self-imposed originality of diction.

SAINTSBURY: But Atticus might have asked himself how we could reasonably expect to find the peculiar aroma of Browning's personality in 'the imaginary utterances of imaginary persons, not his own'.[1] Were Caliban, Sludge, Blougram, Hohenstiel-Schwangau, Count Guido – his 'fifty men and women' [*One Word More*, line 1] – his hundred or more men and women – to speak with Browning's own voice? The surprising thing is that they do, that they inevitably must; that is, their inventor inevitably must. Not even Dickens could come nearer to Sludge – Sludge in his abject self, Sludge in his vile dialect – than Browning does. And yet Sludge remains Browning, Browning remains Browning, in that it is Browning's voice, Browning's ear, that controls the line, the verse. The jargon is but overlaid on Browning's English.

SIBYLLA: But we are used to that failure in mimicry: Meredith's people speak like Meredith, Henry James's like James. It is Trollope's people who always speak (and write letters) like themselves. Hardy's rustics we take on trust. And as for mimicry, the more perfect the more trivial, surely?

COLIN: I wonder if Mr Saintsbury's word 'control' does not give us just what we want, to reconcile Atticus to those fearful monologues. I had found the word 'volubility' for Browning, or rather for his dramatis personae, and have since found that Mr Saintsbury and Mr Symonds had used it already, but I think we haven't Browning's secret till we say 'controlled volubility'. 'Control' is the essential word. He seems to give Sludge and Blougram their head, and one fears they will be interminably voluble –

SAINTSBURY: Yes, you will remember Bagehot's friend who always looked ahead to see how much he had let himself in for – 'what length of intellectual adventure he was about to commence'!

COLIN: – but it is Browning who controls their argument – they think they have freedom of speech, but their creator has foreknowledge absolute.

FRANCES: Or not quite absolute. Dear Sibylla, you have written of the 'uncontrasted ignominy' of Blougram. Browning thought he had given his Bishop a sufficient foil in the incorruptible simplicity of Gigadibs. It is unlikely that he foreknew that in a few years he would be writing *A Death in the Desert*. In that poem, Atticus, each one of a little group of St John's disciples had suffered or was to suffer martyrdom for the faith in which the Apostle was dying. Browning did not leave Blougram uncontrasted.

KER: He reappears as a Cardinal in *The Ring and the Book*, to serve as a foil to the heroic priest Caponsacchi.

COLIN: It is the argument that justifies (and inspired) those poems. Re-reading, after a long interval, *Blougram*, *Sludge* and *Prince Hohenstiel-Schwangau* – one wonders, as one gets nearer and nearer to the end, however Browning is going to explode their sophistries. He knew from the first.

SIBYLLA: But if we speak of volubility and control we must also speak of compression. Surely never, never, in all literature was more compressed into two lines than the anguished appeal of the wife-murderer against the sentence of the Pope:

> Abate, – Cardinal, – Christ, – Maria, – God, . . .
> Pompilia, will you let them murder me?
> [*The Ring and the Book*, XI, 2426–7]

And, Atticus, that is Browning's conception: his creature's abject terror, his own dramatic irony, his the divine satire which is pity.

ATTICUS: "The iron muscle and electric nerve."

SAINTSBURY: But that compression is frequent in Browning. Consider the drama in this "epigram" (in the Greek sense). It is Eurydice to Orpheus:

> But give them me, the mouth, the eyes, the brow!
> Let them once more absorb me! One look now

Will lap me round for ever, not to pass
Out of its light, though darkness lie beyond;
Hold me but safe again within the bond
Of one immortal look! All woe that was,
Forgotten, and all terror that may be,
Defied, – no past is mine, no future: look at me!

SIBYLLA: A kingly gift to Leighton for his picture.

FRANCES: So now we have represented to Atticus that Browning has
a right to his subjects, to his arguments, to his dramatis personae
(with whatever degree of mimicry he found worth while or irresistible). It only remains for us – doesn't it? – to demonstrate the verse
as – well, as *not* predominantly what Atticus said it was.

ATTICUS: Thank you, Frances. It is sweet of you to spare me those
"brickbats"!

COLIN: We will never mention them again. But I should like to
call up a reinforcement on your side in the unexpected person of
Mr Stevenson.

KER: R.L.S.! But he isn't anti-Browning, surely?

COLIN: No indeed! he has spoken of *The Ring and the Book* as 'a
poem, one of the noblest of our century'. But listen to what he has
said of *The Inn Album*, a poem which I think fully deserves the
same description. In an anonymous review,[2] of which he has confessed the authorship, he wrote:

When Mr Browning finds a line shambling out from underneath him in a
loose mess of unaccented syllables; when he finds it, like an ill-made
blancmange, subside into a squash or quagmire instead of standing on
its own basis with a certain sort of dignity or strength – quick, says
Mr Browning, break it up into an unexpected parenthesis, choke off the
reader with a dash, leave him clinging at the verse's end to a projecting
conjunction, cut a somersault before him, flick off his hat with your toe in
true Mabille fashion; in short, do what you will so you bewilder him, and
the limping verse will get away to cover undetected.

ATTICUS: Well, that's pretty spirited!

COLIN: Oh, yes! I can safely offer you Mr Stevenson's support, for
never were accusations more preposterous, more wanton. Precisely
and especially what the verse of *The Inn Album* does is never to
shamble, never to limp. No verse ever trod more firmly, none was

ever more tightly packed – packed tight with the story. Never was story-telling more controlled. No single thing is said that is not meant to *tell* again, later. Mr Stevenson says that it took him five minutes (him! the most parsimonious of story-tellers in prose) to realize that the woman had, at the end of the poem, committed suicide. It should not have done: the verse had told him that, nine times (as I counted). It took *me* five minutes to realize that the younger man would not be charged with the murder of the elder man. It should not have done. Mr Symonds and another writer[3] say that we cannot give the woman our respect. We must. The story answers all the questions we can put to it; and always, always, Browning controls the verse.

FRANCES: Yes, the verse. If we can convert Atticus to that, he will find all the poetry we have found, and more too. Mr Ker, do start us off!

KER: Let us concede to Atticus that a great deal of Browning *looks* like –

Peter Piper picked a peck of pickled pepper

but "it is wrong to take the harsh colliding consonants as a true sample of Browning's art". They are there on the printed page, and only there. They are not in the verse as a lover of verse would speak it.

SAINTSBURY: Yes, Browning as much as any poet teaches us how he would have his verses read; and, so read, they *are* verses; it *is* verse, the verse of a master. His 'harshnesses' prove to be none at all when our voice follows his, by note, as with sympathy and goodwill it learns to do.

ATTICUS: You remind me of Father Hopkins. You don't know his verse yet, but Mr Bridges means to print it some day: I can't think what people will make of it! When I had to tell Mr Hopkins how little I could like his – his – well, in brief, *his* "brickbats" he wrote to me,[4] "But take breath and read it with the ears, as I always wish to be read, and my verse becomes all right." And you would say this on behalf of Browning?

FRANCES: I want to say for him no less than that he was a veritable connoisseur of verbal loveliness – of which, four examples crowd

264

upon me at once. His Aristophanes is trying to recall a girl's name: he remembers that it was –

> some rich name,
> Vowel-buds thorned about with consonants,
> Fragrant, felicitous, rose-glow enriched
> By the Isle's unguent, [*Aristophanes' Apology*, 639–42]

and after making many shots at it, he recaptures the name itself: Balaustion. Then there's another name, that of a Paris jeweller who has given a notable diamond to bedeck the image of Our Lady:

> the liquid name
> 'Miranda', – faceted as lovelily
> As his own gift.
> [*Red Cotton Night-Cap Country*, I, 542–4]

And then a flower's name:

> This flower she stopped at, finger on lip,
> Stooped over, in doubt, as settling its claim;
> Till she gave me, with pride to make no slip,
> Its soft meandering Spanish name:
> What a name! Was it love or praise?
> Speech half-asleep or song half-awake?
> I must learn Spanish, one of these days,
> Only for that slow sweet name's sake.
> [*The Flower's Name*, 17–24]

ATTICUS: I could wish, Frances, that those were my verses, and you reading them. Tell me some more.

FRANCES: Well, a phrase this time: Miss Thackeray's, in Browning's appreciation of it: 'call the land' (it is Normandy) –

> call the land
> By one slow hither-thither stretching, fast
> Subsiding-into-slumber sort of name,
> Symbolic of the place and people too,
> '*White Cotton Night-Cap Country?*' Excellent!
> [*Red Cotton Night-Cap Country*, I, 142–6]

COLIN:

> He who blows through bronze can breathe through silver,
> [*One Word More*, XIII]

and often enough he does.

SIBYLLA: Mr Saintsbury says that our voice must follow Browning's, note by note. I think we can hear in Browning's verse that his was 'a scrupulous precision of enunciation'.[5] His 'usual' is always three syllables; his 'real', of course, has a diphthong, we can hear it. His 'naturally' is always four rippling, undulating syllables; his 'squirrel' always two equal syllables. His polysyllables always ripple, necessarily when one of them fills the second half of an alexandrine:

> he will buy
> Up the whole stock of earth's uncharitableness,
> > *[Fifine at the Fair,* XXXII]

but also habitually:

> soul
> As supernaturally grand, as face
> Was fair beyond example.
> > [*The Inn Album*, II, 279–81]

> sent a-slide
> My folly falteringly, stumblingly
> Down, down, and deeper down. . . .
> > [II, 363–5]

KER: I would instance one line as putting Browning along with Tennyson as a prosodist,

> All in quantity, careful of his motion,
> Like the skater on ice that hardly bears him.

ATTICUS: And that line is – ?
KER: Just this:

> There flashed the propriety, expediency . . .
> > [*The Ring and the Book*, IV, 983]

ATTICUS: Very thin ice! But I agree that it does bear you.
KER: Well, here's another like it:

> Guido, clandestinely, irrevocably . . . [III, 456]

SIBYLLA: But I should have said that Browning, in general, seems "intentionally to ignore quantity".
COLIN: Do you mean that ten-syllable lines of his often have more than five accents?

SIBYLLA: I am willing that you should put it that way.

COLIN: But the line isn't clogged or huddled. The syllables and the accents make room for each other, *mingling like flood with equal flood In agitated ease.* (ATTICUS *shows himself pleased with this application of his own verse.*) COLIN (*continues*): But I confess I could not always mark the accents with confidence.

ATTICUS: What need, if the lines *do* convince the ear? Try a few of them on us.

COLIN: These are all from *The Inn Album*, so that I am putting Mr Stevenson in the dock:

The lady's proud pale queenliness of scorn. [*The Inn Album*, IV, 695]
Should life prove half true life's term, death the rest.
[*Aristophanes' Apology*, 1288]
    Lay these words
To heart then, or where God meant heart should lurk.
[*The Inn Album*, IV, 184–5]

You! leave this youth, as he leaves you, as I
    Leave each. [V, 161–2]

In folly beyond field-flower-foolishness. [II, 251]

Some parson, some smug crop-haired smooth-chinned sort
    Of curate-creature. [II, 293–4]

Sun-warmth, dew-coolness, – squirrel, bee and bird. [III, 66]

ATTICUS: I don't like turning Queen's evidence against my fellow prisoner, but *I* should pass those lines.

COLIN: There is one habit which rules Browning's verse, measures it, makes it verse. It isn't a mannerism, for it is everywhere in literature, but it is so laughably (when one has become conscious of it) ubiquitous in Browning, that it must be his method: a method of accumulation – a string of adjectives attached to one noun, one nominative with three or more predicates, one predicate to three or more nominatives, or a succession of phrases of one pattern, set in apposition. He has most of this in common with every writer, with Henry James, for example, in whose prose,[6] also, it sometimes, naughtily, makes verse:

> unhurried, unflurried, unworried
> sifting, selecting, comparing

or – and this might be Clough –

> dazed a little, no doubt, breathless, no doubt, and bewildered.

But now see how it works in Browning:

> Murder's proved;
> With five – what we call qualities of bad,
> Worse, worst, and yet worse still, and still worse yet.
> [*The Ring and the Book*, I, 168–70]

ATTICUS: Poor Lindley Murray with his bare three degrees of comparison!

COLIN: Oh, Browning can do it again:

> Rare, rarer, rarest, not rare but unique.
> [*Red Cotton Night-Cap Country*, I, 354]

These next lines are notorious, and I know that some Catholics take them in bad part, but I think we must allow Browning the good humour of his ill humour. He hadn't found the librarians at the Vatican sympathetic or helpful with his researches, and the less so that he was a Protestant:

> 'Go get you manned by Manning and new-manned
> By Newman and, mayhap, wise-manned to boot
> By Wiseman, and we'll see or else we won't!'
> [*The Ring and the Book*, I, 444–6]

And now for eight adjectives, six of them hyphenated, to one noun:

> A husband poor, care-bitten, sorrow-sunk,
> Little, long-nosed, bush-bearded, lantern-jawed,
> Forty-six-years full.   [IV, 717–9]

ATTICUS: Yes, that *makes* the verse, as you say, and as it would not in Urquhart's Rabelais.

COLIN: But you must let the "method" make verse in this line although Browning printed it without commas and without my pauses:

a priest,
Smooth-mannered, soft-speeched, sleek-cheeked visitor.

[III, 250–1]

ATTICUS: As Mr Saintsbury said, the reader must bring a great deal of goodwill to such a line. But you read it very well.

COLIN: Thank you, Atticus. But this line reads itself:

The lout-lord, bully-beggar, braggart-sneak.

[III, 637]

ATTICUS: If Urquhart weren't unsurpassable, Browning might have given us a new version.

SAINTSBURY: Since you say that, you must certainly read his *Aristophanes' Apology*.

FRANCES: It is for something the farthest in the world from Rabelais that I want to offer Atticus something from *Aristophanes' Apology*.

ATTICUS: Good! Come on, Frances. Colin has had the argument in his hands long enough!

FRANCES: I suppose one might almost define Browning as a poet who never donned a singing-robe.

COLIN (*quoting* ATTICUS *again*): *To strut on stilts was not his use.*

FRANCES: But if he never wrote in the Grand Manner, he was capable of the great style. Atticus, I am going to show you yourself in Browning.

ATTICUS: I say!

FRANCES: Yes, I am! Balaustion and her husband, after the fall of Athens and the death of their adored Euripides, have taken ship for Rhodes. Now you are to think that Athens was for them what England is to you – to us. You are to recall your own dark forebodings of our future, your stern joy in the well-deserved disaster you foresee for us, your serene certitude in a world once more sane after our empire has perished like all the empires before us:

> *A dim heroic Nation, long since dead,*
> *The foulness of her agony forgot.*

ATTICUS: Frances, you bring the tears to my eyes.

269

FRANCES: No, you are to think of literature only, just now. Is not this in the great style? –

> What else in life seems piteous any more
> After such pity, or proves terrible
> Beside such terror?
>
> [*Aristophanes' Apology*, 174–6]

And would not you be glad – would not Landor have been proud – to sign these lines? –

> Why should despair be? Since, distinct above
> Man's wickedness and folly, flies the wind
> And floats the cloud, free transport for our soul
> Out of its fleshly durance dim and low, –
> Since disembodied soul anticipates
> (Thought-borne as now, in rapturous unrestraint)
> Above all crowding, crystal silentness,
> Above all noise, a silver solitude: –
>
> O nothing doubt, Philemon! Greed and strife,
> Hatred and cark and care, what place have they
> In yon blue liberality of heaven?
> How the sea helps! How rose-smit earth will rise
> Breast-high thence, some bright morning, and be
>   Rhodes!
> Heaven, earth and sea, my warrant – in their name,
> Believe – o'er falsehood, truth is surely sphered,
> O'er ugliness beams beauty, o'er this world
> Extends that realm where, 'as the wise assert',
> Philemon, thou shalt see Euripides
> Clearer than mortal sense perceived the man!
>
> [39–46, 50–60]

SIBYLLA: Thank you, Frances.

ATTICUS: Yes, indeed. But, Sibylla, what was it you had in your mind when you spoke of Browning's argumentative voice breaking in emotion, and softening into music?

SIBYLLA: This, from his early drama, *The Return of the Druses*. "There is some difficulty in the character of Anael with her double love and her half-deliberate delusion, so that much of the verse allotted to her is intricate enough; but where strong single feeling rises in the heart of this exiled Druse girl, what exquisite music sweeps out indeliberately! –

> Dost thou snow-swathe thee kinglier, Lebanon,
> Than in my dreams?" [II, 179–80]

ATTICUS: Exquisite, as you say.

KER: Yes. One used to read Browning for his doctrine, for his fun, for the pride in having read him. Now one reads him for his verse, for its *not* infrequent beauty, because, indeed, "what Browning has to give us is not knowledge only, nor strength, but beauty. The simplest and most satisfactory name for it is poetry."

SIBYLLA: And nothing is more English than magic in poetry. Not even Mr Arnold could call Browning Celtic.

ATTICUS: He has no 'horns of Elfland faintly blowing'?

SAINTSBURY: Not Elfland, and not faintly, but "Childe Roland to the Dark Tower came".

ATTICUS: Yes, I cannot pretend to be ignorant of that wonderful poem. And I won't ask you to match Keats's –

> magic casements opening on the foam
> Of perilous seas in faery lands forlorn.

KER: What of this? –

> the sprinkled isles,
> Lily on lily, that o'erlace the sea,
> And laugh their pride when the light wave lisps
> 'Greece' – [*Cleon*, 1–3]

ATTICUS: Lovely! you embolden me to ask for something comparable with –

> A damsel with a dulcimer
> In a vision once I saw

and the rest of it.

COLIN: *Women and Roses* begins promisingly:

> I dream of a red-rose tree.
> And which of its roses three
> Is the dearest rose to me?

> Round and round, like a dance of snow
> In a dazzling drift, as its guardians, go
> Floating the women faded for ages,
> Sculptured in stone on the poet's pages.
> Then follow women fresh and gay,
> Living and loving and loved today.
> Last, in the rear, flee the multitude of maidens,
> Beauties yet unborn. And all, to one cadence,
> They circle their rose on my rose tree.

But then the poem becomes a riddle that defeats me.[7]

ATTICUS: "One of those things that, as Lord Dundreary said, no fellow can be expected to understand?"

SAINTSBURY: Well, W. P., there's a great deal more that we should like to discuss, or to quote, but I think that you and I should be getting off to the Athenaeum now.

ATTICUS: But will you not, each of you, before you go, to complete my subjugation, read me one perfect thing? Mr Saintsbury?

SAINTSBURY: I think this should fetch you, for it might be your own Sussex marshes:

> Where the quiet-coloured end of evening smiles,
>   Miles and miles
> On the solitary pastures where our sheep
>   Half-asleep
> Tinkle homeward thro' the twilight, stray or stop
>   As they crop –
> Was the site once of a city great and gay,
>   (So they say)   [*Love among the Ruins*, 1–8]

but I need not go on.

ATTICUS: Yes, that could be Romney Marsh. And Mr Ker?

KER: We all read so much, and so quickly, and forgot so soon, and perhaps the metre of *Waring* has rushed us so, that we do not remember how "the verse changes from its loose variety into the sounding 'square' verse – the old heroic measure" – how it changes into this, at the thought of Iphigenia:

> To Dian's fane at Taurica,
> Where now a captive priestess, she alway
> Mingles her tender grave Hellenic speech

> With theirs, tuned to the hailstone-beaten beach:
> As pours some pigeon, from the myrrhy lands
> Rapt by the whirlblast to fierce Scythian strands
> Where breed the swallows, her melodious cry
> Amid their barbarous twitter.   [126–33]

(*And with this, and with New Year wishes, the two professors take their leave.*)

ATTICUS: And so, Colin, Browning has no difficulties for you?

COLIN: O, but he has! Occasionally he has a phrase which one thinks of as one and indivisible, and he divides it between two lines, and then I cannot tell how to speak those two lines as two verses.

ATTICUS: Yes, that is serious, isn't it! But let us have some examples.

COLIN: Here are three:

> So, Pope I meant to make myself, by step
> And step, whereof the first should be to find
> A perfect woman.
>> [*The Inn Album*, II, 431–3]

> I was not my own,
> No longer had the eyes to see, the ears
> To hear, the mind to judge, since heart and soul
> Now were another's.   [VII, 36–9]

> In some Salaminian cave
> Where sky and sea and solitude make earth
> And man and noise one insignificance.
>> [*Aristophanes' Apology*, 910–12]

ATTICUS: They crave wary walking. But now you two young people must do as your elders have done, and each give me one more thing of beauty to be a joy for ever. Frances, you shall have the woman's last word.

COLIN (*whose turn comes first*): Well, Sir, I have heard of a man who could always enhearten himself with this great mouth-filling, heart-stirring fragment:

> Bring forth all my war![8]

But for me, I have two lines of Browning, and they happen to come

273

from one of the very few passages where he speaks in his own person. In Normandy he had become interested in an awful story of real local life. Some poor young fool was drifting towards self-destruction, and Browning thinks: "If only he could have been directed to my friend Milsand who lives only a few miles away!" and then through a page or more he pays his tribute to his friend's probity, his sagacity, his helpfulness: "What hinders that my heart relieve itself?" and then come my two lines:

> O friend, who makest warm my wintry world,
> And wise my heaven, if there we consort too.
> [*Red Cotton Night-Cap Country*, III, 781–2]

SIBYLLA: O beautiful masculine friendship!
ATTICUS: That *is* heart-filling, Colin. Frances?
FRANCES: I have never yet been able to read *Sordello*, but a favourite passage of mine comes from it. I met it in a book of Miss Thackeray's and I often say it over to myself. I don't always get the lines right, because of an internal rhyme, and then I look it up again:

> a footfall there
> Suffices to upturn to the warm air
> Half-germinating spices; mere decay
> Produces richer life, and day by day
> New pollen on the lily-petal grows,
> And still more labyrinthine buds the rose.
> [I, 472–7]

ATTICUS: O dear! I shall never be able to snap at Browning again.

(*After which, the girl and young man make their adieux, and go away together.* SIBYLLA *and* ATTICUS *settle down at the chessboard.*)

SIBYLLA: Thank you, Atticus; you behaved beautifully.
ATTICUS: So did you all. And what a lot Mr Saintsbury knows, doesn't he!
SIBYLLA: And what a lot his "W. P." doesn't say, does he!
ATTICUS: A very sweet nature, I thought.[9]

NOTES

¹ [cf. Browning's prefatory advertisement to *Dramatic Lyrics* (1842).]

² In *Vanity Fair*, December 11, 1875, partly reprinted in *Notes and Queries*, February 12, 1944 [CLXXXVI, p. 102].

³ In, respectively, the *Academy*, November 27, 1875 [VII, pp. 389–90], and *Notes and Queries*, March 25, 1876 [fifth ser. V, pp. 244–5: the writer is F. J. Furnivall].

⁴ Actually to Bridges.

⁵ Cyril Bailey on J. W. Mackail.

⁶ In *The Ambassadors*, not then written!

⁷ [On *Women and Roses* see Geoffrey Tillotson, 'A Word for Browning', *Sewanee Review*, LXXII (1964), pp. 389–97.]

⁸ *Paradise Lost*, VI, 712.

⁹ [See also W. P. Ker, 'Browning', *Essays and Studies*, I (1910), pp. 216–40; G. Saintsbury, 'Browning' in *Corrected Impressions* (2nd ed. 1895), pp. 98–116 (also in *Collected Essays and Papers*, II, pp. 242–52), and *History of English Prosody*, Vol. III (1910), pp. 216–40.]

INDEXES

I: REFERENCES TO BROWNING'S POEMS

Titles in capital letters indicate Browning's volumes of poetry; numerals in bold type indicate the more important entries for each poem

II: TOPICS